The Know-How of Public Leaders in Collective Politics

The Know-How of Public Leaders in Collective Politics

BY

LUCAS DÍAZ

Tulane University, USA

United Kingdom – North America – Japan – India – Malaysia – China

Emerald Publishing Limited
Emerald Publishing, Floor 5, Northspring, 21-23 Wellington Street, Leeds LS1 4DL

First edition 2024

Copyright © 2024 Lucas Díaz.
Published under exclusive licence by Emerald Publishing Limited.

Reprints and permissions service
Contact: www.copyright.com

No part of this book may be reproduced, stored in a retrieval system, transmitted in any form or by any means electronic, mechanical, photocopying, recording or otherwise without either the prior written permission of the publisher or a licence permitting restricted copying issued in the UK by The Copyright Licensing Agency and in the USA by The Copyright Clearance Center. Any opinions expressed in the chapters are those of the authors. Whilst Emerald makes every effort to ensure the quality and accuracy of its content, Emerald makes no representation implied or otherwise, as to the chapters' suitability and application and disclaims any warranties, express or implied, to their use.

British Library Cataloguing in Publication Data
A catalogue record for this book is available from the British Library

ISBN: 978-1-83797-355-2 (Print)
ISBN: 978-1-83797-354-5 (Online)
ISBN: 978-1-83797-356-9 (Epub)

Printed and bound by CPI Group (UK) Ltd, Croydon, CR0 4YY

INVESTOR IN PEOPLE

Contents

List of Abbreviations and Acronyms — vii

About the Author — ix

Acknowledgments — xi

Chapter 1 *Know-How* **Matters** — 1

Chapter 2 **Dimensions of** *Know-How* — 29

Chapter 3 **Knowing the Field** — 63

Chapter 4 **Getting Others to Act** — 105

Chapter 5 **No Directions Given** — 127

Chapter 6 **Without Clear Roles and Processes, They Suffer** — 153

Chapter 7 *Know-How* **Conclusions** — 165

References — 177

List of Abbreviations and Acronyms

ALAAP	Alliance for Language Access for All People
AWI	All Are Welcome Institute
BYHH	Bring You Home Housing Organization
CRT	Citizen Rights Collective
FANO	Finance Authority of New Orleans
HANO	Housing Authority of New Orleans
HJC	Housing Justice Coalition
HTAG	Help Them Achieve Greatness Organization
HUD	Housing and Urban Development
HUNO	Homes for Us New Orleans
IAF	Industrial Areas Foundation
LDPSC	Louisiana Department of Public Safety and Corrections
LHC	Louisiana Housing Corporation
LHFA	Louisiana Housing Finance Agency
NBHI	Neighborhood-Based Housing Institute
NNG	Nearby Neighborhood Group
OCD	Office of Community Development
QAP	Qualified Allocation Plan
RSD	Recovery School District
SAF	Strategic Action Fields Theory
SIP	Strategic Interaction Perspective

About the Author

Lucas Díaz is a Dominican-born immigrant to the United States who has lived in the New Orleans area since the 1970s. He completed his PhD in Sociology from Tulane University's City, Culture, and Community program in 2022 after working 20 years in the local nonprofit and government sector.

Since 2000, Lucas has worked on nonprofit management, community engagement and organizing, government-based public participation programs and policies, leadership development, and nonprofit fundraising. He co-founded and led a New Orleans–based community nonprofit organization serving the Latinx community in 2007, then served as the first director of the Mayor's Neighborhood Engagement Office for the City of New Orleans from 2011 to 2013. During his time in City Hall, Lucas wrote public participation policies and designed community engagement programs that are still in use today.

Acknowledgments

I would like to thank everyone who supported my efforts to develop my scholarly agenda by first offering my gratitude to the City, Culture, and Community PhD program at Tulane University for accepting me into the program in 2013 despite having no prior relationship with sociology and entering as a seasoned professional. I would also like to thank those who contributed to my developing ideas, such as Carol Reese, PhD, who helped guide my early student days; my committee chair and mentor David Smilde, PhD, whose theoretical insights helped strengthen mine; dissertation committee member Eduardo Silva, PhD, whose political science perspective helped keep me focused; Michael Cowan, PhD, whose decade-long community organizing mentorship helped me grow into scholarship; and James Huck, PhD, whose unwavering encouragement provided confidence in times when mine was low. Without these individuals' input over the years, I would not have been able to advance my work. Additionally, the study was aided significantly by the Tulane Center for Public Service, whose support and interest played a large role in helping to bring this study to fruition. A note of gratitude as well goes out to all my colleagues in New Orleans who agreed to participate in my research, with particular thanks to those who gave more of their time than they could have imagined. Finally, I would like to thank close friends, family, and my wife, Lauren Boudreaux, especially, who encouraged me when the writing wasn't coming.

Chapter 1

Know-How Matters

A Bit of Background First

Let's begin with how my personal story informs this book. Not the most academic beginnings, to be sure, but it merits consideration since a good deal of the data I use come from my own experiences as a complete member of the fields in New Orleans that I analyze (Anderson, 2006b; Pensoneau-Conway & Toyosaki, 2011; Toyosaki, 2011).[1]

In the months leading up to hurricane Katrina, I made a living as a professional fundraiser in the New Orleans area for a music organization that focused on providing live performances. My work kept me relatively focused on corporate and private donors who cared about the recovery of New Orleans and the role music could play in that recovery. Professionally, I was not inclined to engage in the type of activities that challenged government to change, no matter how dire social justice issues appeared to me in the city. My personal experiences, shaped as they were by working-class Dominican immigrants who were singularly focused on achieving economic stability in the New Orleans area, contributed to the belief that my responsibility as a human being was to focus on "making it" in the United States. I viewed my position as an immigrant as being better served by avoiding confrontation with authority and focusing on getting ahead as an individual.

There was no mention in my upbringing of ever being or ever becoming activists, or any mention of unjust systems during my childhood, contributing to my early-life beliefs that the street demonstrations on TV, or the vented anger folks showed in city council chambers (made available on public access television), couldn't possibly lead to any change. According to my family, people in power don't offer the average person the opportunity to steer the ship. It's not our place, so the average person should just focus on doing what can be done to improve economically. Such was the way I saw the possibility of change before hurricane Katrina.

Two years after the hurricane, I co-created a Latinx-serving nonprofit that did in fact engage in activities that directly challenged local and state government. I experienced the same civic "activation" that many others after the storm experienced in New Orleans (Weil, 2011).[2] I felt compelled to help the newcomer immigrant Latinx community (Fussell & Diaz, 2015) interact with the pre-Katrina general population with which I was familiar.[3] This compulsion fueled a strong desire to build something that could play a meaningful role within the shifting landscape in post-Katrina New Orleans. However, my knowledge and skillset certainly did not fully position me well to take on such a challenge.

Aside from the combined experience-based knowledge of immigrant life in New Orleans and my practice-based knowledge of fundraising strategies for nonprofit organizations, I had no additional knowledge or skills relevant to initiating any form of social service or social justice organization. I reached out to others who could help me form a new organization and embarked on learning what I believed I needed to know to achieve any form of impact. In embarking on this work in 2007, I engaged with three different community organizers in the New Orleans area, all of whom were trained to conduct their work as professionals by the Industrial Areas Foundation (IAF).[4]

The IAF has trained thousands of professional organizers who have worked throughout the United States as part of a tradition that dates to labor organizing in the early 20th century in Chicago. Organizers in this tradition train future prospective community organizers who will take up this work as professionals, as well as organizational leaders who become lay organizers. These professional and lay organizers are trained in concepts and strategies gleaned from years of field practice and internal critical reflections about the nature of the work and how to best pursue it. Through my relationships with the organizers I met in New Orleans, I was afforded the opportunity to participate in two different community organizing trainings, one conducted by IAF in Los Angeles in 2007 and one conducted by IAF trained organizers in Chicago in 2008. It was in these trainings that I learned how regular people such as myself have fought for and secured the desired change they want to see in their communities.

I entered the first training with complete skepticism about what people who are not in power can do to affect the public decision-making of those in power.[5] I learned how organizers go about helping people build power and take calculated, public action steps as part of contentious collective politics that move them toward achieving the social justice changes they seek.[6] After completing my second training, I had no doubt that I could put to practice what I learned from IAF to push for change in New Orleans.

Not long after this training, I engaged in a series of activities that my pre-Katrina self would have thought pointless and doomed to fail. Six years after Katrina, I had either led, co-led, or participated in post-Katrina efforts that resulted in: limited improvements to the New Orleans Police Department's efforts to work with the new immigrant Latinx community in a nonthreatening manner, adoption of professional interpreter standards by the State of Louisiana Supreme Court, and defeat of anti-immigrant bills in the State of Louisiana 2008, and 2010 legislative sessions.

From these experiences in the field, I began to wonder if other groups deployed similar lessons to that offered by IAF and if use of this knowledge helped them achieve the outcomes they desired. Of course, it's not that straightforward. I also experienced various failed actions, which helped illustrate in my mind that possessing the skills and knowledge espoused by IAF as critical to building power didn't always equate to a group achieving their desired outcome. And yet, the marked differences I experienced between those collective actions in which the leadership knew something about what they were doing when compared to leadership that maybe could have benefitted from a little more knowledge and practice is undeniable. It's a qualitative difference that can be understood best via comparison. Alone, without any reference to anything different, a particular approach may seem, on its own merit, to be good enough. It isn't until a previously deemed adequate approach is compared to a more effective one that we begin to perceive such qualitative differences.

Over many different experiences as a practitioner in New Orleans between 2007 and 2018, I observed how these qualitative differences interacted within collective actions. I began to consider how differences in execution between groups pushing for change in New Orleans appeared to align with the level of capacity a group possessed.[7] In activities in which I participated between 2007 and 2018 in the New Orleans area, I observed that groups with high levels of capacity were able to build power and participate in opportunities to affect public decision-making scenarios, whereas groups with low levels of capacity were less successful in their efforts to affect change. At the same time, there were also instances when groups appeared to possess the type of capacity (at whatever level) that IAF championed as critical for success and yet repeatedly failed to achieve any desired change.

These practice-based observations serve as the foundation for the focus and research data this book explores. Based on my own practical experiences in the New Orleans area, the work to bring about social justice change at local levels, particularly when it is collective and aimed at public decision-makers, differs in the hands of leaders who have some degree of knowledge, skills, and/or experiences in and with contentious political action when compared to those who do not. I observed during my 11 years in the field between 2007 and 2018 in New Orleans that what leaders know and understand about the types of tactics, skills, and more, which they need for a given action strategy within a given place, varies widely. Not all leaders have the same abilities, and sometimes, there is a lack of awareness by groups about how much they don't know, and there are instances where it is the will and energy of charismatic leaders alone that keeps a group pushing for change in the face of 0 indications of success. These experiences suggest that these differences in capacity do, in fact, matter, which this book explores through the development and application of *know-how* as an analyzable concept in contentious collective politics that can open deeper possibilities in qualitative analysis and practical application.

As I learned from IAF, people do need to know what they are doing if they are going to engage in collectives that challenge power structures and decision-makers, which raises questions about acquisition and deployment of groups' abilities in collective political contention. More specifically, this raises questions about the role that groups' knowledge, skills, and experiences (with bringing and keeping collectives together, deciding upon what form of action to take as a group, and engaging other actors involved in the same spaces in which collective contention occurs, for example) play in their abilities to achieve the changes they seek.

Drilling deeper, this book will focus on leaders of organizations and movements to better understand how *know-how* "showed" up in their work. Using both my own practice-based experiences in New Orleans between 2007 and 2018, as well as 43 interviews with still actively involved individuals between 2016 and 2017, I explore the way that *know-how* potentially interacted with efforts to bring about social justice changes between 2008 and 2016. But before entering into the analysis of these data, which are offered in four separate chapters below that explore different dimensions of *know-how*, I would like to first move through some background information on the academic and practice-oriented literature on contentious collective politics and how these works provide the foundation for how I arrived at the concept of *know-how*. This background information is a sort of brief, and in no way exhaustive, discussion of the trajectory of academic research and other works that pave the way for the next chapter in which I operationalize *know-how* by diving deeply into how the concept works and how it can be used in both academic and practice-based work related to collective political action and more.

Looking Deeper at *Know-How*

So what am I talking about here? What exactly is *know-how*, which I have already mentioned a handful of times above? Simply put, *know-how*, as I use it in this book, is the combination of knowledge, skills, and experiences that comes together in a person and gets deployed in political action.[8] In this regard, I conceive *know-how* as a type of knowing that individuals gain about a given phenomenon that orders action in such a way as to have the potential to increase effectiveness and efficiency in execution within the circumscribed social spaces and processes in which the intended action occurs.[9] For the purposes of this introduction, it's important to establish that *know-how* includes abstract and practical knowledge and skills, which are acquired via a combination of formal instruction, training manuals, and other forms of informal instruction that is then combined with knowledge gained from and skills sharpened through real-world practice (relative to a circumscribed social space).

For example, community organizers trained by IAF put the community organizing concepts learned in classroom settings into practice in the real world, and in doing so begin to cultivate their own *know-how* about what works and what doesn't work in the spaces in which they engage. Another way to help facilitate a shared understanding of what I generally mean when I use the phrase *know-how* is to invite you to imagine a fictional scenario in which you are a resident in a dense urban setting who begins to have increasing concerns about properties in your neighborhood that have begun to look abandoned. You are concerned about their impact on safety, and you find that you are not alone. Your neighbors would like to do something about it. You call for a meeting on the issue. Everyone agrees that something should be done. But what? Does anyone know where to start? Does someone in the group know the steps for this type of action? Can anyone highlight what needs to happen in the next three steps, and then in the next nine, and so forth? Does your town or city have a clearly responsible department, and if so, what are their processes? Does anyone know what is possible in the end?

If you have ever been involved in, or exposed to, similar work, you may have a general idea about possible next steps, regardless of where you live. You may have, in effect, a certain amount of applicable knowledge that you can bring to this situation, which can be applied as a level of *know-how*. On the other hand, if you have never been involved in anything remotely similar, identifying the possibilities for action may not come as easily, if these come at all.

As should be perfectly clear from this small exercise, pursuing any form of social change in the world (regardless of the issue or political leaning) takes a certain amount of knowledge both about the world in which one intends to act and about what actions must be undertaken that will work within that world. In other words, acting in the world with an intent to change it, however small or large the change, requires a certain knowing that I call *know-how*.

Interestingly, this type of knowing has surprisingly garnered scant historical attention in the theory-making and empirical studies of social movement studies (Van Dyke & Dixon, 2013), which dominates the broad subject area of contentious collective politics.[10] In the world of practice, the idea of *know-how* exists mostly as an assumed quality one creates by developing skills through formal and informal trainings and through experiences in the world of practice. In both academic and practitioner spaces, the concept of *know-how* can serve as a vital tool that can help enrich interpretation and analysis as well as learning, teaching, and application. The aim of this book is to bring the concept of *know-how* to the fore for future scholarly endeavors as a conceptual tool that can deepen and enrich analysis of contentious collective action, as well as to provide a general guidepost for practitioners in and educators of public leadership (Brookes, 2014; Hartley, 2018; Marcy, 2023).[11] While the primary aim is to engage scholars in political science, sociology, organizational development, civic engagement, democracy, public leadership, and more in concept discussion and usage as an analytical device (which can be applied with or without a grand theory), the book also explores applicability in the real world for practitioners, primarily through the analyzed case studies and concluding recommendations.

Now, a warning about *know-how*. I have yet to fully develop the concept, but I have no doubt that you have already ascribed to the phrase your own broad understanding of what it could mean – you have undoubtedly filled in the gaps. For example, you may have already had a thought about your academic *know-how*, such as the idea that you know what it takes to make it in the academy, or maybe you have cooking *know-how* and know your way around a kitchen, or perhaps you have mechanical *know-how* and know what to do with a combustion engine. You may have even already concluded, so what? We all have *know-how*, so no big deal. And you'd be right to think so because the phrase *know-how*, which is common enough in public usage, has existed at least since 1838 when it appeared in a review of a mechanical invention in *The Cincinnati Chronicle* on

June 16, 1838, which asserted that the inventor deployed "a good deal of know-how" in the implementation of his ideas.[12] By the late 1800s, the phrase was well established as a type of knowledge that one gains in the practice of something, as this phrase from *The Engineer* demonstrates: "the '*know-how*' of working men has, in many cases, kept pace with the advancement of science."

With such general, widespread usage, the notion that we all possess some *know-how* about something in the world today falls into cliché. We typically presume that *know-how*, of all types in the world, is a given quality of being a modern human. This presumption is so widespread that until someone tells us directly, "no, I really don't know how to fry an egg," the egg frying world takes it for granted that people have learned how to fry an egg without burning down the kitchen before entering adulthood. Such assumptions can lead into all sorts of unexpected troubles. Consider the following example.

Let's assume you, the reader, know how to change a flat tire. Knowing this could mean one of two possibilities. Either you gained the knowledge of how to do it by necessity, when you absolutely had to do it because you were alone, on the side of a dark road, and had no other alternative, so you "figured it out." Or maybe not under such dire circumstances you have changed a flat tire with your own hands, which means you have flat tire-changing *know-how* developed from practice. Or it could be that you may have learned how a tire is changed from someone, either in person or online, but have yet to practice changing a flat tire yourself, making your *know-how* about tire changing not quite what it could be, but at least you know the steps.

Now with this *know-how* in your possession, if pressed, you can change flat tires on just about any sort of personal vehicle with wheels, axles, and nuts and bolts. In other words, you can now apply this flat tire-changing *know-how* to almost anyone's flat tire you encounter on the roads and become a superhero of sorts when you pull over on the highway to help someone change their flat tire. But there's a catch.

You quickly learn that your flat tire *know-how* doesn't adequately transfer to all seemingly similar tires. Your *know-how* is barely helpful with a large 18-wheeler's tire and is even less helpful with any airplane's flat tire. In your eagerness to serve others in need with flat tire-changing problems you learn, in fact, that your flat tire *know-how* powers have limitations that you didn't know existed until you needed to apply them in strange and unusual spaces and circumstances. This is the crux of this book; the idea that when leaders are involved in contentious collective politics – be that in social movements, organized nongovernment organizational coalitions, civic associations, organized worker actions, or disorganized active citizenship (Cohen et al., 2010; Curtis & Petras, 1970; Forestal, 2016; Westheimer & Kahne, 2004) – they bring to their efforts a certain level of knowing akin to the *know-how* you bring to changing a flat tire, and as observers and practitioners, we should be inquiring about the level of *know-how* we believe we possess.[13,14]

But there's another problem that needs to be considered, namely that the transferability and universality of a person's *know-how* can be misinterpreted. In other words, our *know-how* has limitations and boundaries, as it is not universally and automatically transferrable to all circumstances. This is what I reference in the example above when I say that your personal vehicle-based tire-changing *know-how* doesn't transfer automatically to airplane tire-changing *know-how*. From a practitioner's perspective, misinterpretation of our own or our allies' *know-how* in critical strategic actions can spell trouble. For analysts, regardless of their disciplinary lens, similar misinterpretation can lead to false assumptions about what they are analyzing, which in turn leads to either exaggerated or under-examined claims about what was observed. Let's consider this again from the flat tire-changing point of view.

When we think of others' flat tire-changing *know-how*, we have a tendency to generally assume (1) that such *know-how* is universal and as such others around us also have this *know-how* and (2) that much of it must be transferrable to similar scenarios and circumstances that involve a flat tire, nuts and bolts, an axle, and wheels. But as we saw above, the *know-how* we develop specifically from dealing with our typical personal vehicles only gets us so far. We cannot easily transfer the same *know-how* gained from changing our personal vehicles' flat tire into changing the flat tire on a small airplane.

Similarly, we tend to assume that if we know how to do this, surely many others around us must also know how to do this. In the case of flat tire-changing *know-how*, we assume without deeper analysis or self-reflection that many drivers around us also have this *know-how*. Our only information as to whether others possess the same *know-how* comes typically from our personal experiences. We assume the universal nature of this knowledge, forgetting that until the very moment when we experienced the act of changing a tire ourselves, we had no clue as to how to go about doing this. This is what I call a false universal belief, otherwise understood as egocentrism (Ross & Nisbett, 2011), which I believe has plagued theory-making and empirical observations of contentious collective politics, resulting in decades of work that simply omits this critical element of public leadership in collective contention.

Where Has *Know-How* Been?

If you are in academia and are interested in a brief, nonexhaustive, but informative history of theory-making in and about contentious collective politics, then this next section is for you. If you are a practitioner and would rather skip this part, then feel free to go directly to the next chapter where I begin to develop the concept of *know-how* for analytic and practical application.

As I stated above, we typically bring general (largely unexamined) assumptions about the *know-how* we and everyone around us possess, which seeps into our analysis of, and practice in, contentious collective politics, leaving the unsuspecting (both in and outside of academia) in the full belief that *know-how* must be a given quality already in everyone's possession. This leads to an overestimation of the capacities and dispositions leaders involved in collective contention bring to the table. In turn, this perspective leads to a belief that if public leaders are involved at all in collective contention, then knowledge, skills, and other capacities must be already present, requiring no further inquiry. Unfortunately, in the early days of social movement theory development, there was a tendency to see the opposite in collective contention, focusing primarily on the emotional state of a mob in a large crowd of people asking for change (le Bon, 1931; Smelser, 1963; Turner & Killian, 1972). For example, early social sciences scholarship of political demonstrations perceived these activities as collective behavior that was irrational, focusing on how their collective protest behavior didn't fit normative political participation behavior.[15]

It wasn't until focus shifted toward how collectives mobilize political influence when they are challengers to those in positions of power that scholarship began to consider the idea that perhaps contentious collective political activities were conducted by well-adjusted folks, after all (Gamson, 1975; Gurr, 2016). Even so, when the literature began to consider collective political contention outside electoral politics, analytical focus bypassed what actors know how to do, how they learn this type of knowing, and how they deploy it when involved in contentious collective politics, and instead embarked on a decades-long endeavor to explain this type of social activity via large macro-oriented theories, beginning with the highly influential ideas created by Charles Tilly (1978). Tilly's exploration of how contentious collectives mobilize resources, in particular, had a lasting effect, as it served to steer future theory-making and analysis away from individual actors and toward macro explanations, such as the development of the political process perspective (McAdam, 1982), which arose directly out of and in response to Tilly's work. This new theoretical development moved contentious collective politics scholarship's trajectory solidly into macrostructural analysis of how contentious collectives come to exist and mobilize.[16]

The next major development and research in this direction led to a focus on macro-level political opportunity and threat structures that allow groups to come into existence and openly challenge established spaces of power or that serve to limit what collectives can do (McAdam, 1982; Tarrow, 1998; Tilly, 1986). In moving along the same macro analytical trend now in full swing, these approaches led to further macro-related questions rather than questions about how the individuals know what they are doing. This trajectory is punctuated by the creation of frame analysis (Bourdieu, 1992; Edwards, 2014; Gamson, 1992; Lichterman & Eliasoph, 2014; Opp, 2009; Snow et al., 1986; Verba et al., 1995), which shed light on how social movements frame their issues of contention. Frame analysis, however, did not ask where or how individuals developed the *know-how* (again, this concept refers to a type of knowing that combines abstract and experiential knowledge, which I will more deeply develop in the next chapter) they deploy in their framing strategies, as the focus never drilled down to that level of analysis. If by now you are wondering why not, I would like to offer the possibility that throughout its history, most academic thinking about social action has been couched in terms of rational thinking and large scale, or macro, analysis.[17]

While focus on macro-level analysis led much of the social science theory-making and empirical research between the 1980s and 2000s even further away from questions about what public leaders know how to do when they are involved in contentious collective politics, it did spark a reactionary trajectory that sought to bring the focus of analysis to individuals via attention to the subjective dimensions of contention (Goodwin & Jasper, 1999, 2004; Johnston & Klandermans, 1995).[18] This reactionary trajectory sought to focus on the activities and internal dynamics of contentious collectives, particularly as regards the role that emotion plays within these groups (Goodwin & Jasper, 1999, 2004), which indeed directed attention to actor-level capacities. At the same time, however, even these efforts failed to account for the *know-how* that individuals deploy within these dynamics.

In the early 2000s, a new effort to connect macro and micro levels of theory-making and research emerged in sociology and political science called the dynamics of contention approach, which sought to combine macro- and micro-level factors intertwined in dynamic interactions over time (McAdam et al., 2001). This approach offered a broader possibility from which to view previous theories by calling for a more interactive analysis between leaders and structures via a focus on mechanisms and cycles of contention over time. In calling for a focus on the relational contexts between movement-based individuals and the social structures in which they operate, there was an aim to maintain the merits of macro-level social structure approaches while adding how individuals interacted within these structures over time. As promising a shift as this may have been, it failed to adequately conceptualize and problematize the role of individuals' *know-how* when analysis focused on strategic decision-making. In other words, an unexplored assumption remained about what public leaders know how to do and how they use this type of knowing when making strategic decisions within contentious collective politics.

At the same time, between the 1990s and 2000s, scholarship in sociology and political science began to view contentious collectives, particularly social movements, as independent variables in governance changes rather than dependent variables in political processes and structures (Arce et al., 2019), marking a significant shift toward seeing the activities of collectives as the creators of change. The result of this shift was a new trajectory that focused on outcomes. With this shift toward outcomes, the implication arose that leaders must be intentional in their decision-making, and yet, insufficient attention was paid to the *know-how* leaders bring to their work.[19]

If a group mobilizes for the purposes of affecting some form of public decision-making, and it does so with some intended or desired outcome in mind, then decisions about what strategies to implement and what actions to take require some level of *know-how* related to the desired outcome. While outcomes-focused scholarship did not substantively explore how public leaders' know-how interacted with desired outcomes, this line of research did pave the way for a more strategic interaction approach that connects leaders and their environments in relation to their targets and desired outcomes via the strategic decisions they make.

The dynamic interaction approach continues to be used widely in current contentious collective politics research.[20] Analysis along these lines has, indeed, enabled improved understanding of how individuals within organized structures strategically interact among themselves, with allies, and with the targets of their political participation activities, paving the way for three theoretical developments that build on the dynamic interactive approach and provide an analytical framework within which I situate and operationalize the concept of *know-how* for analysis in this book.

In sociological theory-making since 2010, the Strategic Action Field (SAF) theory by Fligstein and McAdam (2012), the Strategic Interaction Perspective (SIP) by James Jasper (2015), and the Civic Action Theory by Paul Lichterman (2020) move closest toward an exploration of what public leaders know and do in collective contention without quite moving into a usable conceptualization of *know-how*. All three provide an analytical framework that incorporates individuals and their decision-making within the context of their own groups, other groups, and the broader social contexts in which they operate, and all emphasize the interaction between individuals and their contexts over time. From a purely analytical view, this is a positive step forward in providing today's social scientists with a more applicable lens to real-world phenomena. I say more applicable because I am also considering the needs of practitioners, who would benefit from theoretical frameworks that can help them improve their practice.

In developing *know-how*, I rely primarily on SAF theory (with some interaction with Lichterman's Civic Action Theory) as a launching point because it provides a seamless framework in which *know-how* can be operationalized as an analytical concept but also because it helps provide a viable lens for practitioners to consider when applying the concept in capacity assessment of their own efforts. For this reason, I reference the theory often in this chapter and the next in which I explain and operationalize *know-how* as a usable analytical concept.

In broad strokes, SAF theory establishes that mechanisms at play in contention between movement actors, general society, government actors, and government institutions and processes (and other spaces of public decision-making) all take place within fields that are constructed by a complex and dynamic set of individuals acting upon organizational and societal factors across time (Fligstein & McAdam's, 2012). For example, when SAF theory states that it explores "how stability and change are achieved by social actors in circumscribed social arenas," this is understood to mean that the social arena can be viewed as a field and the change achieved by social actors as the strategic action field created via action, which Fligstein and McAdam define as a middle-level social order that serves as "the basic structural building block of modern political/organizational life in the economy, civil society, and the state" (Fligstein & McAdam's, 2012). In other words, public leaders create new strategic action fields within existing fields as a direct attempt to either circumvent or diminish the influence of an existing field. For SAF theory, fields are made up of real-world social structures and processes that shape and give meaning to how people engage in either individual or collective activities they believe will bring about some desired social change.

The view outlined above by SAF theory implies a certain knowing or knowledge that public leaders must undoubtedly bring to the actions they take. While there is no shortage of accidental outcomes in the world, often any achieved outcome, be that intended or unintended, is more likely to be linked to people who know something about what they are doing rather than not. Consider it this way; if I am in the business of generating leads for sales and I am adept at the skill of persuasive communication, as well as being deeply knowledgeable about consumer buying habits and market competition, then I bring to the work a certain level of knowing that plays a role in the number of sales I close. Using SAF theory language, I am an actor who generates new action fields by simply deploying what I know how to do upon the existing consumer fields, which is filled with numerous consumers who are not thinking of buying my product until they meet with me. But after meeting with me, some of these consumers will begin to think of buying my product, which results in a changed field, one in which a nonbuying person becomes my customer, all because of the action I took to persuade them.

The same would apply in contentious collective action in which a group will push for change within a given field. For example, in this book, I explore how public leaders in New Orleans pushed for change post-Katrina and how their *know-how* played a role in that work. Wherever *know-how* demonstrated itself to be present at any significant level, the same assessment can be made that leaders' actions paved the way to changing the field upon which they pushed. In one specific instance that I explore in depth in later chapters, public leaders advanced substantive changes in various government practices post-Katrina in part because they generated the fields' very potential for change through the challenge fields they created. This observation may or may not feel radical, depending on what you, as a reader, may or may not have been exposed to up to this point in terms of real-world change work experiences, but my experiences in the field have shown me repeatedly (and perhaps history has also shown this, too) that any change in social structures, including those maintained in governance systems, tend to change primarily when pushed to change by challengers (be that from within or from external spaces).[21] But the key to this notion is that even in seemingly immovable social structures, such as those in place within governance systems and their ubiquitous bureaucracies, public leaders who bring a high level of *know-how* can and do affect some form of change, which is something IAF trainers fully embrace as a given truth.

While I believe that SAF theory enables me, as an analyst to place *know-how* within this interaction between public leaders and the fields in which they operate, I do want to point out an important voice that offers a slightly different view. In Paul Lichterman's development of what he calls Civic Action Theory (2020), he focuses on what he terms styles.[22] For Lichterman, SAF theory fails to adequately conceptualize actors, arguing that SAF theory relies on a limiting conceptual box that looks at actors from an outdated model that fails to perceive how actors behave "in action." In Lichterman's view, Fligstein and McAdam's SAF theory problematizes social skills as a utilitarian ability that entrepreneurial actors deploy, which he finds inadequate for understanding the varied and contradictory ways in which actors behave. This is an important observation worth discussing here because it involves how we conceptualize human action in both the academic and practitioner worlds.

There is little to no debate that our academic and practice-based concepts of human action rely on the longstanding, now taken-for-granted, rational model of human action.[23] It's important to highlight this and its implications in contemporary theory-making and research because to fully grasp how *know-how* works both in the real world and as an analyzable factor in contentious collective politics, we have to come to terms with the limitations that the rational model of human action has given us, particularly when thinking about both how to better study and teach public leadership. Lichterman argues that we need what he terms "a bigger conceptual box" through which one can understand human action. He establishes that such a bigger conceptual box moves analysis beyond the confines of the rational model (2020). I agree with this observation but disagree with him that SAF theory does not offer this "bigger box" possibility.

So what exactly is the problem with the rational model when it comes to its usage in analyzing, explaining, and/or practicing contentious collective politics? There are many salient arguments, from the utilitarian approach to life as untenable to the fallacy that humans actually calculate in the manner described by the proponents of rational action (Colapietro, 2009; Joas, 1996). For action in contentious collective politics, an unquestioned belief in rational actors leads one to expect to find public leaders who have amassed the complete set of necessary skills, which they then apply in order of appropriateness to a known outcome, or end, that they pursue at all costs without deviation. But this is not the case in the real world.

Both SAF theory and Civic Action Theory rely on Deweysian pragmatism, bringing Dewey's end-in-view model of the actor, which I discuss in more detail below, as a more viable model for researching and understanding public leadership in contentious collective politics. The end-in-view model of the actor offers the idea that every human being can create, and in fact does so through action, which Hans Joas terms creative action (1996) of both the intended and unintended variety, which echoes ideas offered by Dewey (2016, 2017). Creative action walks away from rational action (understood as the entrepreneurial actor by Lichterman) and serves as an underlying, if not explicitly stated, model for the actions of public leaders in both SAF and Civic Action Theory.

According to Hans Joas, creative action is a more viable lens to better understanding human actions in collective contentious politics, and it is his work on creative action that best articulates the limitations of rational action as a model (1996). I rely heavily on Joas' understanding of creative action, which for him is the type of action that we all conduct in our daily lives when confronted with the limits of what we know about a given situation. In other words, every person can create a new direction, a new social circumstance when confronted with a moment in which what we know isn't allowing us to move forward in the world, be that in a board room, our family dining room, or the public spaces where people gather to create social change. Joas relies, as do I in conceptualizing *know-how*, on John Dewey's ideas about creativity in public actions, which for Dewey exists everywhere and anywhere that conflict about the public good arises because each politically circumscribed space in which people engage encapsulates the known world for a given group, in a given time, in a given location (2016, 2017).

In other words, when public leaders find themselves confronted with challenges in their work to push for change that causes them to pause and consider that they may not have the answers for their next move, they enter into a re-evaluation, or reconsideration of what is and is not possible, and often create new possibilities that did not exist beforehand. This happens often because public processes and structures are dynamic, replete with shifting grounds, requiring public leaders to react and respond to these shifts in ways that are often particular to a given situation, in a given time, in a given place.

By using a Deweysian view of creative action, both SAF and Civic Action Theory establish that public leaders may or may not have ends in mind, but as Dewey establishes, they may have ends-in-view, but such ends may shift, as the need arises, out of engagement within the very spaces in which the desired ends are to take effect. In this way, I perceive both SAF and Civic Action Theory as providing the "bigger box" that Lichterman offers. However, both SAF theory's focus on social skills and Lichterman's focus on styles miss the mark in the same manner by each failing to adequately explore how these creative actions are related to *know-how* (as conceptualized in this book).

Both theories do provide, however, the analytical jumping-off point from which to expand and develop the concept of *know-how*. For example, in Civic Action Theory's assertion that analysis of civic action leads to observation and understanding of styles deployed by actors (2020) and in SAF theory's assertion that interaction with mid-level structures and processes requires social skills (2012), both frameworks could be said to ignore that social skills and styles either require, or are involved in, or contribute to the development and deployment of *know-how*. While I agree that a bigger conceptual box is needed, I find that even Lichterman's styles leave unanswered questions about where any given public leader acquired the *know-how* behind their style.

I disagree with Lichterman's assessment that SAF theory offers a "limiting" box based on the rational action model when thinking about how public leaders engage in strategic action.[24] In fact, it's quite the opposite; as stated above, SAF theory relies heavily on Deweysian pragmatism, as well as lessons from organizational and institutional theory-making, which offer the possibility for a view of public leaders' actions as moving away from the rational model. Both theories, however, represent how the sociological and political science literature to date largely fails to adequately incorporate knowledge from practice, which has been primarily captured in literature about public leadership, civic skills, and community organizing.[25]

Before engaging the academy, it was my IAF training and leadership fellowship experiences that exposed me to the idea of capacity development in public leadership skills. From this exposure, as I shared at the beginning of this chapter, I began to have interest in just how such knowledge is created, acquired, transferred, and practiced, which led me not just to the academy, as I highlighted above, but also back to those works and ideas that informed my own practice, as well as works not typically considered as part of contentious collective politics. In terms of theoretical approaches, I rely heavily on pragmatism in couching *know-how* as a usable analytical factor, as well as concepts gleaned from community organizing trainings and writings.

When groups of people engage in challenging the decisions made by those in power (whether in government or other institutions), rarely does the observable behavior follow any predictable pattern. With the social sciences largely focused historically on wanting to predict when large-scale collective contention will take place, we have missed for too long the opportunity to further understand how people in a group involved in political contention may or may not know how to do what they do.[26] As I mentioned before, such an oversight for the larger part of the 20th century may be due to a tendency to assume public leaders' *know-how* as a given, as if individuals come ready-made with everything they need to engage successfully in contentious politics. However, a shift away from this did take shape in the last 25 years, with a good deal of research forgoing prediction to focus on interpretation and explanation of the complexity of individual and group interactions in dynamic political participation settings (Ganz, 2009; Goodwin & Jasper, 2004; Jasper, 2015; Jasper & Goodwin, 1999; Paschel & Sawyer, 2008; Stahler-Sholk, 2010). The development and application of *know-how* in this book sits directly within this promising direction. For example, research in the social sciences has provided some insight into how individuals' use of communicative skills and emotional and relationship-building abilities within a given social space interact with the activities and actions that organized groups involved in contentious politics undertake (Benford & Snow, 2000; Ganz, 2009; Jasper, 2006; Kirlin, 2003, 2005). In other disciplines beyond sociology and political science, the contribution to helping develop a robust understanding of what public leaders know and do to affect change is slightly better, though problematic in different ways.

Literature on community organizing primarily stems from practitioners, who focus on a wide range of skills, tactics, and strategies for public leaders involved in bringing about some form of social justice change in their communities.[27] These writings are primarily written by professional community organizers who have worked in the field over a period of decades, providing rich actor-based conceptual considerations that can and should be added to mainstream contentious collective politics literature. At the same time, scholarly attention to community organizing that does exist does not fully problematize and conceptualize *know-how* as an important factor to consider relative to a group's achievement of (or failure to achieve) desired outcomes.[28] Community organizing literature authors do highlight, however, that individuals involved in contentious collective politics do know something about what they are doing and that this knowing is translated into intentional action in service of the political changes desired.

Beyond community organizing, a growing literature about participation in democratic processes points to the need for developing civic skills.[29] For example, Verba, Schlozman, and Brady point out that "the institutional origins of skills have implications for American democracy," which they consider playing a role in mediating other factors, such as income, race, and ethnicity playing potential causal roles in political participation inclusion (1995). In their eyes, "civic skills are part of a larger package including knowledge, motivation or interest, connections to networks of engaged people, and resources..." (Verba et al., 1995).

Such a view tends to be under-observed, if considered at all, in the contentious collective politics literature discussed above. In these works, skills are required for engaging in democratic activities, but what remains unexplored is how these skills contribute to the type of *know-how* I have so far highlighted and how such knowing interacts with public leaders' efforts to challenge for change in contentious collective politics.

Indeed, civic skills and knowledge are found to be associated with civic competencies, which a body of literature argues is required for any type of political participation (Agre, 2004; Bottery, 2003; Daas et al., 2016; Dahlgren, 2006; Shmueli et al., 2009). These findings and observations (and hundreds more too numerous to include here) from the civic engagement and democracy literature help contribute additional foundational components to the idea of *know-how* playing a role in understanding that people do indeed know something (or don't) about what it takes to engage in political spaces and that this knowing matters. Much of the work on skills, however, tends to focus on categorization, which I do not find very fruitful in analysis here as such lists can easily become unwieldy. However, Kirlin's four dominant skills categories (2003) do provide a usable framework, which I loosely adopt in how I operationalize *know-how* for analytical purposes.

Kirlin identifies four dominant categories of skills: organization, communication, collective decision-making, and critical thinking, found in the work of civic engagement, education, political and social science, and psychology scholars who have described some type of civic skill observed in their research (2003). Based on a tabulation from existing research, Kirlin's categories begins to move toward conceptualization of a factor that can be used in contentious collective politics theory-making and empirical analysis, providing for this book, in particular, the contours of a workable framework that eschews skills categorization as its focus. As Kirlin's work highlights, a growing attention to civic skills is developing, which is creating new sets of questions about the role these skills play in enhancing democracy, particularly as it relates to the types of activities that take place beyond and between the vote and their effects on government, specifically in contentious collective politics.

One Final Piece of the Story

So far I have highlighted, in broad strokes, the story of some of the more mainstream academic and professional/practice-oriented theories and ideas created to date that has sought to better understand what it is that public leaders know how to do when challenging for social justice change within collectives. This is a story that is still under development as we continuously strive to understand human actions better, but it is a story that has been overly influenced by the limiting framework of a rationalistic worldview, both in our daily social understanding as well in our academic and professional applications.[30] As I alluded before, developing and using *know-how* as a viable analytical concept and capacity-development tool requires that we "walk out" of the ideas of rational action and enter in the conceptually "bigger box" that Lichterman offers (2020). The "bigger box" that both Lichterman's Civic Action Theory (2020) and Fligstein and McAdam's SAF theory (2012) offer relies on the pragmatist tradition that dates back to the turn of the 20th century, punctuated by John Dewey's later works. Without going too deeply into all of the contours of this body of work, I will highlight below some of the key ideas from this tradition that help provide a broader conceptual framework from which *know-how* is developed and applied.

A key underlying idea that differs greatly between rational and pragmatist perspectives has to do with how knowledge works and what it is that we think constitutes true knowledge. In the pragmatist view, knowing something about what is to be done in a given situation relies both on whatever formal knowledge has been gained (think of passed down knowledge, such as that found in books and training manuals) and what has been practiced in a setting that is similar to the one in which action is set to occur. Here, there are two key ideas conveyed that represent major departures from the rational action view, the idea that knowledge from practice is knowledge at all and the idea that location has something to do with knowledge. Consider it this way when thinking about public leaders; the more depth and breadth of experiences a public leader has in a particular field, the greater the potential for higher degrees of *know-how* development relative to the particular field in which that public leader is engaged. Broadly speaking, this means that once a public leader is exposed to some form of formal/static knowledge about what she needs to know to act, *know-how* then develops in practice in the place where she acts. I will explore in more detail below how these views on knowledge support the development of *know-how* as a concept, but first consider the following example about sports.

Let's consider the *know-how* that a professional basketball player possesses after several years in a professional league. This *know-how* will have developed generally by degrees via practice in the professional league setting in which he has now spent several years. When this same player entered this professional league, his *know-how* of basketball was considerable yet insufficient for this particular league. Why would this be so? Similar to our *know-how* in changing tires, his *know-how* had some of the transferrable knowledge but none of the applicable knowledge to the new situation. We knew enough about what it takes to change a tire with our personal vehicle-based *know-how*, but this wasn't completely transferrable to more complicated types of vehicles. The same applies to the basketball players' *know-how*, as well as to management *know-how*, teaching *know-how*, political *know-how*, and so forth.

When this same professional basketball player was in high school, his level of *know-how* of high school basketball as a senior was far greater than it was as a freshman. However, when this same basketball player joined a university team, he found his high school-based *know-how* suddenly insufficient for university-based basketball. Only through practical application at the university level, both through the team practices and the official games, did he gain the additional contours of knowledge that would be required for him to further increase his level of *know-how* until such time it became sufficient for it to serve him well in meaningful games. Following this example of *know-how* brings to mind the practical wisdom described by Aristotle as *phronesis*, which I incorporate in a brief discussion of knowledge below that brings in other thinkers on how a different way of knowing must inform our analysis and practice of public leadership.

The first launching point is the pragmatist tradition's development of the idea of public leaders' social knowledge in political action, which asserts that there is a socially developed knowing or knowledge that actors involved in political action use to inform decision-making within the fields and arenas in which they operate. This type of knowing, which Fligstein and McAdam term social skills in SAF theory (2012), is what I offer should be understood as part of what helps develop the *know-how* I operationalize below and use in the analysis chapters. In the pragmatist tradition, knowledge development occurs dynamically among public leaders engaged in social action, a key idea developed by John Dewey (2016, 2017) that has been explored in the sociology of knowledge and philosophical literature that informs this book (Colapietro, 2009; Douglas & Wykowski, 2011; Emirbayer & Maynard, 2011; Gross, 2009; Kilpinen, 2009; Levine, 2007; Pedwell, 2017; Romania, 2013).

Let me begin by saying that the academic debate on what constitutes knowledge is a centuries-old debate that remains heated to this day. I certainly will not presume to answer what constitutes knowledge in any definitive manner in this book, but I do decidedly embrace the side of the debate that argues for the inclusion of embodied, practice-based knowledge as equally meaningful to other forms of championed knowledge.[31] At the heart of this debate is the issue of the nature of knowledge and whether human beings have the ability to acquire true knowledge, or how human beings can and do acquire such knowledge, as compared to attaining false knowledge (Douglas & Wykowski, 2011; Emirbayer & Maynard, 2011; Kilpinen, 2009; Kuklick, 1983; McCarthy, 2000; Romania, 2013). Pragmatists such as Dewey definitively sided against traditional philosophical views, which maintained the abstract Kantian-Platonic conceptualization in which knowledge exists in its truest form outside of human consciousness (2016, 2017).[32] For Dewey, knowledge can be created in a given social setting arising out of action created specifically to meet the needs of that time and location (2016, 2017), an idea he recognized as having practical implications for the maintenance of democracy via political participation and action.

If knowledge in its truest form is something that exists outside the everyday person's ability to grasp, as was and continues to be held in the classical view of knowledge that still influences contemporary thinking, then democracy indeed requires the development of "experts" who develop such knowledge in societies where democratic governance grows in complexity if it is to succeed into the future.[33] The intellectual influence of these traditional assumptions on knowledge can be seen in how political engagement outside traditional, legitimate governance channels, processes, and structures was originally perceived in the social sciences in the United States as a behavioral issue.

Dewey's challenge to traditionalist perspectives on knowledge established a counter view that proposed that knowledge was contextual, situated in social experiences both temporally and spatially, and arising primarily out of social action (Baranowski, 2019; Colapietro, 2009; Dewey, 2016, 2017; Gross, 2009; Joas, 1996; Lichterman, 2020). Such a view provided the foundation for ideas about the social construction of knowledge in everyday life that would become the focus of social science interested in how human beings develop the needed knowledge to participate in society in such a way as to contribute to the maintenance of social order.[34] Of course, such view of knowledge as socially constructed has implications for what anyone, not just the elite "experts," involved in political processes and activities know, how they come to know it, and how such knowing gets deployed in political action. Dewey elaborated the implications of this view on politics by conceptualizing the "public as the permanent space of contingency in the sense that there can be no a priori delimitation, except as it emerges from individuals and groups that coalesce in the service of problem solving" (2016).

From this view, people involved in political action are more than simple recipients of the socially constrained possibilities afforded by the social structures in which they live and instead are themselves creators of the knowledge they deploy in action. Training by IAF exemplifies this idea. In both instances in which I participated in IAF training with a group of strangers, we were given a reading that we were tasked to read before arriving to the training. No instructions were given beyond simply to read the material. In our very first session, after reviewing basic administrative and group facilitation information, as well as introducing ourselves, we were randomly ordered into three groups, the Melians, the Athenians, and the Chorus. For a quick refresher, the Melian Dialogue tells the story of how the Melians came to be destroyed by the Athenians.

Our facilitator, in both trainings (which were not conducted by the same group of people, nor were these trainings related to each other organizationally in any fashion beyond the fact that both were IAF based), offered one simple rule, which was that he, as facilitator, had the power to do as he wished. After stating this, he simply said, "begin," without any instructions, no explanations, no rundown of how we were supposed to engage the material. In both trainings, I noticed the same pattern appear. People were left confused, prompting someone in each group to begin to ask about what to do, which in turn led to idea generation about what the instructor wanted, which in turn led to various discussions about potential actions. As individuals surfaced who demonstrated some ability to lead the group toward some clear action, another instructor would pull that person out of the room. This repeated itself over three cycles, and in both experiences, at least one of the three groups decided to change the narrative of the exercise by the third cycle, going so far as to physically hold on to the colleague who was being asked to leave the room.

I share this example of how IAF typically begins their training of lay organizers to highlight how IAF wants individuals to understand that they have the ability to act creatively and change the direction of action, even if such direction breaks from established norms. Of course, IAF wants public leaders to also understand that forging new paths comes with the real risk of bodily removal, which the act of pulling a person from the room signified. This example highlights what Dewey understood about the political arena, that there are ever-present opportunities to forge new paths, and that people involved in collective action typically do just that.

In conceptualizing *know-how*, I also include other thinkers who complement Dewey's perspectives on knowledge, specifically Pierre Bourdieu's theory of practice (1977), Michael Cowan's description of practical wisdom (2017), and Jason Stanley's (2011a, 2011b) philosophical argument for *knowing (how)*.[35]

While Bourdieu's theory of practice differs from the Deweysian pragmatist tradition in many respects, upon closer inspection, his concepts of *habitus*, capital, and field articulate similar concepts found in pragmatist thinking (Bourdieu, 1977; Power, 1999).[36] For both Bourdieu and the pragmatist tradition, knowledge arises out of socially circumscribed spaces (Bourdieu's field concept) from-and-in which actors are habituated (creating Bourdieu's *habitus*) with the knowledge that exists in these spaces and through which actors can then interact and potentially contribute to the creation of new knowledge through action, which in Bourdieu's theory is aided by the accumulation of what Bourdieu terms social and/or cultural capital (Bourdieu, 1977; Power, 1999).

Knowledge, then, arises out of practice, out of the habituated ways in which individuals interact within a circumscribed social space (which SAF theory calls fields) that offers shared habituation among those who also live, work, and participate within shared social spaces.[37] Such a view on knowledge is echoed by Cowan's description of practical wisdom and Stanley's concept of *knowing (how)*. For Cowan, in particular, his research on barrier-crossing leaders shows that these individuals rely on a practical wisdom that the leaders developed through practice (2017). This practical wisdom gained from "doing" action in the world, Cowan asserts, is the equivalent of what is often recognized as expertise in more academically oriented, abstract knowledge (2017). Drawing a direct connection to ancient views on knowledge, Cowan establishes practical wisdom as the equivalent of Aristotle's "wise actor" or *phronesis* knowledge, which is a type of knowledge that arises out of "the particulars" that comes from doing, or acting, in the world. Such knowledge is different from *theoria*, which for Aristotle is "about knowing, not doing" as compared to *phronesis*, which is "the kind of knowing based in experience that makes it possible to act well."

A similar assertion is made by Jason Stanley (2011a, 2011b), who makes a philosophical argument for an elevated recognition of *knowing (how)*, which is the equivalent of the pragmatists' practice-based knowledge from action, Bourdieu's theory of practice, and Cowan's practical wisdom. For Stanley, there is a type of knowledge about *knowing (how)* to do something that individuals develop by doing, which is the equivalent of the *knowing-what* type of knowledge learned from intellectual endeavors (2011a, 2011b). The development of *knowing (how)* takes place in practice, in doing, and through this doing, an individual increases his knowledge about this doing (which includes trial and error, accumulation of information, evaluation, and integration of new knowledge), which Stanley explains as occurring beyond simply being able to explain how to do something. That is to say, one can certainly learn how to explain how to do something (as many millions of textbooks and how-to guides attest) by simply observing and reading, but this is not the equivalent of the type of knowledge possessed in *knowing (how)* to do something from practice (2011a, 2011b).

Let's talk basketball again. If you have watched a full game of basketball, then you have come away with the basics of the game; dribble the ball on a court with two baskets and try to get the ball in the basket designated for you or your team while the other player or team tries to stop you. Knowing these basics allows you to explain the game, but this small amount of explanatory *know-how* cannot help you much when you step onto a basketball court for the first time. In this regard, Stanley echoes a key idea expressed by the pragmatists about an actors' actions as key to development of the type of knowledge that becomes the practical wisdom Cowan describes, which is also echoed in SAF theory, Civic Action Theory, community organizing texts, and other sources discussed so far.

These views on knowledge, with an emphasis on actor habituation through practice (or what has been termed *doing* or *action*, depending on the description or theory), imply that existing models of the rational actor do not suffice when considering how individuals engage politically and how they bring and deploy *know-how* (as conceptualized below) in their interactions. Dewey recognized this issue and established that actors involved in political action cannot be properly understood under the traditional utilitarian model of rational choice, an argument supported in works that continue to develop the pragmatist view today, found more often in cultural sociology literature (Jasper, 2005; Johnston & Klandermans, 1995; Smilde, 2007, 2013). For Dewey, public leaders involved in political action don't necessarily operate through rational choice-making, as per the traditional model of human action but rather with what he terms an "end-in-view" approach that incorporates a public leader's creativity and a situation's contingency into the development of knowledge-based decision-making (Colapietro, 2009; de Souza Briggs, 2008; Dewey, 2016, 2017; Gross, 2009; Joas, 1996; Kilpinen, 2009; Lichterman, 2020; Rogers, 2016; Ron, 2008).

This form of knowledge through action, which Dewey termed habituation and which Bourdieu termed *habitus*, asserts that there is a type of embodiment of knowledge that can be conceptualized for analysis, such as the "embodied" knowledge actors use in political actions.[38] Embodiment of knowledge in this sense includes both knowledge obtained through habits, or habituation, what is known typically as socialization in sociology, which reflects both temporal and spatial values, and meaning arising from the locations where individuals develop socially and engage politically.

Embodied knowledge also means that individuals create concepts through action (or practice, or doing) that enable them to "relate to the world" and "confront dilemmas in the process of life," developing what Smilde terms an imaginative rationality (2007), which echoes Cowan's practical wisdom, Bourdieu's *habitus*, and Stanley's *knowing (how)*. Additionally, Smilde's idea of confronting dilemmas in the process of life as a way of developing knowledge upholds Dewey's idea of creative problem-solving in political action, which sees actors as actively working out solutions to problems for which they have no prior experience or knowledge (Colapietro, 2009; Dewey, 2016, 2017; Emirbayer & Maynard, 2011; Joas, 1996). Through this view, then, one can begin to perceive how a collective can be guided in its actions by the accumulation of embodied social and political knowledge within its leaders.

Such a view of knowledge can be critiqued as being made intelligible only when seen, creating a *"you'll-know-it-when-you-see-it"* dilemma. To the rational model view, this type of knowing appears teleological, becoming unusable. Such a critique reflects the challenges to more widespread usage of this view of knowledge in theory development and empirical studies in the social sciences, particularly in literature that focuses on political participation, of any sort. The effort remains a challenge precisely because the very critique of practice-based knowledge as being teleological misses the very argument the pragmatists and other thinkers and researchers offer.

It would appear, from a classical (rational) view of human agency, that such knowledge development is dependent completely on utilitarian ends. In other words, when applied directly to the field data analyzed in this book, it would appear we can only know such knowledge when we see it in successful outcome attainment. Thus, pragmatists are typically misinterpreted as offering a *"we'll-know-it-when-we-see-it"* type of conceptualization of practice-based knowledge, when in fact pragmatists offer a much more robust understanding of knowledge that relies on comparison to distinguish degrees of knowing.[39]

Such a critique misses several key ideas developed within the pragmatist tradition and in community organizing practice that offer other contributing phenomena to the type of knowledge this study argues helps develop *know-how*. The first of these ideas is the social nature of such knowledge, which implicates a learning from practice-in-place (Berger & Luckman, 1966; Bourdieu, 1977, 1992; Cowan, 2017; Dewey, 2016, 2017; Lichterman, 2020; Smilde, 2007). This means that there is a reciprocal relationship between place (or the field, as described in SAF theory, which itself is borrowed from Bourdieu's idea) and actor, and as such the knowledge that is deployed is less end-related and more context-related, something Lichterman asserts is a key element missing in traditional contentious collective politics that his Civic Action Theory offers (2020).

Another key idea often not considered, but certainly developed within the pragmatist tradition, is that this type of knowledge is created from experience, from the practice-in-place mentioned above, and as such includes episodes of practice in which development of the knowledge arose from failure (Alinsky, 1946, p. 1072; Chambers, 2003; Cowan, 2017; Dewey, 2016, 2017; Joas, 1996; Stanley, 2011a, 2011b). Failure, in this conceptualization of knowledge, is just as much a great developer of new knowledge as success, and as such undermines any teleological critique as it is not so much the outcome that matters in trying to understand when and how actors deploy this type of knowing, or practical wisdom, but the actual deployment of this knowledge in action, which is why Lichterman argues we need to "follow the action" (2020) to better understand how actors interact in contentious collective politics.

Thirdly, a key idea often missed is how knowledge of this type, once developed out of practice-in-place, can be transformed (and often is, but not always) into social knowledge that transcends specific fields. This is precisely what practice-based authors involved in community organizing attempt to do when they write books that try to capture and disseminate the knowledge they have gained from practice by distilling this into transferrable lessons that can be "taught" to others in different fields but who are engaged in similar endeavors.[40] What makes it possible for such knowledge to be transferrable in this same way? I argue that it is our ability to discern commonalities across fields. Remember the tire-changing *know-how* that you have and how you may have assumed its ease of transferability until you were asked to help change the tire of an airplane? Well, part of your tire-changing *know-how* was certainly transferrable; it just wasn't sufficient for the new application, or new field, if you will, of airplane tires.

In IAF's community organizing world, the tactic of using one-on-one meetings to ascertain enlightened self-interest in potential political action-oriented relationships is viewed as a key tactic that can be taught to others wanting to engage in political contention, no matter where they live in the world.[41] Trainers in IAF teach others how to conduct one-on-one meetings, transferring what they can that corresponds to the static aspect of that knowledge, but it is up to the recipients of this transferred knowledge to turn it into their own *know-how* through practice. In this regard, once again, deployment of this type of knowledge is less dependent on a desired end if it is to be understood or perceived but instead relies on the ability to understand how such knowledge is created and practiced in particular spaces.

Lastly, another key idea offered in this view of knowledge that also undermines any teleological critique involves the modeling of actors. As discussed above, the works explored in this section agree that the traditional modeling of human agency via rational choice concepts acts as a hindrance to our abilities to understand and explain what public leaders do, and know how to do, in contentious collective politics (of any type, from local neighborhood association battles with city hall to large-scale social movements). Teleological concerns arise when this type of knowledge fails to make sense in the rational actor model view. Knowledge can be (and is) created without clarity of ends, and as discussed above, such knowledge created out of practice-in-place can be (and is) then transferred by other actors across fields not for the purposes of achieving a political end in its own right but for the purpose of increasing the capacity of others so these others can then act accordingly within their own fields. Certainly, there can be some degree of *desired-ends* style of calculation in the decisions actors involved in contentious collective politics make, but this is not always the case, which the rational actor model fails to recognize.

For example, in a scenario I describe in one of the data analysis chapters, an organized group finds itself involved in work that was not on their radar but which nonetheless required action once it was presented to them. What action was required and for what purpose was complex and contested, and particular to each member of the group, but collectively they formulated a shared set of actions that needed to be undertaken, regardless of particular ends desired by individual members. And it is the intellectual and empirical work conducted in the pragmatist tradition that most directly provides the foundation for developing *know-how* as a concept that can be applied within contingent scenarios and interactions.

The Rest of This Book

While I specifically focus on developing *know-how* in more detail in the next chapter, this section has begun to lay the groundwork by highlighting some of the more general contours. First, conceptualization of *know-how* requires its differentiation from the concept of *knowing what*. All *know-how* is practice-based, while *knowing what* is more abstract, generally.[42] This is important to note because conceptualization here does not constitute incontrovertible truths, but rather rules of thumb that appear often enough to warrant conceptualization for the purposes of observation, analysis, understanding, and explanation. Now, because *know-how* is practice-based, this does not mean that some aspect of the development of *know-how* cannot be abstract. This is exactly why community organizing practitioners write books about their work, and precisely why the IAF has developed an entire epistemology about how political action *know-how* can be transferred from those who have more of it to those who have less of it via formal and informal training mechanisms.

Public leaders' *know-how* can be assisted via formal and informal training, *a la* IAF, for example, and more acutely developed in practice, becoming embodied creative knowledge and/or practical wisdom that can be deployed in dynamic situations. Additionally, *know-how* occurs in degrees, with more depth and breadth of practical experiences generally contributing to more *know-how* (though not 100% of the time, as there can be many instances in which actors simply fail to learn from their actions). The field in which public leaders are engaged, as well, contributes generally to the degree of *know-how* an individual or a group develops relative to the field in which they operate, as we learned in the tire-changing and basketball examples.

In the following chapter, titled **Dimensions of *Know-How***, I fully develop the concept into an operationalized variable that can be used within existing theoretical frameworks that focus on social action or as a stand-alone factor that researchers may be interested in exploring further. Practitioners are encouraged to explore this chapter to gain a fuller understanding of how the concept can be applied to practice but can certainly skip to the final chapter segment that focuses on practice-based considerations. This chapter is then followed by four data analysis chapters that explore each of the four dimensions of *know-how* developed here. In **Knowing the Field**, I analyze how public leaders' *know-how* about the field in which they engaged in New Orleans interacted with their abilities to achieve their desired contentious collective politics. In **Getting Others to Act**, I analyze aspects of social *know-how* and how these interacted with their abilities to achieve their desired contentious collective politics. In **No Directions Given**, I analyze strategic *know-how* and how this shows up in contentious collective politics. In the final data analysis chapter, titled **Without Clear Roles and Processes, They Suffer**. I analyze how operational *know-how* interacted with public leaders' abilities to achieve their desired contentious collective politics outcomes. A concluding chapter offers points for further discussion and application for both academia and the practice-oriented world.

A Final Note About Names

The original names of individuals and their organizations are protected via pseudonyms and other relevant changes designed to protect interviewed subjects, as set forth in the original Institutional Review Board (IRB) approval. There are instances where the provision of pseudonyms was not used, such as the naming of actual laws and policies passed in the State of Louisiana and/or the City of New Orleans. I also opted to identify the New Orleans area field in which post-Katrina activities took place rather than creating a fictional space, as this detail was necessary for situating analysis in a field known to have been disrupted by a major climate event and human-made disaster. In all interview content quoted in this study, I served as the interviewer, and as such, I am labeled by my actual name "Lucas." Additionally, in recounting events in which I participated as a complete member fellow advocate, I make every attempt to refrain from identifying any particular individual in order to protect former colleagues who may not have been contacted for this study. If individuals are named in recalled events who were not interviewed, such as an interviewee recalling an interaction with another person whom I did not contact, pseudonyms are applied.

Notes

1. I use autoethnographic methods (Anderson, 2006b), specifically complete member and automethodological ethnographic methodology (Pensoneau-Conway & Toyosaki, 2011; Toyosaki, 2011) to inform the data I analyze in the study I conducted.
2. See Frederick D. Weil's "Rise of Community Organizations, Citizen Engagement, and New Institutions," in *Resilience and Opportunity: Lessons from the U.S. Gulf Coast after Katrina and Rita*, pp. 201–219 for a discussion of this widespread "activation" across New Orleans neighborhoods.
3. According to demographer Elizabeth Fussell, Latinx newcomer immigrants comprised over 40% of the post-Katrina Latinx workforce that arrived to help clean up and then rebuild the city (see Fussell & Diaz, 2015).
4. The Industrial Areas Foundation (IAF) is a national community organizing group in the United States that dates back to labor organizing traditions out of Chicago in the 1940 and 1950s. Founded by Saul Alinsky, IAF has trained professional community organizers, developed an organizing methodology and epistemology, and has served as one of the major influencing organizations on subsequent US-based community organizing groups, such as ACORN, Gamaliel, and PICO. Notable leaders trained by IAF include Cesar Chavez and President Barak Obama (see https://www.industrialareasfoundation.org/history for a brief history of this organization).
5. This phrasing refers to decisions made by governance entities or their designees (such as quasi-government bodies or even private institutions acting on behalf of government) that decide on the distribution of public goods for a given location. As such, the term is inclusive of local, state, and federal decision-making spaces wherever public goods are at stake, but it can also include corporate decision-

making when it involves commercial control of public goods, such as is the case with energy companies.
6. I use the term contentious collective politics as a broad concept that includes all types of groups involved in contentious activities that challenge public decision-making, but with a focus on unarmed struggle for change conducted via political activities that take place outside the normative electoral processes of the United States. Examples of groups that engage in contentious collective politics includes social movements, local associational groups, advocacy coalitions, and other similar collectives of individuals and organizations at local, regional, or national levels, and even organized units of people within a company.
7. I use the term capacity here as an attempt to capture expertise variances, be they internal to an individual or a group. A group with people who have high capacity in political activities has more knowledge and experience than a group with novice levels of capacity. This is akin to a person with expert-level communications skills having more communications acumen than someone with little to no such skills. The word capacity is also standing in for the concept of *know-how*, which I introduce below.
8. I will develop the concept in more detail in the next chapter, but it is important to note here that I couch the concept as a tool that can be applied to Fligstein and McAdam's Strategic Action Fields theory, described in *A Theory of Fields* in any form of collective contention, from social movements to interorganizational units.
9. This sentence relies on a combination of social sciences theories that I discuss further below.
10. Dyke and Dixon assert that social movement literature until this 2013 publication had historically neglected how actors acquire skills. As I show below, skills are part of the acquisition process through which public leaders develop *know-how*.
11. I use the phrase public leader to broadly denote people engaged in activities that will result in some form of public good rather than some form of direct personal gain. While this book does not dive into what can and cannot be considered a public leader, a good place to explore how public leadership is viewed academically is the *International Journal of Public Leadership* which sees public leadership similarly in that public leaders can be found in government, corporations, civic associations, churches, neighborhoods, and everywhere else people are working together to achieve a public good.
12. I relied on Google's free, public-use AI language model called Bard to help me locate the earliest recorded usage of the phrase *know-how* in the United States.
13. As the literature points out, active citizenship does not mean having legal status within a given nation-state, and instead refers to the active participation of a person in all aspects of political life, both electoral and nonelectoral.
14. I discuss levels in the next chapter, but as a way of introducing this idea, consider that *know-how* can be acquired at very novice levels, and it can be developed into more robust expert-like levels.
15. The following section focuses primarily on sociology and political science contributions. Contributions from other disciplines are explored further below.
16. This type of analysis focuses on large-scale social structures, such as governance units or governance types, or large social movements in which thousands of people are involved, allowing for sufficient scale to which macro analysis can be

applied. As such, analysis of smaller scale collective contention became relegated to civic studies, as both sociology and political science tended to focus primarily on large social movements between the 1960s and 1990s.
17. See Hans Joas' exploration of the rational action model and its influence on social movement theory in *The Creativity of Action* (1996), which I rely on for an understanding of this trajectory.
18. This move was not just about shifting toward micro, or individual, analysis but also about bringing in a cultural analytical lens to collective contention that came out of what is now known as the cultural turn in sociology. As the phrase implies, the cultural turn brought more cultural analytical lenses to bear on all aspects of social life. For an explanation of the cultural turn in social movement theory, see Jasper, 2005.
19. This statement does not exclude the possibility that there are instances in which contentious collectives achieve their desired outcomes almost as if by luck, when there is little to no evidence of the types of *know-how* this study argues plays a role in a group's success or failure. However, it should be noted that fortuitous circumstances should be considered the exception if efforts by contentious collectives are to be viewed as possessing any form of intentionality in the decisions and activities they undertake (which has been the view of scholarship since the 1970s).
20. The dynamic interaction approach, first espoused by McAdam et al. (2001), has continued to be applied and developed in various studies, with three of these theoretical efforts (described below) within the last 10 years moving closer to connecting what actors know, which I use for conceptualization of *know-how* in this book.
21. This is also an assertion made by Fligstein and McAdam in SAF theory.
22. See Lichterman's introduction chapter for an in-depth discussion of his focus on civic action in collective contention as constitutive of this bigger box, which is able to include actors' abilities in analysis of meso-level processes.
23. The rational action model was initially developed in Western Europe during the Enlightenment and further solidified in usage during the industrial revolution and then becoming foundational in the rise of capitalism in western societies. See Hans Joas' 1996 work (cited above) for a detailed exploration of rational thought in the development of our understanding of human action and the limitations such thinking has created in our ability to better understand creative action.
24. I believe that Lichterman simply missed how the pragmatist perspective informs SAF theory.
25. The term *civic skills* in this study is not synonymous with *know-how*. As discussed further below, attainment of civic skills contributes to the development of *know-how*.
26. For example, articulating predictive social movement theoretical models based on linear causal factors has been a mainstay of contentious politics research (McAdam et al., 2001; Opp, 2009; Tarrow, 2011). In contentious collective outcomes scholarship, much of it has focused on identifying and predicting causal links among political activity, structural factors, and outcomes with the bulk of this research dedicated to policy changes, such as new policy creation, removal, or revision (Amenta et al., 2010; Arce et al., 2019; Bosi et al., 2016; Bosi & Uba, 2009; Gamson, 1990; Giugni, 1998; Silva, 2015).

27. See Alinsky, 1946, 1972; Chambers, 2003 for the tactics and strategies professional organizers use to build an organized body of people; Beckwith and Lopez, 2013 for the organizational/institutional strategies and tactics required for building power; Gecan, 2002 for how professional organizing work achieves change in local communities; and Alinsky, 1972; Chambers, 2003; Garza, 2020; Freire, 2005 for explorations of specific concepts requiring attention in teaching and learning about how to build power.
28. See Andrews & Edwards, 2004 for an exploration of the types of policy processes advocacy organizations participate in and what organizational skills they bring to the effort; see Gamson, 1990 for what group strategies are connected to outcome success; see Ganz, 2009 for how professional community organizers conduct their work differently from union organizers in achieving change, and see Warren, 2001 for how professional organizing can help strengthen democracy at the community level.
29. For example, see Bingham et al., 2005; Fung, 2004; Lafont, 2015; Ryfe, 2002; Yang & Pandey, 2011 for explorations of increasing opportunities for civic participation in governance decision-making, and see Agre, 2004; Boyte, 2000, 2004, 2005; Carpini et al., 2004; Chambers & Kymlicka, 2002; Cohen & Arato, 1992; Cuthill & Fien, 2005; Dahlgren, 2006; Edwards, 2014; Kirlin, 2003; Van Dyke & Dixon, 2013 for explorations of the various skills and aptitudes that individuals use to engage in any form of civic activity that has a public good as its rationale.
30. See my earlier comments about rationality's role in shaping our understanding of human action, and in particular Hans Joas' 1996 work.
31. I will dive a bit deeper into what this means below.
32. See Hans Joas for an excellent analysis of this argument. Also consider de Freitas, 2020; Douglas & Wykowski, 2011; Emirbayer & Maynard, 2011; Kilpinen, 2009; Romania, 2013 for discussions of this topic.
33. This idea of experts to make democracy work was championed by one of the fathers of sociology, Max Weber (1946). See also (Dewey, 2016, 2017; Douglas & Wykowski, 2011; Emirbayer & Maynard, 2011; Kilpinen, 2009; Levine, 2007; McCarthy, 2000; Romania, 2013) for more discussion on this matter.
34. There is rich literature in sociology that explores the idea of knowledge as being developed out of practice, or habit. See Berger & Luckman, 1966; Bourdieu, 1992; Douglas & Wykowski, 2011; Levine, 2007; McCarthy, 2000 as good places to start.
35. Stanley offers the term *knowing (how)* in a 2011 article titled "Knowing (How)" but then later amends this term to *Know how* in a book titled *Know How* also published in 2011. I use his original term *knowing (how)* to differentiate his explanation from my concept of *know-how* throughout this paper.
36. See Gross, 2010 for an exploration of this.
37. Consider the idea of the American dream in the United States as the kind of cultural knowledge that 300+ million people share who live their lives within the confines of US society. Here, the socially circumscribed space is both temporal and spatial, as ideas about the American dream and what it points to have basic similarities across the United States, but with variations according to time and place. By simply living within the United States, an individual "picks up" this knowledge (which can be acquired through social interactions, content reading in

books, cultural reproductions in the arts, social media content, or other forms of communication).
38. See Bourdieu, 1977; Dewey, 2016, 2017; Emirbayer & Maynard, 2011; Fourcade, 2010; Smilde, 2007 for discussions on embodied knowledge.
39. See Joas, in particular for a robust discussion of the nonteleological framing of the pragmatist view.
40. See books by Alinsky, 1946, 1972; Chambers, 2003; Cowan, 2017; Ganz, 2009; Garza, 2020; Gecan, 2002; Warren, 2001; Whitman, 2018 as good places to start.
41. The concept of enlightened self-interest is also referred to as common self-interest, an idea developed by Dewey and other pragmatist thinkers that influenced Alinsky, who taught it as the type of interest that enables human beings to work together through each other's shared enlightened self-interests, those interests that move beyond the private and into the public, which generally imply a benefit to all, or to the common, rather than to a single person.
42. See Stanley's 2011a, 2011b article and book for a more thorough philosophical articulation of this difference.

Chapter 2

Dimensions of *Know-How*

Is It Public, or Is It Private?

Before diving into the heart of this chapter, I would like to discuss a critical lesson that serves as one of the foundational concepts for community organizers in the Industrial Areas Foundation (IAF) tradition – the idea that humans have private and public relationships. In the IAF tradition, public/private relationship is a linchpin concept that both professional and lay organizers are taught. Why is this concept so important to them and why bring this up here? And more importantly, what do they mean when they teach people to distinguish between private and public lives? Let's imagine a scenario together to get us to a shared understanding.

You're a housing coalition representative who goes often to local government public meetings because your work requires you interact with officials about various housing-related issues. Your advocacy has often led you to lunch meetings with one decision-maker, in particular. The lunch meetings have been very fruitful, giving you a platform to educate the individual on a key policy solution that your coalition has been advocating for more than a year. However, this same decision-maker has been very astute, often asking you to rethink a component of your collective's policy, or asking for additional research, and so forth. You begin to suspect that some form of stalling tactic is being deployed, so you decide that for your next lunch meeting, you will confront this person about that. When the meeting comes, you do confront the decision-maker, making him visibly uncomfortable. He changes the subject and makes any talk about policy reform impossible. At the next public meeting, he avoids looking at you and thereafter ignores your phone calls, effectively ending the lunch meetings. What do you think happened?

This sort of situation happens often in contentious collective politics, leaving organized groups to dissect such moments for clues when answers aren't being freely offered. Much of the interactions between groups who push for change and public decision-makers often create similar challenging situations. In an IAF training session, such a scenario would be acted out in a role-play exercise and then debriefed to use the experience to elucidate the idea that two relationships were at play, one private and one public. The public relationship was the one established at public meetings, in which both the advocate and the public official fully understood that their interactions with each other were of the public variety. At the lunch meetings, however, it becomes questionable as to whether the same public relationship remained intact for either of the individuals. It could be that at least for one of the individuals the relationship was friendlier, and thus, perhaps in transition from public to private.

We can't say for certain, but what we can say from the scenario is that either one or both individuals mistook the lunch meeting to be a "safe" space. In other words, a space in which the challenges of the public meeting, and therefore the very public interactions between the two, could be put to the side, which would explain why the public official was willing to listen, learn, and ask questions but not act on demands. What I hope should begin to surface is that public and private relationships operate on two different modalities. In the IAF tradition, these two different modalities exist at opposite ends of a logic continuum. On one end of the continuum sits the private relationship with its desire for affection, intimacy, and friendship. On the other end of the continuum sits the public relationship with its need to establish boundaries and social order through transactional exchanges. It doesn't necessarily matter from an analysis perspective if it was the public official or the advocate who thought they were in a less public relationship mode during the lunch meetings. What is clear from the example is that one of them, if not both of them, confused these two modalities, and when this presumed but unreflected shift in the relationship was challenged by the advocate, the public official retreated.

This distinction in the two types of relationships we encounter is critical not just to organizers and advocates in the field but to academic analysis, as well. As an academic analyst, we must understand this distinction and approach our observations of social life with clarity on the matter. Chantal Mouffe established that an analytical distinction between private (individual liberty) and public (republic goals and needs) life exists that must be considered when discussing public life, democracy, and the public good (1991). The concept of individuals living a public versus a private life has a history in sociology (Sennett, 1977; Smelser, 1963), but it is the IAF's epistemology that I rely on the most in conceptualizing and operationalizing *know-how* for analytical usage. For the IAF, understanding the differences between one's public and private relationships meaningfully serves as a tool that professional and lay organizers can use to maximize effectiveness in political action by ensuring that all actions in public life are undertaken in line with public life logics (Alinsky, 1946, 1972; Chambers, 2003).

In teaching this to lay and professional organizers, IAF leaders hope to diminish the pitfalls that many first-time advocates experience when engaging in political action equipped only with the social norms and practices learned from private life. This intentional training signifies the IAF's epistemological position that individual actors can develop the needed knowledge and abilities (and contribute to an individual developing a type of social *know-how* that I describe below) via intentional training designed to give them the tools they can use in practice. By problematizing and conceptualizing *know-how* in contentious collective politics by first establishing this distinction, I can then focus on how public leaders engaged in contentious collective politics deploy *know-how* in public life as a distinct phenomenon that does not necessarily equate with what may or may not happen in one's private life.

Professional organizers trained by Alinsky and his subsequent protégés in the United States understood this distinction, perceiving that action in public life was like art, one that required not only formal training but training through practice in actual public activities in which the stakes extend beyond personal or individual gain. This view aligns with both Dewey and Joas' views on how creativity is involved in political action (Dewey, 2016, 2017; Joas, 1996).[1] For example, IAF encourages its trained organizers to practice countless cycles of relationship building, followed by research, public action, then evaluation (win or lose) as key to improving effectiveness as organizers, and as instrumental to developing *know-how* in collective power-building techniques and strategies. As I've highlighted so far, the concept of *know-how* expands on concepts of skills, such as Strategic Action Field's (SAF's) concept of social skill, which is too limiting a concept for the purposes of analysis. The concept of *know-how*, as I highlighted earlier, implies a combination of knowledge about something and knowledge about how to do something in its given context, which is developed from both abstract knowledge and practical experience in a socially circumscribed place. Additionally, developing *know-how* involves a certain amount of creativity, as it is through exploration of new solutions for given circumstances that gives rise to new actions.

Creativity, Fluidity, and Power Positions in the Fields

Creativity enters this process when organizers continue to evolve their levels of *know-how* through practice, with each unique instance presenting an opportunity to confront the limits of their *know-how* and from that limit create solutions for a given circumstance that then becomes part of a person's toolbox for future application (Dewey, 2016, 2017; Joas, 1996).[2] This is the same process we discussed earlier with the basketball player or the tire-changing person. In the instance of being confronted with a scenario in which *know-how* proves to be insufficient, we create new *know-how* through our own practice in that given situation, sometimes in a single moment or other times over a long period of practice. In this way, *know-how* can be viewed as a factor in public life that can be applied in a given field and that can creatively emerge from application in a given field.

If you recall, in SAF theory, a field is a social arena in both temporal and spatial sense. In making *know-how* an analyzable factor, it must be operationalized as something particular to the observed time and space in which the *know-how* is being deployed. In other words, the *know-how* that public leaders deploy in each field can best be understood within the context of that field in that given time. While an individual may build up *know-how* over years of experiences across many different fields and bring that *know-how* to bear on actions in which she engages, when observed by a researcher, that researcher must be able to contextualize the *know-how* analyzed relative the field and time in which it was deployed. Bear in mind, as well, that no field is permanent, as change occurs regularly within fields due to a nearly unlimited variety of internal and external factors acting upon them.

As such, I adopt a conceptual model in which all forms of social structures (from government agencies to community-based organizational and informal groups) are perceived as social fields that are in constant flux at all levels of society, from the super local to the national or global. The idea of fields in flux in which individuals engage, from the contentious collectives in which they are involved to the local or national fields in which they take action, implies that public leaders can, and do, imagine possible changes to these fields (Anderson, 2006a; Fligstein & McAdam, 2012). Indeed, the outcomes that public leaders in contentious collective politics pursue (in whatever fashion and toward whichever target) represent a collective's imagined changes to existing social structures and processes within target fields. For people in democracies such as the United States, the very act of imagining a different future relies upon two allowable ideas; firstly, that a better society can exist tomorrow, and secondly, that regardless of position in life, an individual can perceive oneself as having the power to fashion or create (via some form of political participation) a better society than the one currently in existence, be that at the local, national, or global level. Such allowable ideas are cornerstone components of a free democratic society, enabling more individuals, at any level, to engage in this activity. This is not to say that such activity doesn't occur in more repressive governance systems; it does, but when it does occur, it takes place in hushed, clandestine spaces, as such thinking could easily be considered threatening to a repressive regime.

Additionally, large fields, such as a nation-state, are perceived as containing within them all manner of social fields across all sectors of society, from national to local governance fields and from national to local people–initiated or institutionally created fields in commerce, charity, education, arts, social justice, and more. In this regard, a nation can be operationalized as a field in which other fields exist. In the discussion below, analytical design applies this perspective from SAF theory and augments the conceptual framework with additional theoretical concepts from the pragmatist scholarly tradition, civic engagement, and organizational theory, as well as practice-based community organizing concepts developed by IAF.[3]

One of the key concepts developed in SAF theory that I use to operationalize *know-how* is the idea of strategic action fields, which the theory describes as the mechanisms through which changes in a field can happen, as it is human creative action that puts a strategic action field in motion, and it is (I add) through a public leader's *know-how* that such a strategic action field occurs. All analysis in this study adopts this understanding of fields as important to perceiving *know-how* being deployed in action. In other words, whether a public leader has the sufficient *know-how* to meet a given situation can only be analyzed from within the field in which *know-how* is deployed; otherwise, it is meaningless – one cannot analyze the *know-how* of a great cyclist when that cyclist is having lunch or even when pedaling a paddle boat.

Within SAF theory, fields then do not occur in a conceptual vacuum, abstracted for the purposes of intellectual argument, but rather are conceptualizations of real-world social structures that are understood as shaping and giving meaning to how actors engage in either individual or collective activities, which they believe will bring about some desired social change. Through middle-level fields, which are themselves embedded in larger macro-level fields, analysis can perceive individual and/or organizational fields as being in relationship with, being influenced by, and/or influencing larger macro-level fields (such as those maintained by state or national government agencies). Strategic action fields occur within these levels of embeddedness, emerging, stabilizing, or deteriorating over time (see Fig. 1 below for a conceptual map of this analytical framework).

Using recollections, notes, and published media from my years as a complete member, peer practitioner (Pensoneau-Conway & Toyosaki, 2011; Toyosaki, 2011) from 2007 to 2013, as well as interviews conducted between 2016 and 2017 of individual actors who engaged in social justice change efforts in the years after hurricane Katrina in the New Orleans area, I operationalize occurrences and activities as taking place not only in local (meso-level) fields but also within larger regional, state, and national (macro-level) fields. First, it's important to consider that a substantial number of fields along the southern portion of the State of Louisiana were disrupted by the hurricane, creating field instability in just about every facet of socioeconomic and political life along the Louisiana gulf coast.

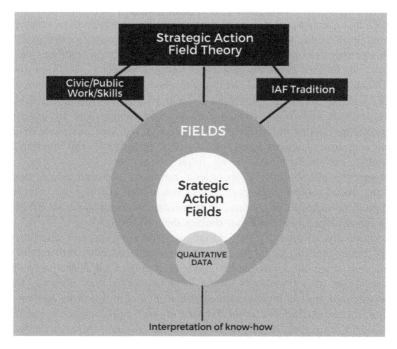

Fig. 1.   Conceptual Map of Analytical Framework.

Using SAF theory, analysis perceives the city of New Orleans as an unstable field that took longer to stabilize along socioeconomic and political lines than the remainder of the State of Louisiana.

At the same time, as a field within broader, overlapping fields delineated by region, such as the metro New Orleans area (broader than the city proper), the southern gulf coast field (broader than the metro area but not as broad as the entire State of Louisiana), the State of Louisiana, and the US nation field (both in terms of its government and social structures), analysis can also differentiate how proximate and distant fields interacted with the New Orleans field, and by extension with the actors engaged in social justice change work within this field. This embeddedness of fields is a key SAF theory characteristic.[4]

In SAF theory, strategic action fields are created by individuals or groups to affect some form of change upon an existing field, or to create new fields, or to eliminate a field. Any creative action in public life aiming to have some influence on a field is then viewed as a strategic action field, and this strategic action field (or creative action in Deweysian pragmatist language) is created by some level of *know-how* that is deployed by a public leader or group of public leaders. All manners of formal institutions and informal groups, at all social levels, create strategic action fields in their public efforts to affect change in the fields in which they are embedded. Using this concept, observation or analysis of *know-how* being deployed to create strategic action fields in the real world requires understanding the embeddedness of these actions within multiple layers of embedded sociostructural fields. This means that when actors engage in contentious politics, whether in collective or individual form, they can be viewed as creating, or attempting to create, a strategic action field that can disrupt an existing field.

This perspective on fields, which builds on the theoretical traditions, in large part, of John Dewey, Pierre Bourdieu, and Anthony Giddens, establishes strategic action fields as the conceptualized circumscribed social arenas in which public leaders' actions are made intelligible because it is precisely their actions that create, stabilize, destabilize, or transform fields (although there are times when exogenous shocks that impact fields may be nonhuman, such as natural disasters, which of course describes hurricane Katrina, included in this analysis as a nonhuman exogenous shock on all fields in the New Orleans area).[5] This understanding allows for the operationalization of strategic action fields as dynamic social orders that participants are either creating or entering or attempting to stabilize, destabilize, or transform, requiring some set of abilities and/or knowledge (*know-how*) that enables them to do this.[6]

Additionally, strategic action field creation, stabilization, and destabilization can be understood as social activity aimed toward collective rather than individual ends when the goals benefit either a circumscribed collective, a demographic subset of a population, or the broader public. For example, when I created Pueblo Inc., a Latinx-oriented nonprofit organization in 2007 in New Orleans, the end goal wasn't for me to create my own employment or establish my professional trajectory in community building (though these certainly were tangible benefits I enjoyed), but rather to have an institution that could address New Orleans metro area-wide Latinx issues in housing, voting, criminal justice, and language access. What I did and how I did it to achieve any level of success between 2007 and 2011 (when I served as executive director of this new organization) can be understood as oriented toward collective social justice change goals for the Latinx community rather than as oriented toward my personal, individual needs and interests. Such a perspective then enables me to operationalize my work and the *know-how* I developed and deployed during my work in this organization, as creating strategic action fields within various social justice fields, making it relevant to this study.

This is not to say that deeply personal goals oriented toward individual benefits do not occur within collective activities. In my own practice, I observed both at play in my experiences. I pursued personal goals that intertwined with my organization's public goals but not always, as I certainly experienced instances in which my personal goals were at odds with the public goals my organization pursued. As I will point out below, individual needs and interests often can be in constant tension with collective needs and interests, sometimes conflicting and sometimes aligning within a single individual's publicly stated purposes and/or observable actions. The point here is to articulate analytical criteria for what is and is not considered action/activity that can be interpreted as related to strategic action fields and thereby as being able to say something about *know-how* in the field. Individually oriented agendas, interests, desires, and expectations are not considered for analysis unless these can be directly connected to collective ends, or these play a significant role in field dynamics, such as when a personal hatred between actors who care about the same issue undermines a group's ability to be effective in its pursuit of change.

However, even when my activities and actions as a complete member advocate met the above criterion of collective vs. personal gain, not all of my work could be categorized as constituting new strategic action fields. Using SAF theory to locate my own work, I can say that some of the work I engaged in simply took place in "unorganized social space" (Fligstein & McAdam, 2012) that had little to nothing to do with participating in, maintaining, challenging, or transforming a field, even when the desired ends were collective in nature. Two examples of collective work that I led during my years as a nonprofit director can help clarify how this level of operationalization works.[7]

In the first example, I created and led a conversational group focused on strengthening Black and brown relations among leaders in New Orleans. In 2009, I brought Latinx and African American leaders who were engaged in the New Orleans field together to dialogue and get to know each other as people. In the second example, I led a newly created subcommittee on language access in criminal justice that I helped codevelop for a local language access collective, also in 2009. While the Black and brown dialogue collective always remained open to the possibility of future action, the ongoing gatherings and the work I conducted to coordinate meetings during the time that I led them never rose above the level of conversational gatherings, which cannot be operationalized with SAF theory as work that either took place in or created a strategic action field.

The criminal justice language access work, on the other hand, engaged from the onset in activities and actions aimed at tackling language justice issues in Louisiana courts with the express purpose of addressing existing inequities in the court system. This work, under SAF theory, can be operationalized as an activity that created a strategic action field because activities had the express intent of enabling the collective to enter and challenge the existing New Orleans criminal justice field, as well as potentially creating a new language justice field within, or tangential, to the criminal justice field.

Finally, in SAF theory, strategic action fields' dynamics are such that they are: (1) always jockeying with other strategic action fields, (2) always in flux, and (3) created out of shared understanding of the actors involved (Fligstein & McAdam, 2012). More than anything else, strategic action fields are about collective contention, in which actors within fields are perceived as jockeying to improve status quo social orders or defend stable social orders from undesired change. In today's complex societies, no strategic action field can be conceptualized as being created in a social vacuum whereby actors can engage in field creation and challenge without other fields having effects on their efforts. Such constant jockeying means that strategic action fields cannot be operationalized as static, and the *know-how* that gets deployed in order to create strategic action fields relates directly to that point in time and space. Though fields can, and do, achieve some form of stability, this stability cannot be equated with some form of static existence. Fields are always in flux as they deal with exogenous shocks, fend off challenges from other fields, or fend off challenges from public leaders within. This constant fluctuation in field structure and stability means that field boundaries are also in flux.

For example, the housing field in New Orleans, which is the operationalized field this book analyzes, not only drastically changed in the aftermath of hurricane Katrina when compared to what the field looked like before the storm, but it continued to change regularly between 2007 and 2013, particularly as a seemingly endless new crop of public leaders challenged all aspects of housing during these initial rebuilding years, including the observed main case in my analysis, which sought to transform the housing justice subfield within the larger housing fields. Within the New Orleans area housing field, distinct subfields that were traditionally separated by differing housing interests (housing affordability, housing ownership, housing development, to name a few) can be conceptualized as overlapping during the instability years post-Katrina, influenced largely by the exogenous shock of the storm, but also by new public leaders, such as the main housing justice case, that sought to use these years of instability to bring greater attention to the issue of housing affordability and equitable access.

However, as creators of a new strategic action field focused on housing justice, the main case in my analysis (a housing collective) met with (as is discussed in analysis below) numerous roadblocks that over time affected the affordable housing strategic action field the collective created. This resulted in fluctuations within the field that culminated in unexpected outcomes for the collective (see analysis below for in-depth exploration).

Conceptualization of the creation of an affordable housing strategic action field also demonstrates the third point highlighted above about shared understanding. Actors in the housing field came to agree upon and develop a shared understanding about housing affordability and the need for a new action field focused on this issue within the greater New Orleans housing field. Without a shared understanding of what constituted affordable housing, a strategic action field could not have been created, as this required collective imagining, agreement, and action to bring it into existence. This collective imagining underscores the role that meaning making plays in collective behavior broadly, and collective contention specifically (Brubaker, 2009; Fligstein & McAdam, 2012; Jasper, 2006), which in itself requires a type of social *know-how* (described in detail below), which in turn informs the type of framing work that social movements were found to conduct in previous theories (Benford & Snow, 2000; Snow et al., 1986).

As an analytical tool, Fligstein and McAdams' SAF theory helps me place *know-how* as critical to the dynamic interactions and interplay of existing societal structures, meaning making, and public leaders' actions, enabling analysis to focus on the individual and small group level not as isolated but as part of, embedded within, various interlocking and competing fields. When a collective is perceived as creating a new strategic action field, work by public leaders is perceived as first establishing what is being defined and how it should be understood within the context of the fields in which the individuals operate (Fligstein & McAdam, 2012). Relying on Jürgen Habermas' theory of communicative action as a foundational framework, the SAF theory's inclusion of shared understanding enables me to insert *know-how* as that which public leaders deploy in creating this collective imagining (Fligstein & McAdam, 2012).[8]

Within these interactions between public leaders and the fields in which they engage, SAF theory provides different orientations from which to view individuals relative to their positions within a field. These three orientations include incumbents, challengers, and governance units (Fligstein & McAdam, 2012, p. 13), which are power-relevant positions within fields that SAF theory calls categories, which themselves build on Gamson's (1990) perspective on incumbents versus challengers. I use the term power-relevant because these three positions reflect power relationships within a given field that are in constant flux.[9] For example, incumbents and governance units tend to have more power relative to challengers within a stable field. Challengers tend to have more power when they create a new strategic action field that is accepted by the general public and results in destabilizing incumbents. Challengers can have more power than other challengers (or even than governance units) when advancing a new strategic action field that includes incumbents of a broader or adjacent field as allies or when transforming existing fields in which incumbents operate. These relationships captured as categories, or orientations, help elucidate how *know-how* about the field can be deployed in service of some planned action.

In this analytical framework, incumbents tend to be those who are perceived as having some disproportionate position of power over stable fields and "whose interests and views tend to be heavily reflected in the dominant organization of the strategic action field" (Fligstein & McAdam, 2012, p. 13). Challengers are perceived as tending to have a less dominant position within a field, wielding less influence than incumbents, but can articulate and understand, with the relevant *know-how*, field power dynamics as well as field logics, and often challenge existing fields by creating new strategic action fields within existing fields dominated by incumbents (Fligstein & McAdam, 2012, p. 14). The third group, governance units, is perceived as tending to be internal to a field. Not to be confused with state-related entities, which certainly can be actors within a field, governance units tend to worry about field maintenance, ensuring field stability, and in this regard tend to align with incumbents in terms of field norms, values, and priorities (Fligstein & McAdam, 2012).

Fitting Analyzed Cases Into a Working Framework

Members of the housing justice collective case that I analyze are operationalized as challengers within the New Orleans and Louisiana housing fields, as the housing collective they created is perceived as a new collective in the unstable post-Katrina housing field, which aimed to create a housing affordability strategic action field both in New Orleans and at state levels. Incumbents within the New Orleans housing field in 2008, during the time this collective was taking shape, are perceived as not only government officials who oversaw certain aspects of housing-related policies and programs but also new and old housing groups, as well as new government programs created in response to the storm, which dominated the direction of housing initiatives. Governance units with interests in field maintenance and stability of the New Orleans housing field are perceived as associational groups of real estate developers, lenders, real estate agents, and construction companies, as well as government regulatory agencies, such as city planning, finance, and permitting.

The main housing justice collective case that provides the bulk of data from interviews is compared directly to another housing justice collective case that is also an actor in the housing field, with some limited, tangential participation in the affordable housing strategic action field. This collective case is a neighborhood association that is interested in housing as a strategy for bringing the neighborhood back after hurricane Katrina, but only as a sub-strategy to the work of creating a new strategic action field in the municipal governance field. Through their strategic need to participate in the New Orleans housing field, which they entered as new actors in the years after Katrina, members of this collective are classified as challengers. At the same time, this collective case is also operationalized as a challenger in the New Orleans housing field on other fronts not directly related to housing affordability, as will be shown in analysis below. The third case, which is a second comparative case to the main housing justice collective case, is a housing organization that is also a member of the main housing justice collective case, but which also engages in its own strategic action field creation in its housing work within a targeted area in New Orleans, and compares to the neighborhood housing collective case in that this case also embarks upon new strategic action field creation within the municipal governance field.

Operationalizing individuals within the cases highlighted above as challengers implies that actors have some level of recognition that their contention is directed toward some person or group of persons in decision-making positions within the field they are challenging. In other words, when public leaders are operationalized as challenging an existing social order in whatever fashion, operationalization also includes an understanding that there is some level of awareness (this may differ, as will be shown in analysis below) about the field and its incumbents by public leaders who are challengers.

With occasional exceptions, public leaders are perceived as having the understanding that bringing a challenge forward in the hope of advancing some social justice goal requires confronting someone or some group in a position of power to deny their challenge. No new idea for programming, budget allocation, or legislation, for example, will simply be implemented based on a group or pubic leader's wishes, as any call for change carries with it the potential that something already in place must go, and with it the potential that someone or some group will be attached to this status quo and have no interest in losing it. I operationalize the colleagues I either engaged with as a complete member (between 2007–2013) or that I observed/interviewed (between 2015–2018) as challengers. In categorizing them as challengers, I am also asserting that they know they are challenging decision-making targets, which implies having some form of *know-how*.

As I established in the first chapter, theoretical scholarship has failed to adequately theorize how social skills matter in contentious collective politics. To date, scholarship on civic engagement, organizational theory, and community organizing, typically divorced from contentious collective politics theories and their traditional analytical foci, has explored a number of social skills that actors may or may not deploy in public engagement, which are typically referred to as civic skills. For example, civic skills are deemed as required for individuals' engagement in civic spaces in any form of activity benefitting the collective or public good (Boyte, 2004). Similarly, institutional theories have a history of investigating what individual actors do and/or know how to do to achieve institutional success (Battilana et al., 2009; Chrislip et al., 2022; DiMaggio, 1988; DiMaggio & Powell, 1983; Hartley, 2018), but as Fligstein and McAdam point out, even when research focuses on the individual's actions, there is a failure to provide an adequate theoretical framework through which the analyst can establish a public leaders' agency in direct relation to that actor's circumscribed social spaces and circumstances (2012).

Are we simply following the contours of norms and practices laid out before us by the social structures in which we live, as robots, devoid of free will? Or are we agentic individuals, after all, fully capable of carving out our own paths, regardless of structural limits? SAF theory provides the most critical theoretical component for operationalizing *know-how* in this regard by defining the term social skills as "the attempt by social actors to create and sustain social worlds by securing the cooperation of others" (Fligstein & McAdam, 2012, p. 17). Unlike theoretical approaches that would describe such work by social actors through the lens of power and preference (which are certainly components, just perhaps not *the* root of such actions), social skills in SAF theory are "inextricably linked to the distinctive human capacity and *need* to fashion shared meanings and identities to ensure a viable existential ground for existence," which Fligstein and McAdam refer to as the "existential function of the social" (2012, pp. 16–18). This is to say, power and preference (the usual analytical framing for examining strategic action) can only be understood as being bound up by larger issues of meaning and identity, which I find is a highly useful framing for operationalizing *know-how* as an analyzable factor through which public leaders attempt to engage in and change existing structures of power.

This theoretical perspective helps me as an analyst better conceptualize and analyze my own work as a complete member advocate in the years between 2007 and 2013. For example, any decision I made or action I took in the language justice work aimed at Louisiana courts between 2009 and 2011 that enabled the collective's efforts to advance our group's targeted social justice agenda can be conceptualized as related to our relative power and preferences, certainly. This is made more intelligible by SAF theory's framework on shared meaning making, in which the work, and our desired ends, aimed to fulfill a shared vision of a better society in which we wanted to belong, one with better language justice in the courts.

What I and my fellow collective leaders did and how we did it, as well as what we knew about what we did, what we knew about the field we were challenging, and how this knowing helped decision-making and strategic action, can thus be operationalized as demonstrations of certain skills, abilities, aptitudes, and/or knowledge and experience (in other words, contributing elements to the development and deployment of *know-how*). This combined *know-how* enabled us to create shared meaning for ourselves, perceive actionable steps that would be needed to bring this shared meaning to the greater field of criminal justice, and implement the needed activities and supportive structures that would bring this shared, envisioned better society into existence.

By bringing attention to the shared meaning-making role that social skills play in contentious collective politics and by establishing their direct relationship to the fields in which they are embedded and to which they are directed, SAF theory enables operationalization of social skills in strategic action fields, as this is where they are perceived as being deployed by actors who are either building, stabilizing, maintaining, or destabilizing strategic action fields (2012). Additionally, these social skills are assumed as widely distributed in SAF, whereby every individual has the capacity to acquire and deploy such social skills. This assumption of equal distribution implies that any public leader has the potential to engage others in collective strategic action. However, it is worth highlighting here that actors are not equally exposed to the types of opportunities in which these social skills are typically acquired. As such, the possibility of equal distribution of social skills is not fully realized in practice due to a variety of reasons, which are explored in more detail below.

It is when I can perceive public leaders as being involved in strategic action fields with others, creating shared identities, political coalitions, shared interests, and then fashioning these into agreements, transforming collectives into "framing lines of action, and mobilizing people in the service of broader conceptions of the world and of themselves" (Fligstein & McAdam, 2012, p. 17) that I can fully operationalize social skills being deployed relative to field creation, stabilization, or destabilization.[10] This in turn means I can place *know-how* as a central component to the very pulse within any politically contentious collective unit, be that a social movement or a neighborhood group. Echoing Dewey's ideas about public action (Dewey, 2016, 2017), SAF theory establishes that social skills are deployed according to the situations perceived by actors, who actively engage in "reading" the field, as well as other actors in the field, and making decisions about what is needed for a given desired action trajectory in the target field (Fligstein & McAdam, 2012). These social skills show up as *know-how* in action.

While I am interested in exploring how social skills can be perceived in collective contention and how the deployment or failure thereof interacts with outcomes' success or failure, this book does not focus on enumerating and categorizing lists of social skills and finding their frequency. Nor do I enter into a list-building endeavor, as this can get unwieldy, as I mentioned earlier. Instead, I simply take the concept of social skills out of SAF theory and "plug" in *know-how* as a more suitable concept for analysis. I make this move because it helps me demonstrate how a researcher can utilize *know-how* within an existing, relevant theory in contentious collective politics. I also do this because I wish to shift the conversational focus from social skills to *know-how*, which I perceive to serve both practice and research better in its ability to connote creativity and application that relies on both static/formal knowledge and knowledge gained in practice. In doing so, I amend SAF theory for my analysis by locating the theory's concept of social skills as previously learned abilities that contribute to the *know-how* that gets deployed in a given situation. For example, in my work on language justice issues in New Orleans, my previously learned skills of communicating with diverse leaders, gathering their ideas, and being able to summarize their key agreements contributed to the *know-how* I was able to deploy in various moments of group-building work. My analysis focuses less on enumerating the numbers of skills I relied upon, or on how many of these are needed to constitute some level of ability, and instead focuses on how *know-how* was deployed and how it affected group actions.

I use the concept *know-how* as a more expansive conceptualization of what I analyze, connoting knowledge attainment combined with experience and action in the fields in which they are deployed, where *know-how* means both knowing the truth about something as well as knowing how to do something, given the knowledge in hand, within a prescribed field in which a particular type of doing occurs in a particular manner because it fits best for a given situation and desired outcome. Again, think about the basketball player or your own tire-changing *know-how* and how such *know-how* becomes potentially limited in a new field. As such, the concept of *know-how* refers to knowledge being applied in a specific way for a specific situation (which can include a combination of previously learned social, intellectual, communicative, and emotional skills). Now, this previously learned set of skills may come from any aspect of life, but a good deal of it comes from formal learning, what Stanley differentiates from *knowing how* as *knowing what* (2011a, 2011b).

For example, when I first started the Latinx nonprofit in the New Orleans area in 2007, I brought to the endeavor a certain level of *know-how* about nonprofit fundraising that served me well, enabling me to move the organization from a startup with $0 annual income to one with over $400K annual income in 4 years. This *know-how*, in order for it to be conceptualized as such, included a good amount of *know-what* of a specific type (Stanley, 2011a, 2011b) – namely fundraising techniques, strategies, and tools that experts use, which are standardized by the National Association of Fundraising Professionals in the United States. What is the difference between the two? Let's use my *know-how* in fundraising to further describe how I apply it in my analysis below.

Some of the foundational elements of fundraising include basic knowledge about the components of a grant, the types of donors that are possible in the philanthropic field, the legal structures in place regulating philanthropic activity, and the types of activities the Internal Revenue Service allows charitable organizations to conduct. This basic knowledge is an example of some of the *know-what* of philanthropy, but it hardly makes one a professional fundraiser. I can easily find summaries about this information online to satisfy my curiosity, but it will not make me an expert fundraiser or even an entry-level professional fundraiser. Additionally, tips, or expert advice on blog posts, and newsletters by professional fundraisers provide additional *know-what* information of a different sort. Such *know-what* items might include examples of good *moves management* database practices, do's and don'ts of online annual fund solicitation and strategies for creating a bequest program, to name a few. However, it isn't until I apply this *know-what* specifically in social action within the philanthropic field that *know-how* emerges and plays a meaningful role.

In my early experiences as a professional fundraiser, it was my demonstrated *know-how* in writing that helped me enter the field of fundraising as a writer for a fundraising team. Once in the fundraising field, I learned the *know-what* of that field and enhanced it with practice over time, aided by professional trainings, peer learning, mentorship, and on-the-job experiences, which all combined to help me develop the needed *know-how* to become a professional fundraiser. Let's consider just the grant writing aspect of fundraising to further explain.

My own *know-how* about grant writing could be described as increasing exponentially in my first 4 years as a professional grant writer between 2000 and 2004. From extensive practice over time, I understood more and more how to write compelling grant narratives for different audiences and different purposes to the point that some of this could be described as *know-how* becoming automatic, almost taken for granted. I learned, for example, how to assist principal investigators who were less adept at program design and help them bring their ideas into focus, a type of *know-how* I couldn't have demonstrated when I first became a grant writer but had. Most individuals with proficiency in writing can write a grant, but they won't always know how to help a principal investigator design a decent program. Such lack of *know-how* would most likely be reflected in what type of grant narrative is created. There are many grant writers in the world whom I have met who simply don't build this type of *know-how* because most of their work revolves around simply writing a narrative from what has been "said" to them by the people seeking the funds. The practice of cocreating with someone on their project enables grant writing to develop a deeper *know-how* about program design (in each instance being specific to the program being worked on, but through accumulation revealing generalities that can be broadly applied, similar to basic tire-changing *know-how* generalities).

Is basic knowledge of the components of a grant without any experience in producing a grant considered *know-how* in this example? From the perspective under which it is operationalized in this study, it is not. Knowledge of the components of a grant and the ability to write do not combine to create grant writing *know-how*, if the assumption is that such *know-how* is a type of demonstrated expertise developed through real-world practice. As such, for a grant writer to develop and deploy *know-how*, that person would have to possess some knowledge about the "truth" of the *know-what* (about grant writing) combined with the "truth" of how to use this *know-what* in an expert fashion in a given situation – which Cowan refers to as wisdom (2017) and which Stanley asserts is "knowing how to do something [that] amounts to knowing a truth" (2011a, 2011b).

There are also levels of *know-how* that can be ascertained via comparison. Levels of *know-how* can range from having developed zero *know-how* relative to the action one is implementing, to having some *know-how* of the somewhat sufficient variety, to having a significant amount of *know-how* based on vast experiences.[11] In the grant writing example, someone who writes their very first grant for a small sum of funds that will be used in 1 year demonstrates a certain level of *know-how* on par with getting the job done for the first time. However, the same *know-how* has the potential to be of an insufficient level for a more complicated, multimillion-dollar, multiyear, and multi-organizational grant request. Some of the applicable *know-how* will transfer, of course, just as it did in our tire-changing example, but the new field of bigger stakes will demand more *know-how* than is currently possessed by our hypothetical grant writer. This is not to say that this same fictitious grant writer can't be up to the task; she very well may be. In tackling a new field in which her *know-how* is deficient, she has the opportunity to develop the needed *know-how* by simply diving in and tackling the problem. In other words, not having the sufficient *know-how* for a given field is not a death note but instead an opportunity for public leaders to gain the needed *know-how* that can help them achieve their desired goal. Central to this issue for any given public leader, and for analysts to consider, is asking whether public leaders become aware of their limited *know-how* in a given scenario, and if so, do they forge forward anyway, or do they slow down to ensure that they have developed sufficient *know-how* to better tackle their objectives.

Let's consider another example, which I hope can help you get a better grasp of how I am conceptualizing *know-how* for both analysis and practice. Let's look at writing, which like tire changing, many of us know a little something about. Above, I shared that I brought writing *know-how* to my work as a professional fundraiser. Using this conceptualization, I can be said to have achieved my level of writing *know-how* after years of formal training and practice in creative writing. But I didn't always have the level of writing *know-how* that I brought to that first grant writing job. When I first attempted to write three-point argument essays for my freshman composition class, I could barely attain a passing grade despite being proficient enough in the skills needed to compose English language three-point essays.

Throughout the United States, entry-level college students struggle with freshman composition, and I was no exception. University freshmen have been writing for at least a decade by the time they enter higher education, only to learn (as I did) that they still have to learn how to write well, particularly those pesky three-point argument papers. Over the course of a semester, students learn the needed *know-what* about the three-point argument and then are asked to translate this into *know-how* by writing an original three-point argument of their own. What is the difference between those who pass and those who don't? It is their deployment of *know-how*, which, according to the rules established by the freshman composition field (maintained by field incumbents that include faculty and graduate students who teach freshman composition), requires that students not only show knowledge of the structural aspects of the short essay, but also that they demonstrate an ability to make a meaningful argument within the confines of the essay form's structure.

Only through some form of assessment can *know-how* of this style of writing be perceived, requiring that the person who determines if *know-how* was deployed also be a person who has a thorough grasp of what *know-how* looks like in a successful three-point essay. In addition, the assessment has to account for levels of difference in *know-how*, such that some who deploy excellence in argument essay *know-how* receive high marks and those who barely do so receive lower marks, with a cutoff in place for those who do not achieve basic *know-how* proficiency, as determined by someone who either possesses expert level or has developed the ability to perceive expert-level *know-how*.

This last portion of the example is important to reiterate. As an analyst who is not involved in any significant way with the observed contentious collective, can this person truly perceive *know-how* being deployed? I believe so, because the outside observer's own level of understanding about what *know-how* looks like and how it differs in terms of levels can be developed with practice. A social scientist with no real-world experience of contentious collective politics at all will have considerably less *know-how* about what *know-how* looks like in his early career but can sharpen his observational skills and thereby increase his level of *know-how* about what *know-how* looks like, even if this person never practices himself. Now, having said this, of course an analyst with real-world experience has the potential to see even more than the person with great observational *know-how* but no practical *know-how* in contentious collective politics. The ability to learn to detect levels of *know-how* develops out of comparison, as it is through numerous comparisons that some amount of truth surfaces about what level of *know-how* is required for a given situation (Cowan, 2017; Stanley, 2011a, 2011b).

However, this is not to say that practice over time is the sole indicator of a high degree of *know-how*, as this is not an absolute but more a general rule. It is possible for a neophyte in any endeavor to demonstrate a higher level of *know-how* in practice over a seasoned practitioner, though these would be exceptions. While this may seem to further complicate operationalization of *know-how*, I argue that it does not, particularly when applied within SAF theory. My ability to operationalize *know-how* in this study relies on recognizing its interaction with field creation, stabilization, or destabilization. As such, strategic action activities and their desired outcomes have a direct interaction with deployment of *know-how*. The student's essay, in this example, is a new strategic action field in the world of essays. Successful creation of this essay is an indication of *know-how* being deployed.

As discussed so far, *know-how* then can be conceptualized as a type of truth, or wisdom, about an action (Cowan, 2017; Stanley, 2011a, 2011b), developed through practice, in which an individual has mastered the ability to combine *know-what* (which is content knowledge) with instructional *how-to* knowledge into *know-how*. This *know-how*, again, is not equitably distributed in terms of proficiency, as there are different levels of *know-how* that public leaders bring to any given social action. As mentioned above, this may not be an absolute, but it is an observable general principle that governs conceptualization and operationalization. Consider the basketball player example once more to help clarify this point.

A player on a high school basketball team can be described as possessing a high degree of *know-how* about the game of high school basketball when she applies this knowledge on the court with other high school players in team competition, which requires deployment of *know-how* in order to both be on the team and play on the court. But this same level of *know-how* becomes insufficient for the same player attempting to play with professional players who possess an even higher, more expert level of game *know-how* relative to the field of professional basketball.

In this example, the relationship between *know-how* and the field in which it is deployed, which is vital in SAF theory operationalization, becomes clearer. The high school basketball field, while similar in many respects to the professional basketball field, operates differently than the professional basketball field on a variety of levels. Dribbling, shooting, blocking shots, and making free throws may look the same, requiring the same motor motion regardless of the two fields, but differences, such as level of all-around play, rules, and court size, matter enough to require more field-specific *know-how* if a player is to be successful within that given field.

Additionally, experience in the field matters, as it will be only through actual play in a professional field that the high school player who may possess the needed *know-what* of the professional basketball field will be able to gain the needed *know-how* to succeed on a professional basketball court. This can be observed when most college players drafted by professional leagues require time to develop their proficiency at the professional level, regardless of the sport. Each field offers unique social structures and processes that someone new to that field must learn and become familiar with, which typically happens via practice and participation within the given field, and it is through this practice and participation in a given field that *know-how* can be perceived.

Consider a new example. This time, let's look at bicycle riding to help further clarify how *know-how* can be conceptualized as differing according to field context. Anybody who has ever ridden a bike more than a few times develops a certain basic *know-how* about bike riding. We learn that to stay upright and move forward at the same time, we must keep our body balanced and centrally positioned relative to the center of the bicycle, and we must pedal continuously. Without thinking about it, we develop *know-how* about these basic mechanics in our bodies, such that it enables us to apply them to any bicycle we mount, regardless of wheel size, weight, etc.[12] Now, for the vast majority of us, our *know-how* on bicycling will end here because it constitutes the extent of our practice, but for people who bicycle competitively, this level of *know-how* will be insufficient. Anyone interested in entering any of the various competitive bicycling fields, where *know-how* must include complex knowledge about bicycle configurations, performance specifics of certain designs and materials, physical limitations of the human body, and so on, will require more practice and participation in the relative field of competition in order to develop *know-how* that will help that person succeed in that given competition. As described in the basketball example above, the requisite *know-how* that will enable successful action in bicycling depends on the field in which the *know-how* is being deployed. One can't simply jump onto a mountain bike and roll down a rocky hill without any experience of downhill biking and rocky terrain and expect to make it to the bottom of the hill without falling, or worse, breaking a few bones.

This same conceptualization of *know-how* applies to human actions in contentious collective politics. What people do in contentious collective politics can be analyzed on the basis of the type of field-specific *know-how* in which it is deployed. The analyst, in turn, does not necessarily have to be an expert in the specific actions and activities that can be conceptualized as *know-how*, as one can, through intentional development that is typically guided by others (trainings, experiential exposure, practice, coaching, mentorship, etc.) who possess a high degree of *know-how*, learn how to analyze deployment of *know-how* via comparison within a given field.

For example, critics in the arts typically lack (though not always) the type of *know-how* that they critique in the works of artists. A critic may not be able to play a cello with the same level of artistry as Yo-Yo Ma, but this does not mean that the same critic cannot, by extension, recognize, appreciate, and evaluate Yo-Yo Ma's deployment of *know-how* with the cello on any given score he performs in a given arrangement. This type of analysis is possible because the critic familiarizes herself with what the different levels of *know-how* look like within the field in which she deploys her craft as a critic, enabling her to use comparison to perceive how different levels of *know-how* "show up."

The same conceptual model applies here in terms of how I operationalize, perceive, and discuss the *know-how* that I analyze. My knowledge about, and even level of proficiency in, the *know-how* I analyze stems from a combination of my own training and practice in the fields I observed and analyze, as well as my own analytical development as a researcher in this field, which I not only use in support of my analytical observations but also in support of comparisons of how *know-how* is deployed across all cases.

Thinking in Dimensions of *Know-How*

I use a deductive approach that is informed by my own experiences between 2007 and 2013 as a nonprofit complete member advocate in the New Orleans field, a trained community organizer practitioner and educator, as well as a government bureaucrat in charge of public participation. I then combine with SAF theory to enumerate a short list of nine types of *know-how* that belong to four broad dimensions of *know-how* that actors deploy repeatedly in contentious collective politics. Why only four? I landed on four from a simple process of reflection about the *know-how* that community organizers try to develop in others and the *know-how* that typically shows up as critical to group organizing and mobilizing. As I stated earlier, I have no interest in enumerating the large number of skills that one can acquire and deploy in practice as a public leader. Instead, I want to look at specific types of *know-how* that are critically important to contentious collective politics. To do that, I have to limit analysis, which for the purposes of this book is a short list of only nine types of *know-how*, which I describe in detail below. These nine types of *know-how* are divided into four large buckets, which I call dimensions. These four dimensions are informational, social, strategic, and operational, with each having the capacity to contain a large variety of other types of *know-how* that I do not explore here.

The four broad dimensions of informational, social, strategic, and operational *know-how* reflect *know-how* that I observed in my real-world practice. These four dimensions were repeatedly deployed wherever public leaders were involved in contentious collective politics, particularly in collective activities that had a specific aim of bringing about some form of social justice change. There is a fifth dimension, emotional *know-how*, that I intentionally omit because it has received a great deal of attention in contentious collective politics and civic leadership literature, as I highlighted in the previous chapter. It suffices here to simply connect to that literature and the ideas about emotional skills by pointing out that an emotional *know-how* dimension can be understood as an underlying dimension that informs the other four dimensions I explore. For example, analysis focuses on nine types of *know-how* that exist within the four dimensions I list, and for each type of *know-how*, regardless of the dimension in which it is situated, one can make an argument for some level of emotional *know-how* needing to also be present. As such, I assume emotional *know-how* as present for the purposes of analysis in this book.

Additionally, the conceptual map in Fig. 2 below shows how the dimensions relating to each other should be read as having no beginning or end or as being absent of any hierarchical structure whatsoever. One should understand the conceptual map as interlocking dimensions connected together randomly, meaning I could easily move the locations of each dimension, and no level of importance would be gained or lost by this action. A circle would be a better

48 *The Know-How of Public Leaders in Collective Politics*

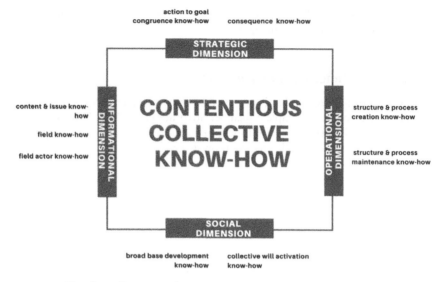

Fig. 2.   Conceptual Map of Dimensions of Know-How.

representation in this regard, but I chose the square with the intention of highlighting the distinctiveness of each dimension over the reciprocal relationships. With this in mind, please consider that to fully understand the conceptual map, you must imagine each dimension of *know-how* as influencing the other dimensions and as also being influenced by them.

Below, I describe each dimension of *know-how*, beginning with informational *know-how*, and explore within each the corresponding types of *know-how* that one can find being deployed through that dimension. The first order of analysis of both the interviews I conducted and the events in which I participated is to look for instances in which one of the nine types of *know-how* was present at whatever level. After identifying the presence of some level of the nine types of *know-how*, I then use my own knowledge about the fields in which an identified *know-how* was deployed or knowledge about the fields offered by the interviewee to establish what levels of *know-how* were deployed and the interaction of that identified *know-how* with the field. I combine these insights to provide interpretations that offer a picture of how public leaders' *know-how* interacts with the work of pursuing social justice change as members of contentious collectives involved in nonelectoral political actions in New Orleans post-Katrina.

The first in order of discussion (but not importance), **informational *know-how***, refers to how public leaders use information about the field in which they operate to create, stabilize, or destabilize fields. Public leaders in a given field who demonstrate any level of informational *know-how* typically demonstrate **content and issue *know-how*, field *know-how*,** and **field actor *know-how***. Each of these types of *know-how* can be extensive from a field-specific perspective, depending on the field in which a public leader operates, but there are some generalities that can be observed across each regardless of the type of field.

I operationalize content and issue *know-how* as referring to usage in strategic action of topical knowledge and its accompanying debated and/or contested issues that provide the core set of meaning(s) with and through which all actors in the field relate and/or identify to the field. Content and issue *know-how* then refers to any form of information created by field experts, field analysts/observers, field regulators (both within and outside of state agencies), or field-adjacent experts, analysts, and observers. For example, the main case for this study is a housing justice collective comprising housing-related organizations and individuals. While I will explore how informational *know-how* for the housing justice collective is deployed and how it interacts with the collective's desired outcomes, an individual generally interested in any aspect of housing social justice does not necessarily have to have any knowledge about the housing field in New Orleans if she wants to simply engage as an individual who is concerned about having access to a safe place to live. Such an individual might join a collective that is advancing a housing justice agenda or may show up to a local council meeting to express concerns about housing or may yell at public officials during any public event in which these officials are present.

These examples represent some of the types of activities that people engage in when advocating for a cause they are concerned about, but it does not get us to any understanding of a person's informational *know-how* about the housing field in which a person may be engaged, in part because fields are not significantly affected, if at all, by the activities of a single individual expressing concern. If concerns by individuals were a sufficient factor in creating or destabilizing fields, the social sciences would be awash in examples of concerned individuals creating change across all fields, and in turn, the world's social inequities would possibly look very different than they do today.

Informational *know-how* is a requisite ability if an individual or a collective is interested in addressing housing justice issues in such a way that the desired outcome has some impact on a respective field. Possessing content and issue *know-how* means that public leaders know the history and debates surrounding an issue, inclusive of political, academic, and public thoughts and writing. This knowledge gets identified in my analysis as content and issue *know-how* when public leaders demonstrate an ability to use knowledge about the field's arguments and histories in the actions they decide to embark upon. For example, when a public leader connects for her collective the rationale of a political action to historical and existing social frameworks within the target field, I perceive this as content and issue *know-how* being deployed.

Content and issue *know-how* is interlocked with field *know-how*, which shows up in being able to put to practice some action that relies on knowledge about how a field is maintained, such as knowing what laws, nonlegislative policies, norms, and practices have contributed to the creation and maintenance of a field. Field *know-how* also includes knowing the subfields and their relationships to each other, knowing adjacent fields and their impact on a given field, as well as field ambiguities and uncertainties.[13] A public leader with field *know-how* has a strong understanding of how different players in an arena interact with each other, which agency has power over what process or policy, and which larger fields influence or even dictate how smaller fields engage in the world. A person who deploys a high level of field *know-how*, for example, about the New Orleans housing world is able to understand the potential limitations of a particular agency or department relative to its location in a larger field, as is the case with New Orleans housing policies and programs and their relationship to federal laws and policies in the United States.

Finally, public leaders have to know who the other individuals are within a field and what positions of power they hold within a given field relative to the public leaders' own position within a given field, all of which constitutes field actor *know-how*. In the IAF community organizing tradition, collectives are taught to research the "players" who make the decisions about the issues they want to tackle and then get to know as much as they can about these players and target them for the collectives' strategic actions. Without the types of *know-how* I just described, which can show up as different types of informational *know-how*, public leaders I interviewed who belonged to the housing justice collective would hardly have achieved the outcomes they pursued, as I show in analysis below.

Now, possessing the type of field information described above can certainly be helpful to strategic action, but to truly recognize it as informational *know-how*, as I operationalize it in analysis, one has to identify usage of the information in service of strategic action. Again, one can intellectually accumulate knowledge about a field and the relevant powerful actors within and do absolutely nothing with this knowledge beyond filling curiosity. Such activity does not qualify as strategic action within SAF theory, and hence eliminates learning for learning's sake from being interpreted as an example of informational *know-how*. In my analysis below, I discuss an episode in which the housing justice collective decided on a specific strategic action that set the collective toward a more politically contentious path (as compared to previous activities up to that moment) and which was possible primarily because of key members' application of informational *know-how* in strategic action aimed at affecting the New Orleans housing field, enabling me to interpret this *know-how* accordingly. However, informational *know-how* is just one of four dimensions of *know-how* that actors require if they are to successfully create, stabilize, or destabilize a field.

In the dimension of **social *know-how***, which refers to any number of *know-how* that individuals use to engage, communicate, and/or coexist with others, I operationalize two types of *know-how* that I focus on for analysis: **broad base development *know-how*** and **collective will activation *know-how***. As can be imagined, the list of what people know how to do socially that enables them to engage each other, create groups, coexist in communities, and so on can be quite vast. However, in using SAF theory in my analysis, combined with knowledge from my own practice, particularly via concepts taught and practiced by IAF, I limit operationalization to the two broad types of social *know-how* I named above.

Broad base development *know-how* is operationalized as *know-how* that is demonstrated in what public leaders do to bring other leaders and groups together for a shared, collective cause based on shared interest. A broad base simply means a diverse mix of people and organizations linked together into a collective that is working on a shared agenda (Alinsky, 1972; Chambers, 2003). Here, the term *broad* applies to a diversity of peoples, groups, and interests and not necessarily numbers (though this matters as well for other reasons not discussed here). The marks of a broad base can be understood better in comparison to a thin base. A thin base typically reflects a more homogenous grouping of people and/or ideas. Whereas a broad base includes members of a collective who reflect diversity in interests, institutional types, political ideologies, ethnic orientations, geographic locations, and so on.

Developing such a base of diverse actors, as one can imagine, does not happen by happenstance, nor does it happen easily. Such coalescing of various peoples and institutions undoubtedly requires a leader or a group of leaders who have the requisite *know-how* to bring people together.[14] Analysis of the cases I observed and interviewed focuses on broad rather than thin base development *know-how* because it offers more analytical meaning. A focus on broad rather than thin base development enables analysis to eliminate mediating factors, such as deeply held shared interests, which can serve to enhance engagement in group participation of similar-minded people when compared to a group of diverse interests. This is not to say that thin base development is simple, which it certainly is not, but rather the distinction here is an interest in how public leaders bring together diverse interests, groups, and people to focus on an agreed-upon line of strategic action that challenges a field.

Many of the skills often referenced in collective behavior or organizational studies, whether called social skills (Fligstein & McAdam, 2012), emotional intelligence (Jasper, 2011), civic work (Boyte, 2000, 2004), soft skills (Brungardt, 2011; Hurrell et al., 2013; Jain & Anjuman, 2013), or civic capacities (Chrislip et al., 2022), are used in the service of broad base development *know-how*. As stated earlier, I do not focus on enumerating a laundry list of skills, but it is important to highlight a few examples of the types of skills actors do bring to bear in deploying broad base development *know-how*.

For a public leader to successfully bring people together to form a collective around shared interests, this person must know how to socially engage and communicate with a diversity of people. Public leaders who are able to do this typically know how to build meaningful one-on-one relationships with targeted individuals by communicating in a way that builds trust and confidence and/or by identifying and establishing shared self-interests (Alinsky, 1972; Chambers, 2003). These two abilities incorporate a host of social, emotional, and intellectual normative aptitudes that are often the subject of how-to management and leadership blogs, popular articles, and training manuals. Also, the combination of skills deployed in any singular effort to build a meaningful one-on-one relationship can differ from encounter to encounter.[15]

By way of example, my ability to actively listen may be more crucial for a given meeting with a target individual, where in another meeting with a different target individual, it will be my position within the field that plays a more important role in adding this person as an ally to the collective.[16] Similarly, establishing shared interests can be accomplished via a variety of aptitudes or fortuitous circumstances.

In one instance, shared interest can be intentionally established by a highly skilled public leader who knows how to pry appropriately without offending the target individual while at the same time building trust, all of which combines as a demonstration of broad base development *know-how*. In another case, shared interest can happen because two public leaders share a similar exogenous threat and intentionally seek each other out to meet this threat collectively, in which case, broad base development *know-how* is not demonstrated because the "coming together" required no specifically targeted action used in the service of strategic action.

My ability to interpret broad base development *know-how* then depends less on identifying and cataloging every specific skill used and more on how this type of *know-how* is deployed in strategic action (as per SAF theory methodology). When it is deployed, I must identify the most salient components of this *know-how* that is being deployed in that instance. As such, operationalization of broad base development *know-how* limits coding it to instances when such *know-how* is deployed in strategic action that is creating, stabilizing, or destabilizing a field. By way of example, the conversational group I organized in 2009 (mentioned above) to discuss Black–brown relations does not get interpreted as a demonstration of broad base development *know-how* (though it certainly is a demonstration of this type of *know-how*) in this study because it does not occur in the service of strategic action, as established in SAF theory. Again, this differentiation applies here only for the purposes of the analysis I conduct in the succeeding four chapters. Outside of SAF theory application, the same example above certainly demonstrates broad base development *know-how*; it's just that for the purposes of my analysis via SAF theory, it does not meet the criteria.

The other type of social dimension *know-how* I analyze is collective will activation *know-how*, which refers to a public leader or group's ability to take new relationships and turn these into active participants in a collective endeavor. As the second type of *know-how* within the social dimension, collective will activation *know-how* incorporates SAF theory's social skill category of story framing and convincing others via brokering, as well as what actors do to establish a collective identity that resonates with members, which can include such abilities as effective public speaking, defining and filling roles, and helping would-be participants anticipate future benefits. Again, it is less critical for this study to enumerate the many types of abilities or skills that actors display in service of this type of *know-how* and more important to identify salient skills or other opportunities and/or circumstances that enable and/or support collective will activation *know-how*.

It is important to note that this study does not focus on when and why such activation happens, which was one of the initial, significant threads of inquiry in mobilization research, where the interest was on people's rationale for involvement in contentious collective politics (Gurr, 2016; Smelser, 1963). What is clear is that once actors embark on inviting people to form and/or join a collective, they then have to get the collective to engage ***as a collective*** toward a common goal. Doing this requires collective will activation *know-how*, which can include any combination of abilities and/or skills that enables an individual to get others to compromise, cooperate, and participate actively by taking up a role within and for the collective.

Operationalizing this type of *know-how* then also aligns with SAF theory's methodology of connecting what public leaders do to the respective fields in which they are doing it. Knowing the field and its players, as well as knowing how to build and activate collective will, are requisite *know-how* if actors are to lead collectives in strategic action aimed at some form of social justice change.[17] However, it isn't enough to know the field and mobilize folks to come together in shared anger. Once a public leader has successfully brought people together, what next? Public leaders must also know how to engage in strategic action, a type of *know-how* that they demonstrate when making strategic decisions about what actions to conduct to achieve a desired outcome, particularly when engaging in strategic activities that require in-the-moment strategic decision-making.

I operationalize the third *know-how* dimension, **strategic *know-how***, as an ability to analyze a field or fields and determine field-relevant opportunities and threats, as well as identify field actors who may be supportive or antagonistic relative to a collective's goal and use this information in determining action steps that move the collective toward the agreed-upon, desired outcomes. Similar to the other dimensions of *know-how* discussed above, one can develop a laundry list of strategically oriented abilities and skills that public leaders possess and show, but for the purposes of analysis, again I limit my discussion to the operationalization of two types of strategic *know-how*: **consequence *know-how*** and **action-to-goal congruence *know-how***.

A public leader's ability to make plans and decisions informed by an awareness of how desired outcomes may occur as a consequence of targeted actions is what I conceptualize as consequence *know-how*. In demonstrating consequence *know-how*, collectives make strategic action plans and decisions knowing exactly what they want to achieve, as well as what potentially desired and undesired outcomes may arise, even if these same collectives may not have the full picture of all the steps to get there. When deploying high-level consequence *know-how* in both design and implementation of strategic action fields, actions are selected because of their anticipated value in advancing a collective's work toward attaining its desired outcomes within a specific field, with some consideration (though this will be speculative, at best) about both intended and unintended consequence.

An example of an episode from my time as a nonprofit organizational leader demonstrates how operationalization of this type of *know-how* gets interpreted. During the 2011 Louisiana Senate election cycle, then-US Senator David Vitter's campaign for re-election placed a campaign advertisement that painted border-crossing immigrants in a particularly derogatory light, prompting many in the New Orleans area Latinx community to express concern.[18] As a leader of a Latinx community organization at the time, I was urged by community leaders to use the nonprofit I ran to speak out publicly against Vitter's campaign ad. Initially, I refused to make any form of public statement, expressing fear of political retribution similar to the one that ultimately doomed the Association of Community Organizations for Reform Now (ACORN).[19]

However, as days passed after the initial airing of the political ad, pressure grew from within the Latinx community to say something, and I began to consider and weigh the consequences of speaking out versus the consequences of not speaking out and ultimately determined that not speaking out offered far worse potential consequences for the organization with regards to trust from the Latinx community's leaders. After consulting with the organization's board of directors, I devised a strategy that aimed at maximizing the potential positive consequences (enhancing trust) of a public response while simultaneously minimizing the potential negative consequences (becoming a target of the then-sitting senator). I reached out to other nonprofit leaders in the African American, Jewish, Vietnamese American, and white community and invited them to stand with our organization in a press conference that was held on October 18, 2010, to denounce the anti-immigrant political ads. All four local television news stations covered the event, in which a dozen diverse leaders joined in to publicly denounce the ads, a call that was aired in that evening's local news cycle.

Vitter's ads were not removed, as was requested, but the group I pulled together accomplished what others had asked of us, which was to give voice to the Latinx community's concerns about the anti-immigrant ads in a very public way. Using SAF theory, I can interpret my decision-making and implementation of what I chose to do as a demonstration of consequence *know-how* that is directly related to the New Orleans social justice and Latinx community fields in which I operated as a nonprofit leader, even if deployment of this *know-how* failed to achieve the desired outcome. In this example, I interpret my actions as consequence *know-how* because of decision-making that relied on knowledge about potential positive and negative consequences within the fields in which my organization operated.

It's important to note that it cannot be assumed that individuals who hold some form of leadership role within a collective possess the requisite *know-how* to do most of what they actually do to mobilize a collective toward effective strategic actions. In many instances, public leaders work with the best available *know-how* they have in a given time and circumstance and create from there a situation akin to the person with the car tire–changing *know-how* being asked to help with an airplane tire. In that situation, the person grabs what they do know and *creates know-how* through practical application.

My example about Senator Vitter also serves to demonstrate action-to-goal congruence *know-how*. Action-to-goal congruence *know-how* is deployed when public leaders implement actionable steps (in whatever form of activity this may be, such as making calls, writing letters, holding town halls, lobbying, marching in public protest, etc.) that are specifically designed to move the collective toward its desired outcomes. Additionally, such *know-how* is crucial in situations that have the potential to derail collective planning and implementation.

It cannot be assumed that the path to a desired outcome by any collective is a simple linear matter, as if tracks for the way forward are automatically laid out for those interested in challenging incumbents in their fields. On the contrary, the lack of action-to-goal congruence *know-how* is more prevalent precisely because public leaders can, and often do, lose sight of how flashy, popular, or convenient action steps do little to advance, and sometimes detract from, a collective's longer term goals. In addition, the way forward for any desired strategic action will rely on human decisions, reactions, behaviors, and so on, which no public leader can predict and which can derail even the best plans.

Recognition of action-to-goal congruence *know-how* depends on both the field in which a collective is engaged as well as that collective's stated goals and/or desired outcomes. For example, a frustrated resident angry about a blighted school building in his neighborhood who takes out his frustration by shouting obscenities at a public works crew that is patching a nearby section of street reveals very little action-to-goal congruence *know-how*, as there is no structural or legal pathway for the public works crew to take up a school blight issue. Such an example may sound ridiculously fabricated, but it is precisely this type of misdirected energy and lack of strategic decision-making that repeatedly plagues collective strategic action.

The immediate allure of venting angrily becomes the go-to strategic action, even when such action yields nothing in the way of movement toward a desired outcome. In my example of consequence *know-how*, I accepted the possibility that a public response to the anti-immigrant ads would have had little effect on the removal of the ads or the outcome of the senatorial campaign, despite this being a desired goal by those leaders who pushed me to coordinate a press event. I could have gone ahead with a display of anger and discontent, surrounded by Latinx leaders only. Had I done this only, I would have shown action-to-goal congruence *know-how* if the end game was to vent. The goal was not just to vent but to have an impact on the anti-immigrant ads' runtime and on the future relationship between my organization and the community my organization served. Knowing the prospect of the former goal as minimal, I designed a press event that would maximize a less flashy, but no less important, goal of demonstrating leadership in the social justice nonprofit field and building trust in the Latinx community field.

In this way, I can be perceived as deploying action-to-goal congruence *know-how* when I designed a press event that made it less about the organization I ran and its angry members and more about the collected unity of other leaders in solidarity with the Latinx community, meeting my organizational goal of furthering trust with the community. Indeed, collectives with leaders or groups of leaders who have action-to-goal congruence *know-how* often work diligently to steer away from activities that derail their movement from their stated goals. Such *know-how* is used often when public leaders are actively engaged in strategic action, as the opportunities for derailment are never-ending in the volatile spaces of political contention. However, knowing how to bring people together, activate them collectively, and point them toward activities that have a winning chance to affect a field can, and does, flounder if there is no adequate structure and processes in place that help members of the collective engage meaningfully. Public leaders who demonstrate the final *know-how* dimension, operational *know-how*, do just that.

Operational *know-how* refers to public leaders' abilities to build and maintain functional collectives that provide its members with structural and procedural paths for participation. When people come together in a group around shared interests, it is unlikely (though not necessarily impossible) that some form of organic self-organizing will occur. People do not automatically know how to self-occupy and self-define their roles in a group (Anderson & Brown, 2010; Gist et al., 1987). Someone, or a group of people, with knowledge about structures and processes will organize decision-making processes and internal rules for engaging, at the very least, to enable more effective group functionality. Collectives involved in contentious politics are no different in this regard. Roles need to be assigned, committees need to be formed, capacities need to be directed, and so forth, if the collective is to engage meaningfully on the basis of shared interests, and doing this requires a good bit of knowledge about how to organize people to work in groups. Although SAF theory does not expressly reference operational *know-how*, it is an area of focus in the institutional literature on which SAF theory is partly founded (DiMaggio & Powell, 1991; Meyer & Rowan, 1977). I rely on this tradition, as well as on IAF concepts and my own practice as a nonprofit leader and community organizing trainer, to limit operationalization within this dimension to two types of operational *know-how*: **structure and process creation know-how** and **structure and process maintenance know-how**.

Public leaders who demonstrate structure and process creation *know-how* have comparative knowledge about existing structures and processes used by other groups and demonstrate an ability to implement the needed structures and processes for a group in which they participate. One can make the case that knowledge about group structures and processes is something every human being learns from childhood onward, from family to K-12 education and the workplace. We are surrounded by different types of social structures and processes our entire lives, from which most of us learn something about authority, roles and responsibilities, and even accountability. And yet, it would be an oversimplification to assume that such knowledge is equally distributed among members of society in such a way that anyone can start a collective and get it to function effectively simply because we have all been exposed to the various institutional structures that humanity has put in place.

While there is an underlying assumption here of equal distribution in terms of people's abilities to form groups, which implies some level of knowledge about and ability with structures and processes, even if only at the simplest levels (such as a two-person hierarchy with roles of leader and follower), this does not equal to structure and process creation *know-how*. Any reader of this book can attest to the difference in functionality among groups they've been involved in when there are clear roles and defined processes for decision-making and action when compared to spaces in which these are not so clear.

Regardless of the legal status of a collective, be it a business, an association, a coalition of organizations, or an informal gathering of people, the collective's ability to accomplish what it wants to achieve will rely on its inner structures and processes in some fashion. As such, recognition of structure and process creation *know-how*, as I have described it, requires that analysis looks for a public leader's or group's active involvement in creating group structures or processes that are then used by others in achieving the collective's desired outcomes and/or goals.

In interpreting this type of *know-how*, I am less interested in the intrinsic value of a structure or process, as my analysis does not focus on a comparison of strengths and weaknesses of structures and processes relative to outcome success. Instead, I am interested in understanding and describing when public leaders intentionally created a structure and/or a process that he or she (or they) deemed necessary for a desired strategic action gaining traction and moving toward a desired outcome and/or goal related to strategic action.

Similarly, structure and process maintenance *know-how* is operationalized in the same fashion as structure and process creation *know-how*, only here the focus is less on whether a public leader or a group of leaders created a structure and/or process, but rather on whether a leader demonstrates a need to ensure the ongoing operation or usage of a structure or process by a collective's members relative to strategic action. For example, there are cases where individuals who had no role in creating a structure and/or process used by a collective see the value in ensuring ongoing maintenance of existing structures and/or processes for the good of the collective and its intended outcomes and/or goals. I can interpret this *know-how* being demonstrated in such instances when public leaders either defend the usage of a structure and/or process or when they actively ensure that others use existing structures and/or processes within the collective whenever this is framed as benefitting the collective's intended goals and/or desired outcomes.

Finally, operationalization of both structure and process creation and maintenance *know-how* does limit observation to how these are demonstrated relative to the collective to which a person belongs and does not consider external field structures and/or processes. For example, in my work on criminal justice language access between 2009 and 2011, I pushed for the establishment of committee leadership roles based on advocacy areas, justifying this on the merit of having an accountability/leadership role/mechanism for the work that needed to be accomplished by volunteers. I interpret this activity as a demonstration of structure and process creation *know-how* because of its direct relationship to the strategic action of the collective in which I was involved.

Within this same work, the committee I led explored and discussed opportunities for change in the various structures and processes in the New Orleans and State of Louisiana criminal justice fields. These discussions led to the recommendation of new structures and processes that I do not interpret as a demonstration of structure and process creation *know-how* because it was a solution the group wanted adopted within the local and state criminal justice fields and not so much a needed element for collective functionality. As such, our ability to provide a structural and procedural solution to the target agency gets interpreted as a demonstration of informational and strategic *know-how* (described above) rather than structure and process creation *know-how*.

How Research and Analysis Is Structured

This book analyzes data from a qualitative study that began with a simple question: does an individual's knowledge about (and perhaps skills in) civic engagement play a role in achieving desired outcomes in social justice change work at the local level? This led to the question I explore in this book, how does *know-how* deployed by local actors interact to enhance or limit their desired outcomes in contentious collective politics? To explore this question, I used a qualitative design that includes data comprising my own experiences as an active participant in various advocacy efforts between 2007 and 2013, including my role as a volunteer with one of the organizations selected as a case between 2015 and 2018, along with 43 interviews conducted between 2016 and 2017 of 10 organizations that operate in New Orleans. Below, I provide the brief contours of the research design and analytical framing.

As I mentioned before, I was a member of the community of advocates that I interviewed before I became a researcher, which means that for many of the cases interviewed, interviewees either had a prior relationship with me as a peer advocate or were aware of my different activities and roles as a former nonprofit director or city of New Orleans bureaucrat. For interviewees who either knew me personally or knew of the work I had been involved with, my role as a researcher was new to them, prompting preinterview conversations about my life changes from participant to academic observer before the interview could begin. My complete member status (Toyosaki, 2011) served as both a benefit to the study and a complication, which I fully address in my dissertation methods chapter. At the same time, this connected experience to the data I collected and analyzed provide me the ability to compare information from positions within and outside of various fields, where applicable. For example, when an interviewee discusses strategic action that I am familiar with because of my previous involvement in the field, I am able to use my recollection of events to further enhance analysis of the interviewee's data.

In terms of how data are structured for analysis, I rely on case comparison primarily by comparing what individuals from different organizations say and do. Interviews are compared analytically both within the collective to which they belong and across other organizations. The bulk of analysis focuses on one main case, a collective organization that has a focus on housing justice, which is then compared with two other housing justice involved groups, as well as other groups in the New Orleans field who are not involved in housing justice.

Analysis of data is presented in four separate chapters below, each corresponding to one of the four dimensions of *know-how* discussed above. The chapters' ordering reflects the order of presentation in this chapter, but this ordering is in no way an indication of which dimension of *know-how* is more important. The relationship among the different types of *know-how* and their corresponding dimensions is cyclical and reciprocal, which is why Fig. 2 above depicts graphically four sides that have no beginning or end.

The starting point for discussion can simply be arbitrary, but I do choose to begin with the dimension of informational *know-how* simply because it is the chapter in which I further discuss the concept of fields relative to an actor's engagement in them, which is a key SAF theory element that informs the entire analysis. This chapter, titled **Knowing the Field**, explores how actors' *know-how* about the fields they engage in interacts with their abilities to create, initiate, advance, and/or succeed in their declared political change agendas. The following chapter, titled **Getting Others to Act**, explores the social dimensions of *know-how*, with a focus on what actors know how to do that enables collective formation and activation. In this chapter, various "social skills" are discussed in terms of their contribution to the two types of social *know-how* this study is interested in discussing.

The final two chapters explore strategic decision-making and structures and processes in contentious collective action. In the third analysis chapter, titled **No Directions Given**, I explore the strategic dimension of *know-how* by focusing on what actors know how to do that enables them to make strategic decisions that keep a collective's activities directed toward its intended goal(s). Here, I also discuss how actors' abilities to perceive potential consequences of planned and or desired actions interact with a collective's desired outcomes. The last analysis chapter, titled **Without Clear Roles and Processes, They Suffer**, explores *know-how* of the operational dimension and how this existing or lacking ability interacts with a collective's ability to pursue its change politics agenda. Analysis is followed by a findings chapter that explores this study's findings implications for both research and practice, ending with final concluding thoughts.

Considerations for Practitioners

If you're a practitioner and you find yourself wondering how any of this could be useful to you, consider the following example. A nonprofit leader who has been running a modestly successful advocacy organization realizes at the 10-year mark that most of his successful actions occurred in the first 3 years of the organization's existence. The organization's membership is smaller than it was when the nonprofit leader began his work. Now, implementing any collective action involves considerably less people, and worse, the work is less effective. In this leader's final assessment he discerns that had he spent more time and energy building his staff and community leadership members' *know-how* that this could have had a cascading effect. Had he made an emphasis to build a capacity development program for both his staff and the community leaders who support his organization's work, such a mechanism may have been able to help generate new leadership development, fostering a pipeline of new energy ready to replace outgoing members.

As a practitioner, it is vital to consider what *know-how* exists within your group. Regardless if you're a group of friends, an advocacy organization, a civic association, or some other form of group, you will need to know the levels of *know-how* your group possesses. In this regard, it's important to always determine what talents exist within groups. Who knows how to do what? And who knows how to influence others to act or to listen? And who knows the lay of the land? All of these capacities point to valuable potential *know-how* that any given group can deploy in contentious collective action.

Finally, practitioners are encouraged to read the succeeding analysis chapters, as both analytical and practice-oriented observations are made throughout analysis. While much of the analysis in each chapter uses the SAF theory jargon of fields and actors, it also explores examples and offers interpretations about what public leaders are doing, providing potentially valuable insight to practicing public leaders.

Notes

1. As mentioned earlier, the idea of creativity in action presents an alternative view to the pervasive rational action and one which I consider a more reality-based view on what takes place in social action, and particularly in political action, which takes place at the juncture of competing public values, meanings, and power struggles.
2. See Joas, in particular, for his exploration into creative action.
3. These include, but is not limited to, concepts on public versus private life and relationships, common versus selfish self-interest, and seeing the world-as-it-is versus seeing the world-as-it-should-be. For discussion on these concepts and more, see *Roots for Radicals*, specifically, by Ed Chambers, 2003.
4. See Fligstein and McAdam's first chapter of *A Theory of Fields* (2012) in which they describe "how embedded social actors seek to fashion and maintain order in a given field."
5. For a full explanation by Fligstein and McAdam on how they both build and differ from Bourdieu and Giddens' views on fields and strategic action fields, see the first chapter of *A Theory of Fields* (2012). In particular, how they take Bourdieu's idea of individual action in a field as a springboard, from a theory about individual action to their rearticulation into a theory of collective action, as well as how they rely on Giddens' ideas of structuration to build their key idea of strategic action that changes meso-level social orders.
6. I highlight the dynamic nature of fields as providing both cultural (in terms of meaning, norms, and values) and structural (in terms of social mechanisms, structures and processes arising from government or private institutions, or even society-at-large) factors, referring to them in this study as dynamic social orders to point to a synthesis of structural and cultural analysis, which is certainly an element of SAF epistemology, but one that I want to bring forward as particularly meaningful within the social movement tradition, as it combines a historical chasm between the two perspectives in terms of explanatory power. Structural and cultural factors are at play at all times, and each can create the other in any given scenario. It is not an either/or issue, in terms of explanatory power, but rather a both/and issue with particular dynamics in particular cases.
7. The word "led" here is somewhat problematic because it has the potential to imply that I was the sole decision-maker in all respects for the two groups I describe below when, in fact, the opposite is the case. As I show later during analysis, leading does not necessarily imply leading in everything. Sometimes, as was my case, leading simply means keeping the group together, on task, and making progress, while others within the group take the lead on different tactics and strategies. At the same time, I am choosing the word led because it does more accurately connote my activity as compared to coordinated. I certainly

coordinated others, but in coordinating, I pushed for things to happen in certain ways, summarized ideas, and made requests of others to act.
8. While Habermas's theory of communicative action certainly remains within the rational action model described above, I interpret SAF theory as borrowing the main ideas of communication's role in strategic action without accepting its reliance on rational action. I believe, instead, that SAF theory is more closely aligned with Dewey's creative action model, further elaborated by Joas.
9. Power here refers to the ability to get others to act or do (which is derived from IAF) – the power to establish a strategic action field requires others to agree and to act on this agreement, be that through the establishment of an institution, a law, a policy, or a program, or the allocation of funding, or the recognition of decision-makers, or other such similar actions in which others are "doing" what a challenger group requests/seeks. Power in this study also aligns with Steven Lukes' view of power as established in his book *Power: A Radical View*.
10. Also see Fligstein, 2001; Goodwin and Jasper, 2004; Jasper, 2006; Benford and Snow, 2000; Snow et al., 1986 for the ideas expressed in this sentence.
11. I do not develop these levels into analyzable components of *know-how* in this book but invite others to consider the potential for further development and understanding in this regard.
12. What Smilde calls embodied creative knowledge in Smilde, 2007, which echoes Bourdieau's habitus concept in Bourdieau, 1977.
13. Here is an example of a social skill category that Fligstein and McAdam provide in SAF but which I include as a contributing skill to field *know-how*.
14. Community organizing as a profession, as developed by IAF, concerns itself with this work primarily and conducts trainings for prospective professional and lay organizers in the concepts and tactics learned from decades of practice in the field. It is also worth noting that exogenous threats, such as Hurricane Katrina, can certainly bring people together regardless of what civic skills they have, but I contend that even in this situation, it will be the group who possesses the requisite *know-how* that fares better in outcome attainment when compared to another group in the same community that does not have the needed *know-how*.
15. The term encounter here refers to an event in which a public leader is engaging a potential participant, ally, or adversary in order to build a relationship where one doesn't exist. Such encounter occurs as a direct result of strategic action. That is to say, the need to meet with and engage a targeted person flows out of a set of activities that are strategized as meaningful and potentially helpful to the outcome desired.
16. Active listening is one of the key communication skills that often shows up in community training modules. I have trained others in how to develop and sharpen this skill, relying on training materials developed by NeighborWorks America, a national community development support organization in the United States with whom I engaged for trainings during my time as nonprofit director.
17. I use the term *lead* intentionally because my experiences as an advocate practitioner and my data from observations and interviews point to the notion that collective contention, similar to most group efforts, requires leadership, be that a single person or a small team, to gather, organize, strategize, and make decisions about the way forward. As such, this study takes up the position that leadership is itself an important component of contentious collective politics. See Andrews

et al.'s 2010 article "Leadership, Membership, and Voice: Civic Associations That Work" in the *American Journal of Sociology* for a study that looks at the role of leadership in civic associations.
18. See https://americasvoice.org/blog/vitter_winning_most_racist_ad_of_2010_competition_ignores_latinos_cont/ for reporting on this advertising campaign by the then-sitting Senator.
19. For a description of the events that led to ACORN's demise once it became a target of the Republican Party, see Dreier, Peter, and Christopher R. Martin. 2010. "How ACORN Was Framed: Political Controversy and Media Agenda Setting." Perspectives on Politics 8(3):761–92.

Chapter 3

Knowing the Field

Setting up the New Orleans Situation

In the aftermath of the levee failures after hurricane Katrina, the New Orleans social justice field, along with other social fields in the affected areas, was in shambles. The work of organizations and neighborhoods to push for social justice change in New Orleans prior to the storm was upended, as was everything that actors knew and understood about the fields in which they operated before August 29, 2005, including basic government structures, processes, and capacities. An external shock to the region, the levee failures not only brought death and destruction but also an opportunity for change that may not have been possible prior to the hurricane. While the analysis that follows in this and subsequent chapters is not about Katrina's levee failures, the event looms large in the backdrop. Interviews conducted between 2016 and 2017 with local advocates involved in the New Orleans social justice field share their stories about their work and experiences in pushing for social justice change in the immediate years after the storm's devastation.

Everything these individuals shared during interviews is related to work conducted in New Orleans within 10 years after the storm, making it a significant factor that requires accounting. Analytically, it is sufficient to position the storm within the context of this study's analytical framework as an exogenous shock to the social fields in New Orleans and the surrounding regions. This exogenous shock disrupted existing fields, their structures, and the actors within them. In many instances, the storm unearthed decades of intractable, corrupt, and inefficient systems operating at all levels of governance in New Orleans (Burns & Thomas, 2016). In contentious collective politics literature, such a shock creates an opportunity within existing governance structures, whereby challengers to existing power dynamics and their related systems have an increased opportunity to influence power relationships and affect change. How exactly did Katrina create opportunities for political contention to expand?

Through its complete decimation of most social and physical systems in the city and surrounding region, which disrupted lives, devastated physical infrastructure, and upended the availability of public goods and services, the storm created massive destabilization of all types of social fields, from individual households to local and regional governance.[1] Fields destabilized by Katrina's levee failures offered public leaders a window of enhanced opportunity to pursue their political interests, particularly those actors perceived as challengers to newly stabilizing post-Katrina fields or to pre-Katrina fields attempting to re-establish themselves and bring back old status quo ideas, policies, practices, and norms. Such a disruption signaled to challengers that this could be the opportunity to affect the type of changes that had eluded them for so long.

Fields stabilized at different times across different social arenas and geographic areas, as these were directly related to an uneven, hodgepodge recovery in the region (Burns & Thomas, 2011). Neighborhood recovery is one clear physical example of the patchwork nature of field stabilization. Viewed through Strategic Action Field (SAF) theory, a neighborhood, with its set of associational resident-based groups, businesses, churches, schools, and so on, constitutes a field within a broader field of local or regional neighborhoods. New Orleans neighborhood recovery was anything but uniform (Kamel, 2012).

Each neighborhood, as a unique field, recovered in its own way and in its own time, due to a list of factors, such as the percentage of structural damage, percentage of properties fully insured, and percentage of residents who returned. Neighborhood fields with more residents who were back in their properties were able to stabilize much sooner than neighborhoods that were slower to see their residents and properties return. Neighborhood fields that stabilized quickly were able to then take advantage of expanded opportunities in broader New Orleans fields that remained unstable in the years closest to the levee failures' aftermath, as will be shown below.

By the time the interviews took place, the majority of social systems that had been disrupted by the levee failures were re-established, and their respective fields were relatively stable. Much of the data offered by those interviewed between 2016 and 2017 however reflect moments in time when the fields in which they operated were still in the process of restabilizing between 2007 and 2013, years in which the effects of the levee failures after Katrina were still palpable.

Some Analysis Notes

In this chapter, I explore how actors' deployment of informational *know-how* interacted in such a way as to potentially help or hinder their respective organization's and/or collective's abilities to pursue their desired outcomes within the New Orleans housing field. Analysis focuses on interviews with members from a main case, with the pseudonym of the **Housing Justice Collective (HJC)**. As mentioned before, all interviewed actors and analyzed organizations have been assigned pseudonyms for the protection of study subjects. Similarly, the exact physical location of discussed activities is intentionally presented in generalized terms to further protect study subjects. Factual government agencies involved in the fields analyzed are accurately named. Similarly, government officials who were not part of the study have been accurately named, as well.

The HJC is a post-Katrina collective challenger in the New Orleans housing field that was created in 2007 by another new post-Katrina institutional actor, the Bring You Home Housing (BYHH) organization, a nonprofit housing developer created in 2006. Members of the HJC as of 2017 included nonprofit housing developers, housing assistance organizations, housing educators, housing policy organizations, and even local and state government officials. While not initially intended as such, the HJC gained some prominence as a challenger in the New Orleans housing field in the immediate years after it was founded. Through its efforts, as will be shown, the HJC achieved some of its desired outcomes, affecting the decision-making of housing field incumbents between 2008 and 2017 and potentially affecting normative views on the meaning of housing affordability in the City of New Orleans.

Data from this case are compared with data from two cases that were also involved in housing in the immediate post-Katrina years: the **Nearby Neighborhood Group (*NNG*)** and the **Neighborhood-Based Housing Institute (NBHI)**. The NNG is a neighborhood collective that organized itself successfully to fight the City of New Orleans' 2006 plans to revert certain low-lying neighborhoods into green spaces.[2] The collective successfully galvanized residents into action, accomplishing a significant number of desired outcomes that are explored in this study. NBHI is a nonprofit housing developer that was created by a local church for the purpose of helping residents of a targeted geographic area return home and have affordable housing. While NBHI is not a collective, it engaged in neighborhood resident organizing between 2008 and 2015, helping to create three new neighborhood groups that became new challengers in the New Orleans neighborhood field. Also, NBHI is a long-standing member of the HJC, and its director is a key ally to the HJC leader. It's important to note that I have been directly involved with NBHI from 2015 until the present moment.

While comparison is primarily dedicated to these three cases, I do include in each chapter additional analysis from other cases, where feasible, that provide additional insight on the deployment of *know-how* by other public leaders in the New Orleans social justice field between 2007 and 2016. Analysis in this study follows a generally linear chronology, with this chapter focusing on data about activities that took place between 2007 and 2009, generally, with subsequent chapters exploring more recent events in the New Orleans social justice field successively.[3]

In this chapter, I'll be looking for how informational *know-how* is deployed, looking for how public leaders use information about the field in which they operate to create, stabilize, or destabilize fields. More than just knowledge accumulation, informational *know-how* is an actively utilized capacity that actors deploy in strategic action aimed at advancing organizational and/or collective desired outcomes, which generates a strategic action field. This chapter focuses on three types of informational *know-how*: content and issue *know-how*, field *know-how*, and field actor *know-how*. There is no set order of discussion for the three types of *know-how* analyzed in this chapter, but it generally begins with an exploration of content and issue *know-how* and then incorporates analysis of field *know-how* and field actor *know-how*. Also, public leaders typically reveal deployment of all three types of *know-how* simultaneously in a singular strategic action, but for the sake of narrative discussion, a single type of *know-how* may be explored separately.

Can Challengers Succeed Without Content and Issue Know-How?

Content and issue *know-how* refers to usage of topical knowledge and its accompanying debated and/or contested issues (which provide the core set of meanings with and through which all public leaders in the field relate and/or identify to the field) in strategic action fields. This meaning is established by the public leaders within a given field, along with its supporting institutions and processes, which public leaders put into social practice, bringing into real-world practice the mechanisms that institutionalize and maintain a group's desired interpretation of an idea or a set of ideas. Viewed through SAF theory, contentious politics, of any sort, collective or individual, is an existential fight for meaning, an existential fight for how the world in which challengers want to belong should be ordered, which is typically different than the ordered status quo world in which field governance units and incumbents belong.

This ordering of the world according to incumbents is what challengers desire to change, focusing on the circumscribed arenas of the field in which the strategic action field takes place. As such, this dimension of *know-how* focuses on the core meaning-making and interpretation issues that a challenger views as needing change. In the example below, I use my own experience as a practitioner in the housing field to highlight how content and issue *know-how* interacts with a challenger's desired outcomes.

In 2007, I was working in New Orleans for a music-based nonprofit when I decided to start a Latinx-serving nonprofit organization focused on social justice issues. I had grown up in the New Orleans area as an immigrant, which provided me some knowledge about what new Latinx immigrants faced, but I knew little about the Latinx social justice field I planned to enter. This lack of knowledge about who was doing what to address Latinx issues after the storm didn't hinder my actions, as might be expected.

I made phone calls and requested meetings with Latinx community leaders who could help me. A group of Latinx community leaders agreed to work with me in 2007 because they perceived value in my "outsider" status in the New Orleans Latinx social justice field. Together, we formed Pueblo and focused on first-time homeownership education as the initial priority. The Latinx leaders became board members of Pueblo and shared their knowledge of the field, particularly their historical efforts within the New Orleans area first-time homebuyer education subfield.[4] Making full usage of the information the board members possessed, the new organization planned and took action steps that led to the organization's successful entry into, and slight disruption of, the first-time homebuyer education subfield in late 2008. Achieving this required, among other things, meeting with a coalition of first-time homebuyer educators in the New Orleans area who had the power to certify programs (which was important to lenders). We had to convince them to allow Pueblo to become a certified training program even while the organization's entry to the field challenged the existence of a long-standing for-profit member and increased competition to the coalition (which had unsuccessfully tried to offer Spanish language training).

The aim was to disrupt the first-time homebuyer education subfield and in doing so establish an affordable, nonconflicting Spanish language program for Spanish speakers in the New Orleans area. While we certainly could have created the program without support of the certifying coalition, doing so would not have created the desired disruption, largely because the most meaningful value (beyond familiarizing prospective homeowners to basic ownership issues) of any first-time homebuyer training program is the reduction in mortgage interest rates that accompanies a lender-recognized completion certificate. We could have operated the training program without this certificate, but it would have had no impact on the certifying collective. Moreover, without the board members' knowledge about this subfield's issues, our efforts would have mimicked others that start without certification and result in short lifespans and little to no impact on the field.

In this account, Pueblo's ability to use its board members' knowledge in service of strategic action that was aimed at entering a field and destabilizing it demonstrates how informational *know-how* is deployed. Informational *know-how* reflects both knowing about a thing as well as how such knowledge is used in both planning and implementing a strategic action field. Here, this knowing and doing reflects content and issue *know-how*, specifically. Pueblo's board members' knowledge about the existence of a first-time homebuyer program, its boundaries and its usage, as well as the New Orleans area issues with this program as it relates to the non-English speaking Latinx community enabled the organization to define its desired outcome and plan the needed steps to achieve them, in effect creating a strategic action field.

This brief account also helps to highlight that a public leader does not have to possess all of the needed information about content, field, and other leaders to deploy high-level informational *know-how*. I knew nothing about the content and issues in first-time homebuyer education generally, as well as what it looked like in the New Orleans area, nor did I know any of the leaders in the field. My board members, however, knew about the year-long lack of consistent programming for the non-English speaking Latinx community, the conflict-of-interest issues the for-profit educator presented and how this affected the training coalition, as well as how this issue had become more important post-Katrina with the heavy influx of Latinx people (Fussell & Diaz, 2015). Pueblo used this knowledge and deployed it as informational *know-how* in both designing and implementing a strategic action field that was successful in reaching its goal of disrupting the existing field in such a way as to allow Pueblo's entry as a certified program.

A similar process can occur with new actors who may not have readily accessible information but can research the field's content and issue areas in an effort to build up this knowledge and use it in creating strategic action fields. To clarify, having or acquiring knowledge of the content and the relevant issues within a given field does not automatically become informational *know-how*. It is in the application of this knowledge in creating strategic action fields that this dimension of *know-how* becomes manifest. In the first-time homebuyer disruption narrative above, Pueblo combined the collective knowledge of the group, which each board possessed but had not manifested and deployed it in informational *know-how* when the organization created the strategic action field that enabled it to challenge incumbents in the field and achieve its desired outcomes.

My early work to seek the Latinx leaders out, build relationships with them, and help them articulate a set of desired goals and outcomes within specific New Orleans fields led me to formulate action steps that I took to enable the organization to enter and partially disrupt the New Orleans housing field. I could have engaged, as many public leaders do, in strategic action without gathering the knowledge needed and in doing so could have jeopardized the potential for success. In such a case, lack of knowledge about content and field issues has the potential to limit informational *know-how*'s usage in given strategic action fields. If a public leader misdirects a strategic action field because of inadequate informational *know-how*, for example, by pointing protest toward the wrong decision-maker, such an activity may not only accomplish little, but it may also even serve to deflate any energy and goodwill a collective may have generated.

Actors in the New Orleans Housing Field

Hurricane Katrina's disruption of New Orleans area fields opened the opportunity for new individual and organizational actors to enter as new challengers, and sometimes as new incumbents. In the New Orleans housing field, these actors came as individual leaders and organizational volunteers, justice-oriented people interested in contributing to a just recovery, contractors and subcontractors hired for clean-up efforts, or as national housing or community development organizations looking to establish a foothold on the ground.

A proliferation of new housing-related entities exploded onto the field, with the majority of activities focused on gutting, restoring, and/or rebuilding flood-damaged homes. Most of these new organizations were created by newcomers, but sometimes by pre-Katrina community-based leaders, bringing to the field new actors in housing, both as individual and organizational challengers. Some were only active during the years immediately after the storm, while others continued to exist well into the time of this study's interviews between 2016 and 2017.

The positionality of an actor in the field informs how content and issue know-how interact in strategic action. One of those new voices was the HJC. The person who led HJC, whose pseudonym is Jano, took over in 2008 from his then-supervisor, the CEO of BYHH. He led the HJC through the time of the study and continues leading it at the time of this writing in 2022. BYHH, as an organization, is an interesting story in its own right that is not explored in this study.[5] As a newly created organization, it was awarded a significant public contract to redevelop one of the larger, centrally located public housing units in New Orleans in 2007.

The HJC (which Jano would eventually lead by 2008) was created by the then-CEO of BYHH, whose pseudonym is Sinu (and who was also interviewed for this study). Sinu had some experience in and knowledge about housing when he started BYHH but not to the level needed to undertake a large multiunit public housing development. What he lacked in knowledge about the field and its issues, he more than made up for it in faith and positionality. A man of deep faith, Sinu shared during our interview that his work in the years immediately after Katrina was only possible because of his religious faith. While this study does not explore the intersection of faith and *know-how*, it is an important element that many actors rely on and in many instances use as a type of *know-how* in their contentious politics activities (Alinsky, 1946, 1972; Chambers, 2003; Smilde, 2004).

Sinu relied on others to provide the needed knowledge and *know-how* that BYHH would need to engage in the immense undertaking of developing a large public housing campus. Jano was hired precisely because of his deep subsidized housing knowledge. Despite its nascent entry into the post-Katrina housing world as a newly formed organization, BYHH occupied a significant and powerful position in the New Orleans housing field from 2007 onward, due to its contract with the US Department of Housing and Urban Development (HUD) to redevelop one of the larger, centrally located, shuttered public housing developments in the city. As Jano observed: *"that's what gave Sinu any authority inside of housing, because he had... [the public housing complex]."*

Such positioning instantly situated BYHH as a field incumbent, as their interests were directly tied to those of HUD and the local Housing Authority of New Orleans (HANO) to redevelop public housing as mixed-income communities.[6] Such positioning also put BYHH instantly at odds with community-based advocates in New Orleans who demanded the immediate opening of shuttered public housing units post-Katrina.

Jano reflected both on this positionality and his housing knowledge during our initial interviews (I conducted 11 interviews with Jano) when he discussed a highly publicized and contentious moment in New Orleans area subsidized housing. In the same instance, he also revealed the limitations of informational *know-how* across different areas of knowledge and how such limitations, along with positionality, interact with how public leaders engage in creating strategic action fields.

One of the most publicized and highly contentious moments in the New Orleans area housing field post-Katrina is the December 20, 2007, New Orleans City Council vote on demolition permits of New Orleans' remaining traditional public housing units. On this day, New Orleans City Council faced an angry crowd that wanted the council to put a pause on demolition plans.[7] Housing advocates and concerned residents wanted the housing units reopened immediately so that pre-Katrina residents still displaced 2 years after the storm could return. Both HUD and HANO wanted all vacated units demolished as soon as possible.

Clearly, HANO's interpretation of its role in housing and what this meant in terms of how best to accomplish this as an institution differed greatly from advocates' interpretations, who asked council members to delay demolition permits. These two main opposing sides differed greatly, with a contentious collective will espousing an interpretation based on human rights concerns while field incumbents espoused an interpretation based on future-oriented housing stock improvement strategies. These weren't the only perspectives within the field, however, as others not directly involved in the city council protests that occurred that day held varying degrees of positions that leaned in either direction of the two opposite poles. Herein lies an issue regarding how differences in informational *know-how* present themselves in strategic action across various field actors.

Having worked as a housing bureaucrat in the New Orleans housing field for over two decades, Jano had extensive knowledge about housing decision-making processes, structures, and actors, as well as other fields. As he stated in our initial interview in 2016: *"working at the local housing authority certainly gives you a crash course in all things subsidized housing and government and bureaucracies and also how to fix things. Complicated deals and all that other great stuff."*

In other words, Jano possessed extensive informational knowledge about the New Orleans housing field, particularly the subsidized housing subfield, which was inclusive of the other fields in which this field is embedded, such as the Louisiana housing field and the Washington D.C. housing field, to name the two most obvious and directly related fields that have a direct affect. What Jano offers is an assessment of the potential for high-level informational *know-how* to manifest in a strategic action field when he critiques the now-famous volatile city council meeting on public housing demolition that took place on December 20th, which, according to Jano, was a moot point, as the plan to demolish was already 10 years in the making.[8]

On Thursday, December 20, 2007, a significant crowd descended upon New Orleans City Council chambers, overwhelming security and council staff. More people showed up for this meeting than council chambers could accommodate. Council members cited capacity and fire safety concerns as a reason for removing some individuals already in council chambers, as well as closing any entrance for others outside who wanted to enter. Security reacted violently to activists who attempted to open shuttered gates, using pepper spray and tasers to dissuade anyone from attempting to push or climb over gate entrances outside council chambers.[9] The city council voted on that day to allow the demolition of 4,500 public housing units, ignoring the masses of voices expressing opposition within and outside council chambers.[10] Jano offered the following views on this event over the course of two of the initial interviews, which always took place at the HJC office, which is a large open floor-plan space with one private office. The open floor plan has a 10-person conference table and five cubicles. Jano occupies the private office.

In the selection below, Jano is mostly offering his explanation of what he means when he refers to what he calls misplaced activism. This is a question that I asked Jano to clarify often in the first three interviews, as it wasn't always clear what he meant by it. He offered the following explanation in the second interview:

Jano: Yeah. So, this is my perspective.

Lucas: Because they wanted to stop the demolition.

Jano: Right. All of them are from out of town. You're just sitting going, what is wrong with you people? Something's wrong with you all.

Lucas: So, you're saying that's not a good strategy to get whatever it is that you're saying that you want. Did you even know what they wanted? Were you clear?

Jano: Yeah, they just wanted them to be reopened.

Lucas: They wanted it to be reopened.

Jano: And again, not understanding, number one, where the decisions were actually being made. You're standing there handcuffing yourself to the city council chamber. The city council chamber, they could have voted no for the permit. That wasn't going to –

Lucas: Do anything.

Jano: That wasn't going to do anything.

Lucas: Right.

Jano: Other than delay the eventual redevelopment because the decision was being made at HUD. Go protest at HUD –

Lucas: In Washington, D.C.

Jano: – D.C. go protest at HUD. Go and do that.

Putting aside any debate over what would have worked or what could have worked to stop the demolition of existing New Orleans public housing units in 2007, this exchange reveals some interesting information about Jano's knowledge about the field in which he operates. He indicates, by way of his recommendation to "go protest at HUD," what strategy he believes would have been better than storming local city council chambers. Now, it cannot be known if such a strategy as the one he recommends would have resulted in a different outcome (particularly since attempts were made to engage the HUD secretary to no avail), but it is revealing on several accounts.

As a former housing bureaucrat, Jano was very familiar with the relationship between HANO and HUD, having been involved in meetings and conversations about projects and programs emerging from these two. His observation about where to focus protest stems from this internal knowledge of two of the most significant housing actors within the New Orleans housing field. His opinion on the matter then hints at an assessment about the efficacy of targeting the New Orleans City Council for potentially several reasons. First, as mentioned above, HUD's push for demolition wasn't something that occurred in the spur of the moment (though it certainly was hastened by the levee failure's impact on New Orleans). Rather, the decision to demolish public housing units had been made long before the storm, and it was, to borrow one of Jano's favorite sayings, a train that had left the station.

Second, the three-way relationship among HUD, HANO, and the City of New Orleans (the executive and legislative bodies) had been rife with complicated tensions, particularly in the years leading up to Katrina. These ongoing tensions were certainly at play, influencing decision-making in 2007, which Jano was privy to during his time as a housing bureaucrat, as evidenced by the following observation, which he offered during the first interview: "*Marc Morial, then mayor, had enough power and enough juice and this was under a democratic president to say, 'Don't let HUD take it from me'.*"

Here, Jano references HUD's pre-Katrina plans to maintain some level of control over HANO, which was under more direct mayoral control before the storm. Jano's reference in this quote is about the anticipated legislature that would change HUD policies on subsidized housing considerably, titled the Quality Housing and Work Responsibility Act of 1998.[11] While this act enabled then-Mayor Morial to maintain a small amount of mayoral control via board membership appointment, HUD negated even this measure when it took complete control over all HANO decisions in 2002, 3 years before the storm, due to a perception of ineptitude and corruption, which Jano elaborated on further, connecting the differences between the Morial and Nagin administrations and the changes that occurred in the city–HANO relationship between 2002 and the levee failures of 2005.

> *Jano:* the city had no authority. All of the decisions were being made at HUD. So, the only person who could stop HUD would be Congress. Because the city had yielded its authority while letting the federal takeover happen and not forcing any kind of participatory required relationship or anything like that. The city had no idea what was going on.

Mayor Ray Nagin relinquished this control by simply not fighting HUD's installation of a receivership in 2002 and continued with this stance when HUD pushed for speedy demolition of all remaining public housing units in 2007.

In Jano's opinion, the 1998 legislature was:

> *Jano:* a piece of legislation that totally reformed public housing. It's how public housing works now. That was under Bill Clinton and the Clinton administration, and they actually mentioned the Housing Authority [of New Orleans] by name in this piece of legislation. Which was unheard of.

Here, Jano also references the interesting language included in the federal legislation that highlighted New Orleans, marking what was already a unique relationship with HUD before Katrina. Jano's deep knowledge about this relationship informed his thinking about what might work to affect change. In his mind, any attempt to negotiate any outcome different than immediate demolition would have required working with the appointed receiver and HUD representatives long before the storm in order to have a chance after the storm.

During my tenure at city hall, I witnessed how tensions between agencies, or even departments in city hall, sometimes seemingly petty in nature, could result in decisions that ultimately harm rather than help an agency or department's desired goals. Similarly, there are alliances that sometimes occur among different actors from different agencies, which then show up in decisions that are designed to either overcome or minimize some other actor's unwillingness to support a particular direction.

According to Jano, the relationship to truly consider wasn't HANO's relationship to city hall or city council but to HUD. In Jano's opinion, the history of these relationships was such that HUD saw immediate demolition and redevelopment as key to its national strategy, with HANO serving as the poster child for HUD's vision for the future of public housing in the United States, particularly because of its pre-Katrina failures and post-Katrina significance. Jano's critique points to the need for any challenger to public housing demolition in 2007 to understand the history of these relationships and the issues therein and use this understanding in strategic action. In his own opinion, he did not see this level of informational *know-how* in the city council demonstrators and leaders of people who encouraged everyone to show up and protest at council chambers.

This observation is also interesting because, as he points out, Jano's employer at the time of the city council chamber protests was BYHH, the newly formed organization that had already signed a contract with HUD and HANO to redevelop the public housing complex in its charge. When asked if any of the protestors singled out BYHH during the weeks prior to or after the city council vote, Jano said no, not a single public demonstration was held against BYHH for its participation in the demolition plans at any point during its redevelopment activities.

Lastly, the issue of potential funding loss for redevelopment, which would come from HUD, is included in Jano's observation. In one of its arguments for approving demolition, city council members cited the potential of losing funding from HUD. Jano's observation about protesting HUD in D.C. rather than the city council in New Orleans is partly informed by this knowledge about the relationship of funding streams from HUD to HANO. Without funding from HUD, HANO would have been hard pressed to secure the needed resources to provide public housing services in New Orleans.[12] At the same time, Jano was exposed to internal dynamics and relationships through his various assignments within his former agency over a ten-plus-year stint, as he explained in the first interview: "*...they created a position for me actually called Director of Special Programs.... in addition to anything else anybody wanted to throw at me,*" giving me a sense of other little-known kernels of information, such as potentially unethical relationships between then-HUD and HANO directors and New Orleans area developers that eventually came to some light after the December 20th city council vote.[13] Such relationships point to the potential of a for-profit agenda also exerting some influence in the 2007 demolition decisions on public housing.

According to Jano, HUD was acting on a decade-long push to re-envision and redevelop public housing development at the federal level under its Hope VI plan (see note 8 for further information). In his assessment, any effort to halt the Hope VI momentum on the ground without conducting work in D.C., both among congressional members but also among HUD executives, was an effort in "misplaced advocacy," as he preferred to phrase it.

It's important to reiterate that Jano was a staff member of BYHH at the time of the December 20th city council vote in 2007. In other words, as a staff member in this organization, Jano had a vested interest in HUD's desire to demolish immediately. This is important because it also helps to highlight how an actor's position within the field can play a role in how this actor demonstrates informational *know-how* in strategic action. In Jano's case, this positionality certainly informed his views on what makes for "misplaced advocacy."

Being an actor within an incumbent institution doesn't mean that one is not able to understand or even accept what challengers demand, but it does mean that one's positionally related perspective may hinder a thorough appreciation of the challengers' perspectives and strategies. Put another way, what housing equity and justice means for incumbents in the housing field differs greatly from the meanings associated with these same concepts for challengers, with the two opposing sides proscribing different practices and policies that represent solutions to the social orders each side is trying to establish, demolish, or maintain. Hence, as SAF theory asserts, contentious politics, of any sort and in any social space, is always about groups' interpretations of meaning vis-à-vis the type of social orders that should be destroyed, instituted, and/or maintained.

On how content, issue, field and field actor know-how contribute to new challengers making gains within a field. It would be misguided to assume that everyone involved in some form of political contention is fully knowledgeable about the field in which they are engaged. Some people have more content and issue knowledge than others. Some people have more insights about fields than others. Some know more players within a field than others. And so on.

In the case of the HJC, Jano's knowledge about the subsidized housing field within the New Orleans housing field was much greater than that of Sinu, the BYHH CEO to whom he reported. However, it should be pointed out that it was the CEO of BYHH who had the idea to bring housing actors together in 2007. As the founder of the HJC, Sinu simply wanted to initiate dialogue with other housing advocates and housing providers about the issues they were experiencing in getting the work done.

Seated in the executive suite of another New Orleans nonprofit that Sinu was then running, I began the interview with a question about how the HCJ began. Sinu began his response by "setting the table," meaning that before he could answer, he wanted to establish what was going at the time when he came to the idea of inviting others to come together. For the next 20 minutes or so he elaborated, on the instability of the immediate aftermath of the levee failures. He was occasionally interrupted by one of his staff members. He would address the staff person and then return to where he left off. One statement he made crystalizes his view on why he started the HJC meetings, and how it helped meet his goals for BYHH:

Sinu: ...then the third goal was, how could we work and partner with other organizations and ideally, helping to build capacity for some or shouldering certain things for other? But it was a matter of bringing folks together. So those were our three goals. It wasn't the actual housing units; it was all the aspects of what make our community and the services and the schools and the economics. And then it was third, what do we do as we were brand new? But as a leading non-profit, because we're starting cafeterias and everything up, to bring people together.

What is interesting to note about this quote is that it also points to Sinu's seeming lack of awareness of the powerful position his organization occupied despite describing it as a "leading nonprofit." Regardless of Sinu's own awareness on this matter, being a "leading nonprofit" meant that the BYHH had the ability to influence others, contributing to its ability to convene other housing actors in 2007. As I conducted the interview, there was a desire to push on this matter, but Sinu's intensity was such that it felt prudent to simply not interrupt. Interrupted only by the occasional knock on the door by one of his staff, the interview seemed to ignite a burst of energy, punctuated by Sinu's occasional commentary about how this revisiting of past events brought back so many ideas and memories.

Despite Sinu's seeming lack of recognition on this, simply wanting to work together isn't enough of a draw for many other actors busy with their own organizational issues. When the CEO of a new local nonprofit organization that managed to secure a highly coveted HUD–HANO contract to redevelop one of the largest real-estate sites in the city asks others to join, these others give this invitation some weighty consideration. The true impetus for BYHH forming the HJC was that (despite the contract it was able to secure) it still found itself unable to move its redevelopment agenda in the manner and in the timescale it desired. Thus, the initial impetus for the founding of HJC was not to create a new political challenger within the New Orleans housing field but to simply share information and/or resources that could help housing actors more efficiently do the work of helping residents return.

When I asked Sinu about power, he phrased it specifically in terms of power being built intentionally to achieve a goal. According to Sinu, building power wasn't at the forefront of his thinking, as he shares in the following passage:

Lucas: So, in those early initial sort of creation, that timeframe was early months for the housing alliance, you didn't have any thoughts about, well we need to build power here for example? Did you think along those lines or were you just thinking, we need to collaborate better?

Sinu: Yeah, it was never –

Lucas: Or we just need to help each other.

Sinu: Yeah.

Lucas: That was the initial piece.

Sinu: Yeah. The power's an interesting word.

Lucas: Yeah.

Sinu: It's not a word that ... It may be, I as a white male in New Orleans who'd been here forever, don't use that word. You know, I can jump to the other side. But you never think power because you have power or whatever.

Lucas: Right, right.

Sinu: But no, it never crossed my mind. It was a matter of just really being driven.

Yet, it would be the very power that the BYHH gained as a HUD-contracted organization within the New Orleans housing field that helped propel the HJC into existence. Once other actors accepted the call to convene, however, the HJC began to slowly shift from a loose collection of housing organizations (run by a significant, though new, incumbent) trying to support each other into an organized collective that took on a life of its own, with an interest in exercising real power as a collective rather than as a tool for BYHH within the field. This new direction toward a more politically contentious path (when compared to its original information-sharing goals) occurred primarily because the monthly convenings began to articulate shared roadblocks to progress and shared interests in the equitable affordability of housing for New Orleans' future.

As stated earlier, Jano didn't create nor initially run the HJC. His voice in the initial monthly roundtable convenings was purposefully quiet. It wasn't until Sinu relinquished responsibilities to Jano, who was tasked as the BYHH staffer to continue coordinating the HJC, that his voice came to the forefront of the monthly convenings. Indeed, it had to, as the logistics coordination, group communication, meeting facilitation, and agenda setting was left to Jano. In this role as convener, coordinator, and communicator, Jano became the de facto leader of the HJC within a year of its founding. Once in this role, Jano made full use of the vast housing field informational knowledge he possessed, which he called upon when he perceived a need to challenge the Louisiana Housing Finance Agency's (LHFA) draft of a New Orleans housing needs assessment it had commissioned on the grounds that the draft report findings were starkly incorrect, and if published would have long-term, negative impacts on the work to create affordable housing in the city.[14]

During the second interview in December 2016, I continued to ask clarifying questions about how the HJC made the shift from simply gathering to learn from each other to a more unified contentious collective. After asking if the meetings were still informational at the time when the LHFA issue came to their attention, I asked:

Lucas: Do you remember how you decided to target anything?

Jano: I think the very first thing we took on was, in 2009, I'm trying to pull up my notes, because I can look back through my files. We were recognizing that there were problems. Again, systemic problems, right, and one of the big systemic problems that we identified early on was the Louisiana Housing Finance Agency and their needs assessment. They put together a truly terrible document that said nothing to talk about needs assessment. They pay a university professor at UNO to put together this ridiculous document. We sat down and we tore it to shreds.

His assessment of the situation and his belief that something should be done about the housing needs assessment before it could create long-lasting damage brings to focus Jano's knowledge about the field, its content and issues, and the actors within it that could potentially be affected by this report. However, before exploring how he makes use of this knowledge as informational *know-how* in a strategic action field, it's important to also note that such reports don't often end up in the hands of regular folk, much less in draft form, despite an increased push in the latter 20th century by US government agencies to make their work more publicly available and transparent.[15]

The housing needs assessment was brought into the monthly conversations of the HJC in the early months of its founding by a variety of participants who had relationships with other actors in the New Orleans and Louisiana housing fields who were not participants in the HJC. While Jano does not recall exactly who secured a draft of the housing needs assessment before it was released, he did recall assistance from an individual who participated in the meetings in those early days who worked at a private research firm that was involved in putting the assessment document together. The organized monthly convenings enabled various issues that surfaced to be shared among the different actors, and one of these would have been knowledge about the state of the housing needs assessment and what it was already saying in draft form.

In effect, the HJC received an early warning about the housing needs assessment, which the HJC was able to review, and to which it decidedly reacted. Such early warnings don't typically take place unless someone with some knowledge about the field and its actors, along with established relationships, is able to secure "insider" information. What constitutes being designated as an insider? Anyone who is an actor in the field and has relationships with other actors within that field can be viewed as an insider. The term is not relegated simply to government agency bureaucrats and elected officials and their financial backers, but instead establishes a sort-of "inside game" status for public leaders who are actively participating within a field as compared to those outside of it. Of course, insider knowledge varies according to the actor, with some having more insider information than others. What is clear, however, is that there is a marked difference between those who have and can use insider information and those who don't.

In this regard, Jano (before being tasked to coordinate the HJC) can be considered an "insider" of the New Orleans housing field, as was established earlier, due to his ten-plus years as a bureaucrat at HANO.

Prior to the moment of contention regarding the housing needs assessment, Jano's informational knowledge about the field, its content and issues, as well as its actors, while substantial, largely stemmed from views and ideas belonging to incumbents in the housing field through 2008.[16] After 2008, as coordinator of the HJC and as an individual with a vision for a more affordable housing landscape in the New Orleans area, Jano began to shift his positionality to that of a housing justice advocate, specifically to that of a leader of a collective that occupied a challenger position rather than an incumbent position within the housing field.[17]

As Jano recalls, this shift began in the months before the housing needs assessment came to the attention of the HJC. In the second interview at his office, I am still trying to clarify the timeline on the HJC's movement into collective contention, and how he and other members of the collective are perceiving themselves as they are shifting. Jano recalled a specific HJC member who urged him to do more with the information the HJC was gathering from collective participants:

> *Jano:* And looking at this [information] and making your jobs easier. I know it can make my job easier because as I'm targeting acquisition, I need to know what's what. As you're targeting development, you need to know what's what. And this is great information.... And then we went the next step. And then that was when [Sis] came and said, "You've got all this information. What are you doing with it?" And we explained we need to demonstrate the strength of this.
>
> *Lucas:* She asked that to the full meeting?
>
> *Jano:* No, she was talking to me. Yeah, so I was like, "What?" And she was like, "We need to talk about what everybody is doing."

In this exchange, Sis, a collective participant (not interviewed in this study) who at the time ran one of the few pre-Katrina nonprofit housing development organizations, saw value in presenting a unified front of housing organizations in New Orleans, sensing that telling the story of the housing work that is happening would initiate a move toward such an effort. Jano admits that during this exchange, he is still more concerned about gathering information that can enable the organization he works for, BYHH, to accomplish its goals of building subsidized housing. As Jano put it, he's not seeing himself as an advocate yet (in other words, as a challenger in the field), particularly because his view of advocates stemmed from his incumbent positionality at that time.

At the same time, this long-term incumbent positionality mindset began to change not just because individuals such as Sis urged Jano, as shown in the quote above, but also because Jano's position as de facto leader of the HJC led him to engage in regular conversations with collective participants about seemingly intractable issues that other collective members were also recognizing. The combined informational knowledge of the housing developers, educators, and others who met for monthly HJC meetings to share information and discuss challenges began to steer conversations toward what could be done about these issues, which were increasingly recognized as shared experiences and not isolated situations.

Additionally, Jano attended regular meetings coordinated by federal, state, and local housing government agencies, as well as those held by legislators. He attended these as both a BYHH staffer and as convener and coordinator of the HJC, bringing what he learned back to the HJC. By the end of 2008, many in the HJC realized that the issues being shared in the monthly convenings were symptomatic of larger systemic problems in the New Orleans and Louisiana housing fields. According to Jano, as well as three other collective members interviewed for this study, a concerned group of them saw the need to begin examining housing policies to determine where to push for needed changes. They decided to install structures and processes to do just that (see the chapter titled *Without Clear Roles and Processes, They Suffer* for further discussion on these structures and processes).

The decision to create structures and processes that would help move the HJC into more contentious politics discussions and planning in response to the information shared at the monthly convenings required the ability to interpret the implications of this information on the practice of housing development in New Orleans. Specifically, when public leaders of a group, such as Jano, deduced that the work of HJC members would continue to be challenged due to existing housing policies, he and others deployed informational *know-how* in creating new strategic action fields based on the information they possessed. Forming structures and processes for strategic action constitutes a step toward the development of a strategic action field, as the intention for these structures is to specifically enable the challenger actor (in this case, HJC) to challenge the target housing field(s).

Jano and other HJC members developed a strategic action field that would focus on deeply correcting the errors they perceived in the New Orleans area housing needs assessment, which the LHFA had contracted a third party to conduct.[18] But this strategic action field was not organized by the collective in a widespread collective vote. Instead, a small team of members who both cared about the document and agreed to engage in the work began to put together information to share with the rest of the collective.

Two other HJC members (one with similar housing experiences to Jano as a former bureaucrat at HANO) who were interviewed for this study, and who shared similar concerns about the assessment, were key contributors to the HJC response. Together, they secured support from other HJC actors to publicly respond to the needs assessment with deep revisions by arguing that the assessment established a research-supported narrative in 2009 that the New Orleans housing market was adequate for its post-Katrina needs. As such, there would be no need to build affordable housing units because New Orleans was (*as is* at that time) in a good position to provide such units from its existing, available stock. Such was the overall message of the document they challenged. This assessment, and the decision to challenge it, demonstrates how informational *know-how* is deployed in such a way that it contributes to the design and implementation of a strategic action field that is contentious in nature and is aimed at changing the housing field in which the challenger is taking action.

The HJC actors that convened monthly at this time, with its large number of nonprofit housing developers, agreed with this assessment, enabling the small lead team working on the strategic action field to move forward. Additionally, these monthly attendees (which by now numbered 40+ monthly attendees but was still not organized until this point as a united collective challenger) determined that this would be the issue the HJC could use to publicly establish itself as a collective with a shared agenda, and it would pay off for them in the way they hoped, garnering attention as a substantial challenger in the housing field. Jano offered an assessment of this recognition in our fourth interview, which took place in January 2017. In the statement below, I had just asked Jano to elaborate on the response garnered after the HJC's corrections on the LHFA document.

> *Jano:* It was like the people recognized that we knew what we were talking about, that [the HJC] as a collective, had access to real information, and we weren't just blowing smoke, which again, was something that distinguished us from the typical advocacy conversation.

Prior to this moment, the HJC was no more than a regular monthly convening of curious, like-minded, or interested housing actors who wanted to be in the know, or to simply network and perhaps establish relationships that could benefit individual organizations' work. This was, after all, the original purpose of the HJC, according to Sinu. After this moment a publicly stated intentionality emerged. Jano and other actors who perceived matters in similar fashion purposefully established the group as the HJC, with intentions of challenging government systems on housing affordability policies, programs, and funding.

It is important to note that while the housing needs assessment challenge marked the first public strategic action field created by the nascent HJC, Jano had already engaged in various public meetings in which he introduced himself as a representative member of a new collective. For example, a key activity taking place that would significantly affect the New Orleans housing field was the development of federal (ultimately failed) legislation on housing, one led in the House by Representative Maxine Waters and one led in the Senate by Senator Mary Landrieu. Jano, new on the scene as a staffer at BYHH and the coordinator of the HJC (before it was fully recognized as a collective), participated in meetings held by these two officials and sometimes spoke up when he perceived incorrect assessments and perspectives on the housing problem in New Orleans. For example, in the very first interview, Jano recalls a meeting that he believes marked his transition from an observer to an outspoken speaker:

> *Jano:* The one call, the first call, I'm just sitting there right, listening, taking notes and everything like that.... I didn't know any of those

folks. So, they're on the phone talking. [Senator] Mary's introduced her bill, [Congresswoman] Maxine's introduced her bill, and again I didn't even know the back story that the reason Maxine [Waters] was interested in New Orleans was because of [this national group]. Right? I didn't know any of that. But I do know that I did know that, from my role at [BYHH], that I liked [Senator] Mary's bill. Because [Senator] Mary's bill was a compromise bill...but the advocates are all lining up and this was what was so crazy and how tone deaf all this was... because here's [the Social Justice Group of La] and the [Committee for Housing in La] coming in to being and they're letting themselves be led by extremists on the ground and people from somewhere else. And they're telling them to kick dirt, sand in the face of the senior Senator... And what I normally do is sit back and listen, but I know this shit.

Lucas: Mm-hmm (affirmative).

Jano: I know this game.... This is my world.... This is the world I spent 11 years in....

After this exchange, Jano expounded on the viewpoints he offered in this meeting regarding Senator Landrieu's proposed legislation and how from this moment onward, he felt no hesitation engaging in these multi-housing actor meetings if he felt confident in his knowledge about the subject matter. His energy during this exchange became markedly higher, as if in the retelling he was re-experiencing the frustrations he felt during that time period.

In Jano's estimation, the potential Waters legislation was informed by narratives that would do more harm than good to the cause of housing affordability in New Orleans, a view he shared in the calls with congressional staff, and local, state, and national housing actors. This level of assessment requires not only that Jano possess the ability to discern different ideas being offered, as well as the presumed logics behind these ideas, but also the ability to connect recommendations to real-world application potential within the housing field, a future-oriented understanding that is possible, at its best, when one has a significant amount of knowledge about the field being discussed. While his open opposition to other housing challengers (specifically to those that were in support of Congresswoman Waters' proposed bill) in this meeting may not have been planned, his in-the-moment decision to do so constitutes a form of spur-of-the-moment strategic action field development that relied extensively on informational *know-how* he deployed spontaneously.

Relying on his years as a HANO bureaucrat, Jano understood (in that moment) the value of narratives and how these can be translated into legislation. He used his knowledge about New Orleans housing affordability issues, housing policies at the local, state, and federal levels, and the on-the-ground challenges nonprofit developers were experiencing to decide to speak up. He felt it was important to clarify to Landrieu's team (who was gathering information for their housing bill) that there was an alternative narrative for housing affordability that should be considered. This alternative narrative corrected misinformation that other advocates (in his estimation) at these meetings were offering.

While these individuals were certainly part of the social justice field in New Orleans, they were not regular participants in the housing field, according to Jano. Compared to them, Jano held a nuanced perspective (informed by his content and issue, field and actor knowledge about the housing field) that differed substantively from the information other advocates were presumably feeding Senator Landrieu's team. At the same time, Jano was aware that the developing collective to which he belonged was in the process of shifting toward a more public political challenger role, and as such would want to be recognized in spaces such as this one as a reasonable, trustworthy, and thoughtful voice on housing justice issues and solutions.

In Jano's estimation, speaking up was as much about correcting misinformation as it was about elevating the status of the soon-to-be HJC in decision-makers' eyes, not just in that moment, but for the benefit of future instances in which they, as challengers to the status quo, might find themselves moving forward. Here, Jano relies on his informational knowledge to exercise the strategic move of providing a counter narrative, demonstrating content and issue, field actor and field *know-how* in the process. This instance also serves to highlight how *know-how* should be understood as a precursor to what Lichterman calls styles (2020). Under Lichterman's Civic Action Theory, one can establish that Jano chose a specific style that fit the situation, but choosing any style of action implies that actors know something about what they are doing (otherwise actors are simply fumbling along accidentally in their endeavors, which may be occasionally true about public leaders, but not always), which in turn implies an assumption about some level of *know-how* being deployed in style selection.

The same demonstration of all three types of informational *know-how* is evident when the HJC tackled the housing needs assessment. According to other HJC actors interviewed for this study, correcting the housing needs assessment was a critical step in the development and growth of the HJC as a key challenger in the housing field. It's important to add that the idea to engage in a public challenge with the LHFA wasn't unanimously supported, though a majority of HJC members did agree that something should be done and that the best vehicle for it would be the HJC rather than any individual member organization.

Though the process of critiquing and providing alternate language to the housing needs assessment encompasses a challenge-oriented strategic action field, the HJC did decide to secure a meeting with the LFHA as a first step. They used this step to make the LHFA aware of the HJC's concerns while simultaneously presenting themselves as an ally in the housing development field and offering the opportunity to provide feedback as a favor to the agency (the idea being that it would help the agency save face before catastrophe hit upon publication) before the study moved into its final form.

Here, it is important to point out the value of this type of tactic in a strategic action field, which many organized groups throughout the United States engage in often before moving to more sensational tactics.[19] Challengers in any field have a variety of means to achieving their desired outcomes, from formal lobbying and the electoral process to closed-door meetings and a variety of public protest tactics. There is no right or wrong here about which tactic is better when comparing any of them to each other in a vacuum, but such tactics rarely take place in vacuums. As such, deciding beforehand which tactic will be most effective depends heavily on the level of informational *know-how* a challenger possesses. Having more informational *know-how* may not guarantee successful attainment of a desired outcome, but it will certainly increase this probability when compared to a challenger (everything else being equal) with less informational *know-how*.

Actions aimed at getting an incumbent, or a group of incumbents to respond favorably, or aimed at removing them, if that is the necessary step, often (but not always) occur in public, in spaces where other actors in a field will be aware of the action and will make decisions about their role in it. Different tactics elicit different types of responses from targeted incumbents, other actors in a given field, and the general public. Therefore, challengers in a field have to make decisions about which type of tactics for their strategic action fields are most appropriate for the moment, using the informational knowledge they have about the field to aid this decision. The ability to secure a meeting with an incumbent for the express purpose of influencing decision-making sounds simple, but it is not. In fact, most challengers, collective or individual, often fail to secure this type of activity because incumbents are typically unwilling to meet with challengers.[20]

Additionally, it cannot be assumed that challengers know where to begin when they have an interest in creating some form of change. Without adequate information about the issues, its content, the actors in the field, and field dynamics and contours, public leaders run the risk of planning and implementing fruitless tactics that can backfire and deflate the energy of a collective. In making the decision to pursue a direct conversation as a collective with the responsible actor within the field, the HJC relied on the policy committee's informational *know-how* to both arrive at this tactic and act on it.

This is an important occurrence to note because new collectives don't typically secure last-minute invitations to affect change in this manner. Was there a secret to this taking place? Not really. As Jano points out, the HJC had created a unifying space in which other housing actors saw the benefit of collaboration. Housing actors may have come together for various individualistic reasons relevant only to their organizations, but after a full year of learning about each other's issues and finding similarities, they found new reasons to stay. Much in the same way that Pueblo board members shared information with me, housing actors now stayed in order to share information on strategic actions.

The collection of housing organizations who participated in early HJC meetings did indeed have relationships with other actors in the New Orleans and Louisiana housing fields. It was through one of these members that a particularly favorable relationship enabled the HJC to secure the opportunity to weigh-in on the housing needs assessment. This is not to say that just having a certain kind of relationship alone is what matters in getting things done as a challenger in a field.

Having housing knowledge that is recognized as valuable by other field actors is critical here. The opportunity to review and recommend changes to the draft housing needs assessment would not have materialized if the HJC did not have already within their members the recognized "expertise." In other words, fortuitous field relationships in conjunction with established and recognized housing knowledge combined in such a way to enable the HJC to deploy this via informational *know-how* in a tactic that contributed to a successful strategic action field.

While there are opportunities for public comment that government agencies typically offer the general public on key documents and decisions, such input rarely affect the final outcome of a policy or state document, despite advocates' efforts to make governance more transparent.[21] Getting a copy of a draft study that is to be used to inform housing policy is certainly noteworthy, as this is not something that typically took place in the Louisiana housing field in 2008, nor is it typical to date. More noteworthy still is the allowance offered to the HJC to provide substantive changes to the draft. Viewed from a contentious collective politics lens, the HJC achieved in short order a very important desired outcome, to have the ability to change the housing needs assessment in such a way that it reflected the reality HJC members were experiencing on the ground.

A full appreciation of this win requires reassessment of the assumptions analysis makes. Incumbents, in general, have no interest in listening to challengers when it comes to making changes to their decisions. The reasons may vary greatly from racial and class-based ideologies to partisan distrust and much more, but application of SAF theory steers us to consider questions of existential meaning. As discussed above, challengers in political contention have an interest in affecting some sort of change that will yield a better version of society than the one they currently experience. This implies that challengers perceive their challenges and prescriptions as paths to a revised future social order, one that is different from the existing social order.

In the Industrial Areas Foundation (IAF) tradition, this work shows up in a tension they label *the-world-as-it-is* versus *the-world-as-it-should-be*. Professional organizers in IAF train future organizers about this existential tension so that these new organizers can use this concept as a tool when they go into community to build collectives who will one day challenge incumbents in a variety of fields. In the IAF tradition, the goal is to be aware of where people are on this tension and how this informs political decision-making. As such, political contention, as SAF theory points out, is about what it means to exist in community with others and how such existence should occur.

Given this assumption, we can better understand the very contentious nature of a new field actor (in this case the HJC) challenging an incumbent (LFHA) about the work they are conducting, even on something as seemingly benign as a procured study within a still-in-the-process of stabilizing field. After this moment, it was clear within the New Orleans and Louisiana housing fields that a significant new challenger had arrived. Just how much more success this new challenger would experience in its efforts to ensure and increase affordable housing availability would remain to be seen.

On Two Comparative Cases Showing how Informational Know-How Interacts with Outcome Success. One might assume that informational *know-how* is a simple straightforward matter: the more an actor knows, the more that actor can apply this knowledge to accomplish her goals. Such a view is overly simplistic and cannot inform assumptions used to model actor decisions and behavior in strategic action fields. Our ability as human beings to call up relevant information in a timely fashion and make appropriate strategic use of it exactly when we need it is, at best, an exercise in countless probabilities. The long-standing rational model of human behavior fails in this regard.[22] Despite the best inputs possible at our disposal, humans inexplicably make confounding decisions, sometimes to their own detriment. We do irrational things at the most unexpected moments in the most unexpected ways, regardless of educational attainment, class, ethnicity, gender, etc. While this study doesn't offer a fully developed alternative model here, it does assert that any model for understanding human decision-making and behavior in collective action must account for situational contingency, the varied ways in which a mix of factors interact in a given moment to yield an unanticipated result, including an actor's decisions and actions, and in this regard, application of Dewey's creative action provides the strongest fit (2016, 2017).

Viewing human decision-making and behavior in strategic action fields from a contingent perspective enables analysis to fully appreciate the ways in which informational *know-how* interacts in varied ways with other factors in contentious collective politics. The HJC's ability to garner the attention of the LHFA and secure a productive meeting, be given the go-ahead to address perceived shortcomings in the needs assessment and to actually have their feedback accepted, offers the possibility of informational *know-how* also playing a role in an incumbent's willingness to receive a given challenge.

That is to say, within contention, there can be moments in which incumbents recognize the value that challengers with certain *know-how* offer and as such actively incorporate the concerns and interests of such challengers. Of course, this can occur simply because incumbents may perceive certain actions as beneficial to their own interests, such as listening to challengers on one matter only to then use this gesture to enable shutting down opportunities for change on other matters. A contingent view enables perception of actors in contentious collective politics sometimes benefiting from usage of informational *know-how*, or sometimes not benefitting despite high-level informational *know-how*, and yet at other times benefitting from not having much, if any, informational *know-how* at all.

Post-Katrina New Orleans offers several storied cases of neighborhood activation and hyperlocal collective contention with varying degrees of desired outcomes success that can be used to explore such complex informational *know-how* interactions. One such neighborhood, the Nearby Neighborhood, which fully activated its collective (the Nearby Neighborhood Group, or NNG – a pseudonym) after the storm, ignited the imaginations of many other neighborhood associations locally and nationally, as well as the interests of many national allies in the years after the storm. I interviewed four individuals from the NNG, two neighborhood residents, a neighborhood ally, and the leader of the NNG at the time of our 2016 interviews (he was a university student volunteer in the immediate years after Katrina). All four interviewees corroborated each other's tale of collective activation based on the threat of municipal erasure under then-Mayor Nagin's plans for a smaller post-Katrina New Orleans.[23]

A mixed neighborhood of upper middle class and working-class families, the Nearby Neighborhood, similar to many in New Orleans in the immediate years after Katrina, found itself having to directly challenge city hall just to keep from being erased from the map. Residents self-organized and created a host of action committees dedicated to specific tasks, from locating displaced residents and gutting homes to participating in public meetings and preparing meals, and much more. Residents galvanized around housing issues, first making sure that every home was gutted and ready for renovation, then focusing on building affordable housing stock and ensuring there were community amenities, such as fighting to reopen a local school and library that were shuttered due to the storm.

Neighborhoods, which are fields onto themselves, can serve as a juncture for participation in many other fields that have some say about matters that affect a neighborhood, from crime and education to street flooding and blight. As a challenger, NNG found itself challenging such fields as housing, education, and public safety in the first 5 years after the storm. As has been shown so far, informational *know-how* about a field in which a challenger is engaged can interact in such a way as to increase a challenger's effectiveness in pursuing a desired outcome. Unfortunately, neighborhoods don't typically possess sufficient *know-how* about the many fields that affect them, as knowledge about these fields is often limited in scope, translating to limited informational *know-how* among neighborhood leadership (often exacerbated by lack of other dimensions of *know-how*).

In my time as the director of the Mayor's Neighborhood Engagement Office for the city of New Orleans between 2010 and 2013, I observed how such limitations manifested across neighborhood groups. Despite resident leaders' passions for their neighborhoods and a desire to interact with local government on issues that mattered to them, most New Orleans neighborhood leaders were often at a disadvantage when confronted with the need to understand field processes, policies, and decision-making responsibilities in order to press their challenges forward in the correct spaces and direct these toward the correct incumbent actors. Yet, neighborhoods do challenge local government, of course, and sometimes do succeed in their challenges, even without adequate informational *know-how*, by simply learning from mistakes along the way, doing the public work that Boyte establishes is a path toward building active citizens (Boyte, 2013).

Of course, an experiential, trial-and-error approach to building the *know-how* needed to increase the potential effectiveness of a challenger's contention in a given field may not take place in a timely enough fashion, or there may not be enough time for that to happen if a threat is imminent. For the NNG, the threat of having the Nearby Neighborhood converted into green space in the years after the storm was imminent. Leaders did not have the luxury of time. As Linas (who was the NNG executive director at the time I interviewed him) states, "*I mean obviously, the big fear was, what initially galvanized people was the green dot, you know.*"[24,25]

In many regards, the NNG was not different to similar neighborhoods facing this threat from local government. Many people who were primarily concerned with returning home and rebuilding their lives after the levee failures now entered collective political contention. At the same time, while many neighborhoods experienced the same threat of erasure that the Nearby Neighborhood experienced, most were less successful than the NNG in their attempts to challenge city hall and other local agencies. One key manner in which the NNG differed from others was in its ability to galvanize considerable informational knowledge from outside sources and deploy this effectively in strategic action fields. For example, From his second-floor office located in a community center that NNG had recently opened, Linas explained how he got involved with the work right after the storm. from his second-floor office located in a community center that NNG had recently opened, Linas explained how he got involved with the work right after the storm.

> *Linas:* I graduated and I started in my position as the director of community programming at the school, and I was still able to serve as a liaison for the college and the students…it was a student led program, so they led it, but I was able to be an on-the-ground liaison for them and help them to coordinate and set up the summer program…so it ran and served hundreds of kids every summer….

This ability to secure the needed resources and expertise from non-neighborhood allies and put it to use in different forms of activities within strategic action fields (in the same manner that I discussed above in my role as a nonprofit director challenging the housing education field) speaks to an element of informational *know-how* that requires some attention. When actors don't have the needed information to make effective strategic action field decisions, they need to have the ability to understand where to secure this information, how much of it they need to act, and how to use it effectively in strategic action fields. Not everyone comes ready-made with this ability. Knowing how to "plug-in" recently acquired information into on-the-ground activities in a manner that is beneficial to strategic action is not equally distributed among actors involved in contentious collective politics, which is why I consider it a vital element of informational *know-how*. The NNG demonstrated such an ability in its work to secure the needed knowledge that would enable them to make effective strategic action field decisions.

Unlike the HJC, the NNG lacked the informational *know-how* from among its member ranks to effectively tackle the varied issues it had to deal with post-Katrina. These were residents who did not have any specific experience in the New Orleans social justice field or any of the issue-centered subfields, such as housing, education, public safety, and so on. Similarly, the vast majority of its resident leaders had little to no experience challenging decision-makers.

Yet, residents (such as the two I interviewed) along with Linas engaged in the work to challenge local government on many fronts in their fight to remain and eventually return to full occupancy. In two key instances, NNG actors converted "borrowed" expertise into the informational *know-how* needed for strategic action fields. The main thrust behind their strategic action fields lay in standing up as much of the neighborhood as possible, as quickly as possible, in order to make it harder for the city to rezone the area into green space. This strategy included implementing direct action to return the local library and elementary school back to service immediately, which the NNG identified as pivotal for the neighborhood returning and making it harder for city hall to implement its green dot plan.[26] Both target actions had facilities that were shuttered, still requiring internal debris removal. The local agencies governing these two assets either weren't ready to address this or were already considering permanent shuttering or demolition, which is what occurred in other neighborhoods that were less able than NNG to succeed in their efforts to challenge such decisions by the respective local agencies.[27]

Linas recalls the decision during our first interview in 2016 to illegally enter the Nearby Neighborhood public school campus in order to gut it and abate the deterioration process. He was in the middle of describing the different tasks that he was involved in, from meter reading to knocking on doors, then included this information, which I then interrupted, seeking clarification:

> *Linas:* Um, I did some hands-on work, um, I was involved in gutting the [Turnbull] school, when it was, um…it had been sitting there for about a year, um, untouched…and chain linked fenced, the city was not budging on doing anything, like so many other schools at that time, and so they took it upon themselves to literally bust in there (laugh)….
>
> *Lucas:* Is that what they did?
>
> *Linas:* Yeah
>
> *Lucas:* Did they just break the fence and go in there?
>
> *Linas:* Yeah

By now, the school had become such a central part of the neighborhood strategy to return as quickly as possible that NNG leaders engaged in PR strategies aimed at elevating the need to reopen the school as soon as possible. A 2009 National Public Radio report about the school's opening cites one of the prominent NNG leaders at the time as stating in 2006 that "regardless of who the babies are in the classroom, quality learning will happen" at the school.[28]

Having received little encouragement from the local school board that the school would ever be considered for a fast-track return to service, the NNG took it upon itself to take care of the first step in the process. Of course, the NNG wasn't exactly well-versed in the potential dangers of gutting this type of structure, but to them it didn't matter. In the same conversation quoted above, he continues after my clarifying questions:

Linas: And so, a bunch of volunteers and folks in the neighborhood went in and, you know, the whole Tyvek suits, everything at that time, to protect you from the toxic mold that was in, um, throughout the school building. That was, that made a lasting impression on me, um, it was overwhelming for sure....

It was a calculated move. Gut the property, clean it up, then get someone from the school board to come view the work, with the hope that they could secure support from the school board. As one of the residents who worked alongside Linas, Sammie (a pseudonym), recalled during our single interview in his home. He met with me in April 2017 in his recently renovated living room. His home sat on a major thoroughfare that stands as a divider between the lower income and the higher income sides of the neighborhood. I asked Sammie about the school and whether he was involved in that effort.

Sammie: I don't know what all was involved with the school.

Lucas: Yeah?

Sammie: I just remember that we would talk about it at meetings. At some point there was a principal that was hired, who was a person that I knew.

Lucas: Oh yeah?

Sammie: He was a teacher for a friend of mine who used to run the pre-school. Yeah. Then he was, then we got, kind of, I don't know where we got funding for [Turnbull school], to redevelop it. It took a while. It took some doing.

The NNG was aware that it didn't know anything about the education field beyond soliciting requests to the school board for support. In a stable field nested among other stable fields, this approach would have characterized the typical manner in which most advocates in New Orleans tackled education issues: attack or engage the school board in the hopes of securing school board-initiated change. Before Katrina, such an approach would have easily fit into the school board's normative administrative processes, but after the storm, the very school board itself was in a state of instability. As a field unto itself, the school board managed more than 100 schools before the storm, a number that would be reduced to less than 20 by the state takeover that occurred less than 3 months after the levee failures.

The state takeover created a new actor in the New Orleans education field, the Recovery School District (RSD), which would operate the majority of New Orleans schools until its dissolution in 2018. By the time the NNG sought input from the local school board before trespassing onto the campus, the school had become the responsibility of the RSD, and in this regard reveals NNG's informational *know-how* gaps in their field knowledge.

After gutting and cleaning the site, resident leaders who were tasked to devise a strategy for bringing the school back online actively sought the expertise needed to devise an effective strategy. They learned that they could form a legal entity that could apply for a charter from the RSD, a move that would give the legal entity with the charter the direct control it would need over the site that would be used to operate a school. Having been armed with this information, the NNG deployed informational *know-how* in setting a set of actions in motion that enabled them to secure the desired charter, which in turn enabled them to secure control over the school site.

The effort would prove much more challenging than initially imagined, with NNG leaders having to fight for and win renovation funding while simultaneously operating the school in a temporary home. The operating charter awarded to the NNG-created entity, however, was revoked in 2010, one year after moving into the renovated facilities, due to low performance. Despite this, the NNG had been so successful in establishing the school's connection to neighborhood life that the new charter operator continued the school at the Nearby Neighborhood site, where it operates to this day. Therefore, the strategic decision to gut, clean, renovate, and operate the neighborhood school without government approval until a charter was secured achieved its purpose of helping the Nearby Neighborhood secure its desired outcome of having the school come back to the neighborhood.

The school reopened its doors in the original school site 4 years after the levee failures, serving as a galvanizing project that added value to the group's efforts to fight city hall. It demonstrated locally, as well as nationally, what a dedicated group of neighbors could do to rebuild after a catastrophic event. The notoriety created by NNG's work, culminating in the school reopening strategy, made it almost inevitable that city hall would not, after all, be displacing any of the residents in the Nearby Neighborhood. In fact, the opposite occurred, with the NNG serving as an example case of what neighborhoods could and should do to speed up recovery in similarly devastated neighborhoods throughout the city.

The school reopening occurring within 5 years of Katrina's levee failures was certainly not the norm. Had the NNG not organized efforts to push for this project, secure the necessary government support and funding, and then secure a decision-making role within each step, the school would not have been up and running as soon as it was, if at all. Residents who were interviewed credit their leadership on the strategies deployed and group's ability to stay focused on the goals they set.

Of course, there were many other factors that contributed to the NNG's ability to secure the desired outcomes in this initiative, some of which included field-related dynamics, and some of which included other dimensions of *know-how*. As mentioned above, none of these different dimensions of *know-how* occur in a vacuum, even if this book's structure might imply that. The ability to use information well and deploy it in informational *know-how* requires an actor possess the ability to assess what opportunities the information presents and what actions make the most sense, given what is known. Such abilities are not evenly distributed in the population. One need only peruse civic training programs across the

US to realize that civic knowledge and skills are not evenly distributed or developed. In fact, civic knowledge and skills are not evenly accessible.[29] Finally, a key potential factor to consider that may have contributed to the NNG's ability to achieve its desired outcome is the congruence of interests within the Nearby Neighborhood.

At the time of the interviews with NNG members, the Nearby Neighborhood's luster had somewhat diminished, in part, because of diminishing participation by residents and a growing rift between the needs of the working-class side of the neighborhood and that of the upper middle-class side. Having succeeded as a neighborhood group in defeating city hall and achieving their desired outcomes means that they also succeeded in removing the energy that once fueled widespread participation: a common threat and a common enemy. The impending common threat of a city government potentially converting their entire neighborhood into green space served as the balm that smoothed over any underlying concerns and friction. Thus, Nearby Neighborhood residents were able to unify and rally around the school and other strategies with success, in part, because such targets offered a clear, noncontroversial, nonproblematic focus for all involved, creating a congruence of interests.

It should be noted that this congruence of interests created the space for informational *know-how* to contribute to success in a way that informational *know-how* alone could not have made possible. For example, NNG failed with a strategy to become affordable housing developers as a means of helping low-income residents return. Similar to other endeavors, NNG acquired the needed informational *know-how* from outside sources, but from the onset, this strategy remained mired in setbacks and internal conflict until it was eventually shelved.

The NNG showed that it is possible to achieve desired outcomes in strategic action fields when the public leaders involved do not themselves possess the requisite knowledge and information about the field, its actors, and its content and issues. By simply borrowing this knowledge and deploying it strategically as informational *know-how*, the NNG was able to achieve some of the desired outcomes they wanted, with the main one being the ability to remain in their homes.

As collectives in the immediate years after Katrina, both the HJC and the NNG embarked upon bringing about change that relied on either on-hand or "borrowed" knowledge that was put to use as informational *know-how* in strategic action fields designed to achieve their desired outcomes. Though informational *know-how* did not always contribute to a group achieving its desired outcomes, I have shown that without this dimension of *know-how*, collective contention is hard pressed to accomplish what it wants.

At the NBHI, which is not a collective but rather a small nonprofit housing development organization that is also a member of the HJC, I interviewed three people: Tico, the church's leading clergy; Britan (who was hired in 2012), the second-ever director of the organization; and Phin, a community organizer. This case serves as another comparison that helps illustrate the various ways in which informational *know-how* interacts within an actor's (in this case NBHI) contentious politics and its desired outcome.

Founded by a local church, NBHI was created in the aftermath of Katrina for the purposes of enabling the church to play an active role in housing affordability in the neighborhood where it was situated. Similar to that of NNG leaders, the founding clergy person, Tico, as well as those in the church whom he recruited to assist him in the endeavor, knew little to nothing about housing when they created NBHI. Our interview took place in Tico's vestry offices in May 2017. Seated across from his desk, I asked Tico to start at the beginning of their effort to start NBHI. He began by establishing what he was hearing about what might happen to the community the NBHI would focus on serving:

> *Tico:* I remember they used the phrase that caught my mind, on one of those All Things Considered interviews, uptown New Orleans was going to be even more a Disneyland with drinks.
>
> *Lucas:* Oh wow
>
> *Tico:* That was the phrase. I was new enough to the city, at that point, that I really believed that that made sense. I knew a lot of this property, I had been here a couple of years, I knew the property behind the [church]. That area didn't flood, I also knew it was relatively poor. It seemed like a lot of rental and a lot of people have not come back. We didn't know if they would or not. I thought these developers could just sort of knock all this stuff down. A lot of it was already either abandoned or close to it. So ... the new president of the [Church] Relief and Development ... he happened to come to that meeting right after Katrina. He was new and he brought some money to help with short term needs.... So my first conversation with them was about doing some immediate, using the [church] property to do some immediate triage of water and bleach and that kind of stuff that they certainly gave us some support for. Then I said, "What about this idea of maybe buying up this property so the developers don't get it, and we can kind of be a land bank?"

This lack of knowledge about how the enterprise might work didn't dissuade Tico from advancing the agenda of combating what he was already perceiving to be an eventual land grab. An episode from NBHI's early days brings attention to how informational *know-how* interacts in strategic action fields in much the same way as it does for collective actors who are field challengers.

One of the unknown elements of this endeavor early on for Tico and his founding members was the potential that the founding of a nonprofit organization could at some point position them in a contentious relationship with city hall. Within a couple of years of its creation, this is exactly where they found themselves when the first executive director embarked on the process of securing blighted properties from the city.

Having secured funding from the national arms of the founding church, Tico was able to secure the resources for a part-time director who could steer the fledgling organization. This first director had no knowledge about housing or the housing field in New Orleans, but he did have knowledge and experience in the law. Upon finalizing NBHI's strategic direction of acquiring, developing, and offering affordable housing within their target area, the first director began to attend the requisite public meetings held by the city on available properties post-Katrina. In these meetings, the responsible departments within city hall discussed the various ways that organizations could secure blighted properties. According to Tico, the individuals responsible for designing and implementing this program in the immediate aftermath of Katrina whereby nonprofits such as NBHI could secure an allocation of properties didn't seem to understand the laws and policies that guided their work.

NBHI used the knowledge that the first director researched to push key individuals, including council members who could exercise some pressure on city hall (it should be noted that unlike surrounding parishes, legislators have no direct authority over city agencies in the city of New Orleans governance structure as these are either independent or report directly to the mayor), to act on their behalf.[30,31] Without much more than a few well-placed conversations armed with knowledge about property adjudication legal frames provided by the first director, as well as strategically placed calls to political allies, NBHI was able to circumvent the barriers the city presented to its own program and secure the set of properties and lots it had prioritized.

While this isn't the conventional example of contention in which groups of people engage in tough challenges to obstinate incumbents who aren't willing to relinquish power, it does show how informational *know-how* can interact in a manner that enhances a challenger's desired outcomes. Additionally, contentious situations manifest in various ways when challengers are pursuing any form of interaction with the power holders within a field.

Something as seemingly uncontentious as a local government's open solicitation process for contracted partnerships in the US democratic governance universe is rife with contention. Internal actors involved in shaping the solicitation may push and jostle for their vision for implementation, political insiders (such as lobbyists, close political allies, and campaign funders) may urge elected officials to push on career bureaucrats to design solicitations in a specific way that benefits the insiders, or competing challengers with varying degrees of influence in local government may compete to push their versions of what should be implemented (according to their vision of what will benefit them and their constituents), and so on. In this scenario, NBHI turned from solicitor for properties to a contentious challenger to city hall bureaucrats because NBHI openly challenged these individuals on their interpretations of the laws and regulations in place and even went so far as to increase pressure on these individuals via other political allies, resulting in these bureaucrats giving way to NBHI's interpretation.

Such an understanding of contention in all political activities (I refer here not just to electoral politics but to all decision-making actions that have resource allocation, social ordering, or civil rights implications) is expressed in SAF theory's account of the "existential function of the social" (Fligstein & McAdam, 2012). Using this perspective, all social spaces that constitute a political field (in which decisions are made that affect communities) generate contention because political decision-making never benefits everyone, creating challengers out of those who do not see themselves benefitting from a given decision. Contention, effectively, is varied and occurs at different scales, from a battle of will between two individuals with power within a field to mass demonstrations against large, incumbent organizational actors in government or commerce.

In the case of the NBHI example here, the ability to challenge city hall's adjudicated properties program and exert some influence over this initiative by relying on the knowledge-based legal analysis provided by the NBHI director constitutes a demonstration of informational *know-how*. The desired outcome for NBHI was attainment of targeted blighted properties in their neighborhood, which they planned to redevelop into affordable homes. They learned everything they needed to learn and established all that was required to become eligible to compete for adjudicated properties, as per city hall regulations, only to find they were unable to do so because of the manner in which actors within the different city hall departments were interpreting certain aspects of the program. Here, NBHI, in disagreeing, understood that they could challenge the city's interpretation, which is what they did successfully.

This decision to challenge constitutes a strategic action field, which was designed to not only contend but win the fight. While NBHI, as an organization, still lacked a large amount of knowledge about housing development and other housing related matters, this lack of knowledge did not diminish their ability to successfully challenge city hall on its adjudication program. In this case, general legal knowledge was sufficient for NBHI to convert into informational *know-how* that helped guide its strategic action.

Additional Instances of Informational Know-How Interaction with Desired Outcomes. There are instances in collective contention in which no matter how much informational *know-how* actors bring to strategic action, unanticipated situations simply confound challengers' efforts. An actor may have all the knowledge in the world about the content and issues of a given field and may even have adequate knowledge about the field in general, such as the organizational leaders, the legislation that authorizes certain decision-makers, and budget allocations, to name a few. Despite this, challengers with seemingly adequate knowledge about a field find that deploying informational *know-how* in strategic action fails to enhance the attainment of desired outcomes or are left at a disadvantage when unanticipated outcomes occur.

After the HJC had begun to establish itself as a formidable challenger within the Louisiana and New Orleans housing fields, having accomplished a handful of wins in both fields, an opportunity arose to inform the development of a new state-funded and city-run soft-second program.[32] The newly elected Landrieu administration hired new individuals to oversee housing, and the HJC quickly established relationships with these new bureaucrats. One of the early projects the HJC worked on with these new city hall leaders was the deployment of a pool of one-time funds dedicated to the city-run soft second program, which had been languishing for a couple of years. Everything seemed to be going well for HJC until a wrinkle appeared. As Jano recounts, this wrinkle had to do with providing a special payment allocation to homebuyer educators, which animated him considerably when he talked about this:

Lucas: So you have them (city actors) at the table and the assumption is "we're working together."

Jano: No, I didn't presume that. I presumed they were there to gather intelligence.

Lucas: You presumed that?

Jano: Yeah.

Lucas: How about everybody else in your group?

Jano: Oh, yeah. I think that's what everybody... Well, I think that's why people went back and said, "Oh, yeah. We heard that thing they said over that meeting." We don't necessarily agree with that. So, what could you give me?

Lucas: So, you feel like even though they were there with you, your coalition members understood that even though you were working together, this wasn't a done deal?

Jano: Oh, yeah. Oh, yeah. And we had people like, for example, you know how cool I am with [this lady, right]? She comes to me. She says, "I think we should abandon the homebuyer education people because they need to get their act together and they need to be advocating for themselves."

Lucas: Because you're trying to work with them in this thing?

Jano: Well, also my thing is that I don't know how you do this without talking about homebuyer education. It's stupid. So, it wasn't even about trying to help them so much as, for me, it was this is what makes sense....

Lucas: And so how did you find out that the city decided.... You submitted it but they were at the table designing it with you.

Jano: Mm-hmm (affirmative).

Lucas: You submitted it to Pantu?

Jano: Sent it to [his boss].

Lucas: And what happened when you did that? Like it was just an email? Was it a meeting?

Jano: So we sent him a letter and then we went and met with him.

Lucas: Uh-huh.

Jano: And then he basically told us about the $350.

Lucas: He had a different plan.

Jano: Yes.

Lucas: Already.

Jano: And we were like, "Okay, where'd that came from?" And we [learned] from out back channels, that [Falicia] had gone to them.

The person Jano named, Falicia, is a housing public leader who had considerable leverage within the New Orleans pre-Katrina housing field. Meeting in his office behind closed doors at HJC headquarters, Jano became agitated as he recounted this episode, something he would do often when recounting problematic moments.

Despite the HJC's growing significance and role as a collective that represents housing-related organizations, Falicia, as a leader of another housing organization, acted outside of and in direct competition with the collective, pursuing and attaining a specific program element that directly benefitted her organization, the inclusion of a $350 allocation in the soft second program for homebuyer educators (who presumably would be part of the process for prospective homeowners looking to apply for the soft second benefit).

Such an unexpected outcome, while beneficial to a handful of organizations that participated in the HJC, occurred in such a way that it initially created friction between HJC and housing government leaders. Jano was aware that "old guard" leaders, such as Falicia, could at any moment exert individual influence that could prove harmful to the HJC. Rather than seeking to advance the issue within the collective's overall strategies, Falicia demonstrated to Jano how challenging it could be to build the type of unified voice the collective would need in order to achieve its desired outcomes. While this instance ultimately proved beneficial to the smaller collective of homebuyer educators (some of which were HJC members and others not), it did exacerbate what would be an ongoing tension among housing advocates in the New Orleans field: the extent to which the HJC served (or did not serve) individual organizational interests.

In another case, extensive knowledge about content and issues affecting several fields diminished usage of informational *know-how* in the type of strategic action that achieves some form of desired social justice change. Bana, the leader of the All Are Welcome Institute (AWI), a small nonprofit that operated in the New Orleans social justice field, was deeply knowledgeable about practices in government entities in the New Orleans area that continue to exacerbate and maintain racialized disparities that sustain a school-to-prison pipeline to this day.[33] As a small organization with deep knowledge about a specific practice, AWI participated in a statewide coalition of similar-minded organizations with an interest in ending the very processes and practices that contribute to the school-to-prison pipeline.

Bana expressed during interviews (I interviewed her twice, as well as two other members of her staff in their offices, which were located inside a community center that housed other services, such as arts therapy, yoga instruction, and dance) that one of the long-term desired outcomes for AWI was to see the public entities they focus on, K-12 public schools and criminal justice agencies, change their operations from a largely punitive approach to a more curative approach, in other words, a radical culture shift.

Such a shift would be significant for both the education and criminal justice fields in New Orleans. Unfortunately, such a shift was not taking place when the interviews occurred (2016 and 2017), and the work in which AWI is considered an expert had yet (at that time) to be implemented at any significant scale within these fields. While AWI boasted a handful of independent charter school clients and good working relationships with the juvenile courts, it was not advancing its agenda in the manner it desired. Bana indicated that while thankful for the individual spaces where AWI had been able to bring about some change, the system, overall, had yet to change.

A partial explanation for the incongruity between AWI's desired outcome of field-wide systemic shifts in the school-to-prison pipeline (presumably in both the education and criminal justice fields) processes and what it had been able to accomplish stems, in part, from the organization's inability to use its knowledge in strategic action fields. This inability may be connected to AWI's content knowledge itself, which informs their practical approach to conflict, an approach that is counter to normative modes of action when dealing with conflict. As proponents of a more nurturing approach to problems and conflict, AWI practiced what it preached, and in practicing what it preached, it put into action a test-before-you-drive approach to agitating for change.

Rather than implementing strategic actions aimed at changing systemwide policies, AWI relied on a client service approach. Through this approach, AWI solicited invitations to present their work to organizational decision-makers in target agencies as a professional-development product. If invited back, AWI would teach its alternative approaches to interested administrators, educators, and public safety personnel at a single agency. In this way, AWI engaged in a more subversive form of contention that relied on converting the daily practices of leaders within organizations as a way of influencing them into perceiving the need for broader changes, what Bana often referred to in the first interview as changing the minds and hearts first. When I asked about the broader coalition in which her organization participated, she offered the response quoted below:

Lucas: So, you're providing this technical information on a committee?

Bana: Yes.

Lucas: And they're focusing on trying to push for different actions to change this, and one of them is legislative.

Bana: Correct.

Lucas: Are there other actions they're working on beside that?

Bana: Doing a film, a video, and a web page that talk about the school to prison pipeline, and the impact of the school to prison pipeline, really focusing...for me, though, the way I describe it is as changing minds and hearts, that's what we do first. Change minds and hearts, tell stories that help people understand impact. That's what ... resonate with people, in terms of their heart, have the best impact, I think, in changing feet.

Viewed through SAF theory, Bana's desire to bring about systemic change in the practices that contribute to the school-to-prison pipeline in the New Orleans area is as contentious an endeavor as that of a violent protest in the streets asking for justice. Both are asking for change; both are seeking to reorder the social world in such a way as to have it become a better place for those who are either left out or abused by the current social ordering of the world. What can be understood as contention (by a collective or a single actor) isn't necessarily dependent upon the form the fight takes. Instead, the very act of daring to push for a different reality than the one that exists, no matter how unobtrusive and unassuming the form, can be understood as contention through this lens.

In AWI's case, the type of contention they deploy is subtle, often at the low-man-on-the-totem-pole level, which fails to yield any significant change within a target system in a field. Their "minds and hearts" approach does not include strategic action fields directed at powerful legislators and administrators of large systems. Without deploying informational *know-how* in direct strategic action fields that are aimed directly at power brokers within fields, AWI's strategies have failed to advance the desired change in the scope and breadth they desire.

One final observation worth considering is from another case outside the housing field, which offers additional perspective on informational *know-how*'s interaction with desired outcomes. I interviewed two individuals from the Help Them Achieve Greatness (HTAG) organization, the executive director (Hildan) and a board member (Tamu). The organization works in the juvenile justice field in New Orleans. Prior to cofounding HTAG in 2004, both interviewees worked with other actors from another juvenile justice organization to challenge the State of Louisiana to close one of its most poorly run juvenile correction facilities. Their work before 2004 was openly confrontational with the State of Louisiana Department of Public Safety and Corrections (LDPSC). Both interviewees participated in years of strategic action development and direct-action implementation (which included lawsuits and public demonstrations), gaining invaluable knowledge and information about their target field.

Having succeeded in shutting down one of the worst-run, most violent, and unsafe facilities for juveniles in the nation, Hildan and Tamu, along with two other cofounders of HTAG who were not interviewed, saw a need to fill a gap in services to the target demographic of individuals who were typically placed in such facilities. They formed HTAG and immediately began to engage actors at LDPSC about support for their work.

They contended, successfully, that with the closing of the correctional facility and changing paradigms in criminal justice nationally, Louisiana's lack of prevention and supportive services funding for young people needed to change, as this could contribute to lower incarceration numbers. In succeeding to advance this argument with key actors within LDPSC, they were able to secure state funding for the work they were doing in New Orleans. When asked about this effort with the state, I asked Hildan if he thought of it as a sort of advocate challenge. He did not. In his opinion, he was not engaging in any sort of political challenge, and yet, this is exactly what he was doing in the very act of asking the state of Louisiana to do something it was not doing. Meeting in his office on the second floor of a two-story service center in which the majority of HTAG services were offered, Hildan had this to say:

> *Hildan:* So we actually, and I in particular had always maintained good relationships with the people I worked with whom were high up at the state, so if they were their attorneys, if they were folks in central office, so I always have found that like you get a lot further with honey and so a lot of it honestly comes down to relationships that I didn't personally burn bridges even though there was some skepticism because of the organization that I came from....

Referring back to the earlier observation about what constitutes contention, here, we have another example that can help expand the discussion. Hildan needed a series of meetings and an extensive amount of informational and social *know-how* (discussed further below), paired with an opportunity opening in the greater national criminal justice field, to be able to convince actors within the LDPSC bureaucracy to allocate dedicated annual funding to HTAG. Here, it is important to point out that challengers to the state at local, regional and state levels throughout the United States rarely achieve this form of state response. Such a success in a challenger's desired outcome is rare in contentious collective politics. According to Hildan, the key to his success in this endeavor was his approach as an ally, as someone to be trusted.

This case begs the question: is Hildan right? Did he accomplish what he wanted in securing state partnership in HTAG's endeavors by extending a hand rather than shaking a fist? I don't believe so. In fact, such an approach is unlikely to achieve a challenger's desired results on a consistent basis simply because incumbents in a field rarely extend this form of opportunity and concession to challengers, no matter how much they posture as allies. When such an opportunity is afforded, it is offered to incumbents' existing or known allies, or political insiders who enable incumbents to remain in place, or to elected officials' campaign backers who then impose such decisions upon incumbents and/or governance units within government agencies.

First, contention was indeed an aspect of the scenario that placed Hildan as the HTAG actor in front of state actors. As a new actor in the juvenile justice field, HTAG entered as a challenger, particularly because it sought to change how the state deployed its resources in its efforts to address juvenile delinquency. Contention here lay in the different views on how to best address juvenile delinquency, which reflected contrasting ideas about how to socially order structures and processes that address this within their field. It is possible that HTAG was simply able to take advantage of an opening opportunity in which incumbents were more favorably disposed to consider alternative solution. However, just existing during a time of fortuitousness is not sufficient explanation for HTAG's success. The leader of HTAG had to deploy informational *know-how* in such a way as to take advantage of this moment in time. The old adage of being at the right place at the right time may actually help partially explain HTAG's success.

This case also raises a final question worth exploring. How can opportunity be accounted for in the deployment of any type of *know-how* in strategic action fields? Does *know-how* matter at all in the face of unexpected opportunity openings when it comes to challengers attempting to secure their desired outcomes? Much of the early literature on social movements and civic engagement traditionally focused on the macro social structures that either create or diminish opportunity while the practice-oriented books written by organizers such as Alinsky focused on what individuals can do to challenge incumbents, regardless of opportunities.

Viewed through SAF theory, this isn't an *either/or* issue, but rather a *both/and* issue. That is to say, one can imagine situations in which both *know-how* and open opportunities interact to enable challengers to achieve desired outcomes, whereas situations in which lack of *know-how* combined with closed opportunities interact to stymie success. Simultaneously, one can also imagine the reverse in both scenarios. What the data in this chapter do seem to indicate, and which is also corroborated repeatedly throughout the cases compared and individuals interviewed through this study, is that there is a positive benefit to challengers equipping, or preparing themselves, with as much *know-how* as possible in their political contentions. There is no guarantee that increased, higher level informational *know-how* will bring about a challenger's desired outcomes, but it does increase the potential for success when compared to little or no informational *know-how*.

As this chapter points out, regardless of the degree of informational *know-how* an actor may possess, an actor will deploy this *know-how* in service of her decisions and activities within a strategic action field. Across actors within a field, there are different levels of informational *know-how* that can be observed, with some knowing just enough about a field to conduct confrontation tactics generally aimed to anyone who can help and others not knowing enough to direct their activities toward the decision-making spaces where incumbents and governance units operate. This is where informational *know-how* plays a critical role in challengers' decisions about what strategic action fields will look like, what tactics they will deploy, and toward which incumbents they will be directed, if any. A challenger needs to be able to at least have knowledge about the contours of a field, the actors in that field, and the power and/or authority that such actors have relative to that challenger's desired outcomes. Without this knowledge, a challenger's work to disrupt a field through a strategic action field is likely to prove unsuccessful and (potentially) demoralizing.

Notes

1. For a discussion on the stability of fields as it is used in this study, refer to Fligstein and McAdam's 2012 *Theory of Fields*.
2. See Billy Fields' 2009 "From Green Dots to Greenways: Planning in the Age of Climate Change in Post-Katrina New Orleans" for a discussion of the resilience-oriented urban planning that took place immediately after the storm, which resulted in the type of neighborhood backlash the NNG engaged in.
3. Though not strictly, a chronological order of quoted interviews is not a necessary part of analysis but rather a narrative frame used to facilitate communication with the reader.
4. I will sometimes refer to a field as a subfield when I am referencing a field within the analytical case field. In this instance, I use the term subfield to denote the embedded nature of the first-time homebuyer field within the New Orleans housing field, which is the main analytical field.
5. While this study does not explore the history of how a newly created organization was given one of the largest redevelopment projects in the history of public housing in New Orleans, it is important to briefly highlight this event as it relates to analysis of HJC. In 2006, the local catholic services agency created BYHH in order to serve as the receiver of a contract from the US Department of Housing and Urban Development (HUD) to redevelop one of the centrally located, shuttered public housing developments in the city. This role of serving as a private housing developer of one of the most important sections of land in the heart of downtown New Orleans afforded BYHH a critical position in the conversation about returning residents, as well as among other housing field actors.
6. An independent local government agency, HANO owns and manages all New Orleans public housing complexes, as well as other real estate sites it owns throughout the city.
7. See https://www.democracynow.org/2007/12/21/new_orleans_police_taser_pepper_spray for the documentary about this moment.
8. Jano's statement about this is informed by her knowledge about and work with the HOPE VI program that was approved by Congress on October 6, 1992. Refer to this HUD page for program information: https://www.hud.gov/program_offices/public_indian_housing/programs/ph/hope6/about
9. See the video hyperlink in endnote 7 above for activists' views on the situation.
10. See https://www.democracynow.org/2007/12/21/new_orleans_police_taser_pepper_spray for reporting on this matter.
11. For a HUD summary of the bill, see: https://www.hud.gov/sites/documents/DOC_8927.PDF. Also see http://nlihc.org/sites/default/files/2014AG-118.pdf for a critical review of public housing bills.

102   *The Know-How of Public Leaders in Collective Politics*

12. See https://library.municode.com/la/new_orleans/munidocs/munidocs?nodeId=M7242007-12-20PDF for a transcript of the city council meeting held on December 20, 2007.
13. For a brief news report on this issue, see National Public Radio's report: https://www.npr.org/2008/03/31/89248516/hud-secretary-jackson-steps-down-amid-probe
14. The LHFA (called the Louisiana Housing Corporation as of 2012) is a quasi-government agency that sets policies for housing funding, particularly to development-related tax credits. See their website for more information: https://www.lhc.la.gov/
15. While the 1967 Freedom of Information Act in the United States sets up a cultural and procedural practice of openness and transparency in governance, it does not mandate that agencies aggressively share with the general public every document they create. Some agencies are better than others in any given field at sharing information openly with the general public, but typically such sharing is limited in nature and often provided in such timeline windows that it leaves little time for any potential challenger to mount a substantive challenge, resulting in the open governance movement that continues to push for greater transparency and accountability. Visit: https://www.oecd.org/gov/open-government/ for an example of a movement actor in this field.
16. Jano had extensive knowledge of the pre-Katrina nonprofit housing community, comprising several community development organizations, affordable housing providers, and first-time homebuyer trainers, but he had little knowledge of the myriad of new post-Katrina actors. However, as the lead coordinator of HJC, he was positioned in such a way within the New Orleans housing field that he regularly learned of newcomer actors both in the New Orleans and Louisiana housing fields.
17. This statement is not fully accurate because the housing collective eventually expands to include actors from incumbent institutions, which is discussed in other sections below.
18. The final document that was published was titled, *The New Orleans Market Analysis*.
19. The word tactics, used throughout this study, refers to specific planned or unplanned action activities carried out by actors in a field and that are specifically deployed in order to influence incumbents and/or governance units within a target field.
20. In the IAF tradition, community organizers are trained to understand that power rarely meets with the powerless unless it benefits the powerful fully. Hence, the work of community organizers is to build the sort of power that will warrant a power-to-power type of meeting.
21. One of the issue areas in which I participated as a nonprofit director was a push to make local governance more open and transparent. My organization was one of nine that were brought together through funding from a national foundation (not named for the purposes of protecting people's identities) that wanted to push open governance in New Orleans and Louisiana.
22. One item from this section that informs the same assumption in SAF is the understanding of strategic action as separate from other types of actions, such as action that takes place in what Fligstein and McAdam call "unorganized social

space," which is different than the strategic action that takes place in contentious politics aimed at specific fields (2012).
23. See endnote 2 above.
24. Linas began at the NNG as a university volunteer, then became the executive director until 2017.
25. See endnote 2 above.
26. See endnote 2 above.
27. In other neighborhoods, public infrastructure that was open for service pre-Katrina continued to remain shuttered during the time of these interviews in 2016 and 2017. Many schools, in particular, remained shuttered 10 years after the storm, with the Orleans Parish School Board and then the RSD opting to consolidate and relocate many of its pre-Katrina campuses.
28. For the purpose of protecting these individuals, the source material for this report is not provided here but can be made available upon request.
29. While this study does not address *know-how* acquisition in collective political contention, this is an important issue that requires some discussion. Boyte's claim that public work can serve to bring back the skill building process that once existed in the US does not offer clarity on how this happens, while IAF contends that there are some basic conceptual and action-oriented tools that community organizers require if they are to successfully build power.
30. In Louisiana, the broadest legal jurisdiction after the state are parishes, which are the equivalent of counties in the rest of the United States. Many parishes in Louisiana contain a number of municipalities and unincorporated towns, but the city of New Orleans is contiguous with the parish of Orleans.
31. This is to differentiate from other municipalities in which legislators "oversee" a city manager, putting them in direct oversight relationship of the executive branch. In New Orleans, the only oversight power that council members have is to control the budget approval process and city ordinances but not executive actions and activities.
32. The term "soft second" refers to a second mortgage that is typically forgivable. Nonprofit community development organizations in the United States typically offer these programs, but sometimes city agencies will set aside an allocation for a city-sponsored program. The second mortgage is typically offered to individuals that are below the area median income (usually set at a percentage threshold by program operators) and is designed to enable buyers to get into homes they would not be able to purchase because of down payment requirements without the assistance of this type of second mortgage.
33. The school-to-prison pipeline refers to the systematically racialized systems that contribute to the over-incarceration of Black and brown males in the United States. There are numerous books that have the title "School-to-Prison Pipeline" that offer an exploration into the phenomena, its origins and its policies, but for the purposes of understanding a racialized system (with its processes, structures, meaning, etc.), see Omi and Winant's *Racial Formation in the United States: From the 1960s to the 1990s*.

Chapter 4

Getting Others to Act

One of the ongoing key questions about contentious collective politics, be that in academia or in practice, asks how actors get others involved. Is there some incentive, is it coercion, or is it simple happenstance? There is no shortage of literature that attempts to answer how this happens, but what is not up for debate is that it does happen. And often, there are individuals who do the work of convincing other individuals to participate in groups that engage in contentious collective politics.

Building a cohesive, organized group that develops and implements strategic action fields aimed at changing the political social order, in some regard, can in one instance be perceived as something normative that we all have the ability to do and in another instance as something only special people know how to do. Most human beings, if not all, have an ability, at some level, to convince other human beings to engage in a variety of acts, inclusive of group activities. Usually, the influencing methodology is communicative in nature. That is, there is communication, of some sort, that conveys to a would-be participant that her involvement is desired and/or needed, followed by a rationale of some type that is designed to convince (Habermas, 1998).

This communicative ability, or power, as Habermas framed it (1998), is one of the critical mechanisms human beings use to influence each other to act. Such an ability, as can be imagined, is critical for the creation of any form of group that will take some form of action within a field. Without this ability, human beings would be hard pressed to create shared goals and visions toward which to aim their collective anger. Not to be confused with voice commands, communicative power includes a variety of mechanisms through which individuals relay messages to each other, from physical to electronic. Those with a better handle on how to use these multiple mechanisms increase their potential to successfully influence other actors, placing this ability at the heart of the types of *know-how* that actors in collective contention deploy, particularly in the social dimensions of *know-how*.

Relying on my practical experience as an Industrial Areas Foundation (IAF) trained organizer and former complete member in the New Orleans social justice fields, this study limits analysis of what actors do to involve others to two types of social *know-how*: broad base development and collective will activation *know-how*. I focus on these two types of social *know-how* because they are the most relevant to collective strategic action. Additionally, these two types of *know-how* are broad enough to be inclusive of a wide-ranging set of skills that actors may or may not use in their deployment of social *know-how*.

For example, the ability to build a broad base that engages collectively in strategic action fields requires that a public leader, or set of leaders, possess relationship-building skills, presentation skills, communication skills, and group coordination skills, to name a few. Skills such as these, along with others, are taught by various community development and organizing groups throughout the United States. In the IAF trainings, a great deal of emphasis is placed on specific ways to build a broad base and getting others to participate, such as conducting one-on-one meetings to establish shared, enlightened self-interest. As a practitioner who was trained by IAF organizers during my time as a nonprofit director, I rely on this training to help me perceive when public leaders in collective contention deploy such skills as social *know-how*.

As was discussed above, broad base development *know-how* refers to what actors do to bring other actors together as a collective that works on shared interests. What makes a base broad is a diversity of people and/or groups (this can be formal and informal organizations) and interests (these can be organizational or individual) linked together. Compared to a thin base, which typically reflects a more homogenous grouping of people and/or ideas, a broad base reflects a diversity in interests, institutional types, political ideologies, ethnic orientations, geographic locations, and so on. Exploration of broad rather than thin base development *know-how* is meaningful analytically, as it enables analysis to eliminate mediating factors, such as deeply held shared interests, which can be more easily influenced to engage in group participation of similar-minded people when compared to a group of diverse interests.

Collective will activation *know-how*, which refers to a public leader's (or group of leaders') ability to take new relationships and turn these into active participation within a collective endeavor, focuses on what actors do to encourage participation in ongoing strategic action fields. This type of *know-how* utilizes a wide variety of skills, such as the ability to frame a challenge for others, build collective identity, and secure a critical mass of followers, to name a few. The list of skills that can be used in social *know-how* dimension can be quite large, but as discussed earlier, I do not enumerate the many types of abilities or skills that actors rely on in service of this type of *know-how*. Instead, I focus on observation of deployment of the two types of social *know-how* I just described and their interactions with desired outcomes.

Actors who know the fields and players (the individuals within organizations and governance units) in which they engage as challengers don't just sit back and observe on the sidelines. As challengers, they combine their knowledge about the field with knowledge about, and skills in, dealing with other human beings to deploy informational and social *know-how* in strategic action fields aimed at some form of social justice change. While it is possible for spontaneous self-activation to occur in which there is no identifiable leadership that prompts, motivates, cajoles, or encourages people to engage publicly in contentious collective political activity (as was the case in my personal post-Katrina activation story shared above), this study does not assume this to be the case. In fact, this study assumes the opposite: that wherever collective strategic action of a contentious nature occurs, there is someone or a group of some actors who initiated this action and encouraged others to join in, as this chapter will show.

Analysis of the main case, the Housing Justice Coalition (HJC), and the two comparative cases, the Nearby Neighborhood Group (NNG) and the Neighborhood-Based Housing Initiative (NBHI), in this chapter explores how the social dimension of *know-how*, specifically through broad base development and collective will activation *know-how*, interacts with these cases' abilities to secure desired outcomes related to specific strategic action fields they created within the New Orleans housing field.

Hurricane Katrina and its levee failures, as an exogenous threat to all fields in the New Orleans area, certainly can be said to have served as a significant factor in the mobilization of an entire region into political action by people from all walks of life who prior to the storm had not been as active. My own political involvement as a social justice advocate fits this assessment. However, it would be a mistake to assume that actors who challenged political structures and processes within collective bodies in the post-Katrina-affected fields relied solely on the storm to come together. While the storm may have galvanized individuals to action across all socioeconomic levels, this didn't necessarily translate to the production of well-organized collectives who were successful in pursuing shared interests.

Certainly, anger and frustration over the lack of progress post-Katrina served as fuel for increased participation (Weil, 2011), which I witnessed firsthand during my participation in the city's Bring New Orleans Back Commission meetings organized by Mayor Nagin's administration in 2005.[1] But anger and frustration, as emotional outbursts in meetings, do not in themselves offer any form of usable skill that an actor can bring to a strategic action field that is aimed at challenging incumbents in a field. Instead, actors can skillfully deploy, or develop the ability to tap into, shared anger and frustration to use it to get people and/or organizations to form a collective that agrees on and implements strategic action fields based on shared interests and goals. The formation of the HJC offers some insight into how this type of *know-how* interacts with potential outcomes success.

On the use of broad base development know-how in building the precursor to the HJC. Prior to the occurrence of the first-ever convening of a broad group of housing developers, educators, and advocates in 2007, there was no coordinated effort of any sort that connected diverse housing actors in the New Orleans housing field in the months and years after the levee failures until the HJC was formed. Additionally, there was no such group (outside of a small collective of housing educators) that existed prior to the storm that could have served this role post-Katrina.[2] This is an important detail because it helps highlight that the storm may have been a significant factor in the formation of new housing actors, but it may not potentially be the most significant factor in the creation of a broad-based collective of housing actors.

There were many new actors in the New Orleans housing field post-Katrina, including the Bring You Home Housing (BYHH) organization and the NBHI, which were created to address the housing crisis that citywide flood damage created. The majority of New Orleans' housing stock had to be gutted and rebuilt, which meant increased opportunities not only for traditional for-profit developers and contractors but also for nonprofit developers, housing assistance (such as debris removal, painting and general repairs, and rent support, to name a few) organizations, and individual housing advocates.[3] Almost every major neighborhood in New Orleans had some new organizations that focused on housing. These new actors did not come into existence to affect any systemic issues or concerns in the New Orleans housing field, but rather were created to address direct housing service and development issues within neighborhoods throughout the city.

Individually, these actors found the work of rebuilding or building anew overly cumbersome and slow due to ineffective housing-related processes and systems at the city and state levels after the storm. The BYHH (the founding organization for the HJC), which was tasked with developing a major, centrally located, public housing complex, experienced the same difficulties it was hearing about from other actors. Out of this growing sense that other housing actors were experiencing similar difficulties, Sinu, the CEO for the BYHH, organized the original convening that would later transform into the HJC. During our interview in his executive suite, he offered the following:

> *Lucas:* So, in those early initial sort of … early months for the housing alliance, you didn't have any thoughts about, well we need to build power here for example? Did you think along those lines or were you just thinking, we need to collaborate better?
>
> *Sinu:* Yeah, it was never-
>
> *Lucas:* Or we just need to help each other.
>
> *Sinu:* Yeah.
>
> *Lucas:* That was the initial piece.
>
> *Sinu:* Yeah.

Jano recalled events in a similar, but slightly different, fashion in the first interview, when he answered my question about how it all began:

> *Jano:* So, in the midst of all of that, this stuff is slowly moving. [Sinu's] realizing that, nothing's coming out of the ground. It's 2007. We're coming up on the second anniversary, and bupkis has happened. You know? Nowhere. Everywhere, there is nothing…. Yeah, so [Sinu] wanted to get everybody together to figure out how to move it forward. Should we align? Should we be working together? Blah blah blah blah.
>
> *Lucas:* But this is driven by, because you're not seeing things happening.
>
> *Jano:* Nothing's moving.

Jano interprets Sinu's decision to convene as one being driven by a need to challenge the New Orleans housing field to improve its systems so that BYHH can move its project forward faster. This interpretation differs slightly from Sinu's own interpretation of his actions, which he described as being driven by a need to support others doing the hard work of helping residents return (a perspective Sinu attributed to his faith).

While the two individuals' interpretations of what prompted the creation of the initial convenings that would later transform into the HJC differ in interesting ways, both corroborate each other's assertion that it was Sinu's idea to convene a broad base of housing actors from the New Orleans housing field. Sinu's view regarding these convenings was inclusive, targeting as many actors as possible who cared about housing development (though not inclusive enough, as Jano would later reveal).

While Jano gives Sinu all the credit for initiating the first convening, he recalls that this first meeting happened as a reactionary response to then-Lieutenant Governor Landrieu's interest to bring people in housing together.[4] Out of these conversations, Sinu coordinated the initial meeting with the Lt. Governor's office. Again, in the first interview in 2016, at his HJC office, Jano offered the following insight:

Jano: A couple of banks who are attending the conference… gave us lunch, they gave them box lunches and it was at the convention center. Mitch's [the Lt. Governor] staff arranged for us to have a lunch.

Lucas: Mm-hmm (affirmative).

Jano: So Mitch's staff got us a room inside of the [convention] center. Everybody grabbed their box lunches and then went to that room and we had the meeting.

Lucas: Yeah.

Jano: [Sinu] conducted the meeting, we did an agenda, and we called it the Housing Think-tank.

Lucas: Okay.

Jano: [This] [w]as the first meeting. What's going on? What do we think is happening? What is the problem, blah blah blah blah.

While in this moment the HJC is nothing more than a mechanism to help Sinu achieve his vision (for the BYHH organization) of developing the public housing campus and its surrounding area (according to Jano), this moment helps to set up the HJC for what it would ultimately become. At the initial convening, there is a *"hodge podge of people working on housing"* as Jano phrased it, which includes government officials from the state, banks, developers, housing educators, housing assistance organizations, and more.

As a veteran executive within a large, faith-based, charitable organization in New Orleans, Sinu brought an experienced-based understanding about the type of collective effort that could benefit the BYHH organization's work within the changing housing field post-Katrina.[5] Similarly, as a known and important actor in the New Orleans social justice field pre-Katrina, Sinu possessed extensive relationships not just in housing but other social justice and service fields in the area, positioning him as an influential individual in the New Orleans area.

This positioning is important to note because it interacts with any *know-how* Sinu deployed, resulting in either enhancing or limiting his effectiveness. In this situation, it appears that Sinu's positionality enhanced his deployment of broad base development *know-how*. His position as an important actor in the housing field and as a person who is recognized as an important actor in other New Orleans area social fields, particularly in the faith-based community, generated a sort of sociocultural capital (much in the way that Bourdieu describes cultural capital) that afforded him added weight and significance as a leader in the field.

This added weight and significance is interpreted by other actors in various ways. For some, it's an opportunity to build new relationships, while for others, it's an opportunity to gain exposure, and yet for others, it's an opportunity to "read the room," getting a sense of who the perceived important actors are and what they look like and what they have to say. Regardless of the reasons actors use to respond, such positionality can serve to motivate and influence others to seriously consider participating in a meeting when an invitation arrives. Additionally, Sinu's invitation included a co-invitation from the lieutenant governor, which provided added weight to the value of the proposed convening.

But positioning isn't everything, unless the act of not responding to an actor's invitation is known to result in serious negative consequences, such as might be the case in authoritarian structures. Sinu's position, and the added cachet of his cohost, the lieutenant governor, alone does not account for his ability to bring a large diverse group of organizational actors together, much less continue to engage them and have them return monthly. Instead, this is better understood as resulting from an interaction of broad base development *know-how* with his positionality and the unstable housing fields in which they all operated.

Sinu's reliance on broad base development *know-how* in this account is largely inferred from my own observations of, and experiences with, this individual during his years as a housing actor in the New Orleans housing field. What Sinu was able to do well that many actors fail to learn to do is build meaningful relationships across the aisle with leaders who represent differing beliefs, ideas, and positions on issues. In the IAF organizing tradition under which I am trained, this is a key skill necessary for building any form of collective. One must engage individuals who lead other groups and build a meaningful relationship that is grounded in a reciprocal and relational understanding of each other's interests and how working together might be of benefit to those interests.[6] Sinu had the ability to do just that.

He would sometimes use this ability with a new participating public leader in one of the monthly convenings for the first time who would speak up about a perspective that is missing from the discussion. Sinu would respond with an invitation to discuss further and explore with this leader what could be done to become more inclusive. In Sinu's own view, such an ability stemmed from his faith. Even so, Sinu did not make these initial meetings fully open, shutting out any possibility of local housing government agency participation, which included HANO and the city's office of community development. As Jano recalls, this decision was solely Sinu's:

> *Jano:* The rationale was, it was for the non-profits to be together by themselves…. We didn't ask the membership. This was [Sinu] saying "No. The HANO people can't come."

In Jano's estimation, the base could have been even broader from the beginning, inclusive of the very agencies that the collective would eventually challenge in the near future. Indeed, HANO and other city actors were invited later on after Jano had become HJC's leader:

> *Jano:* … it wasn't until they started to ask that I was like, "Oh, they want to talk to somebody at the city about this," so …
>
> *Lucas:* So, they started to ask? They started to say "Hey, we'd like to learn something about this from someone in the agency?"
>
> *Jano:* And to be frank, "asked" might be over-speaking it, overreaching.
>
> *Lucas:* Yeah? Did you …
>
> *Jano:* No, it came up organically… and then I suggested, "Why don't we get these people?"

In the IAF tradition of community organizing training, the same ability to engage difference of values, ideas, and beliefs and arrive at a shared, reciprocal, and relational relationship can be taught and put into practice and serves as a key skill or tool in the work of building a broad base. Sinu's approach in initiating the early convenings of the HJC shows that broad base development *know-how* played an important role in building the type of collective that represented diverse interests and actors.

However, because his positionality was such that it bears accounting, it is likely that in this instance just having some ability to deploy broad base development *know-how*, even if not at its highest levels of practice, was sufficient to interact with his position and result in broad participation of different housing actors. Additionally, just having a great turnout at a single convening isn't sufficient to classify the event as successful development of a broad base. Rather, it is in the ongoing intentionality that Sinu practiced in creating an open, inclusive space, in conjunction with his ability to build relationships across the aisle, and to then do this monthly until the HJC began to move forward without him, that broad base development *know-how* can be assessed as having played an important role in the

HJC's initial strategic action field (which occurred well after he had stepped away).

On the mixed results the HJC achieved when attempting to activate collective will for strategic action fields. After a group has been brought together, be that by an unfortunate (or fortunate) set of circumstances or by capable leaders, getting individuals to act collectively in a shared strategic action field does not necessarily happen just because those involved have agreed to form a collective. Forming the collective is just the first hurdle that many encounter who build groups for political contention. The members of a social justice collective may all agree that society is inequitable and unjust, but the ways to address the many concerns that members typically raise can vary even more. So how do collectives motivate participants to engage as a collective when the natural expectation would be for small groups of like-minded individuals within the larger body to push for their own concerns, causing splinters within the group?

While it may be possible that collective will activation in strategic action fields can occur organically, what is more likely to take place is that within a collective, there is a group of leaders (or sometimes a single leader) who design and implement different approaches to getting people to act. There may be a provision of incentives, or a discussion of potential avenues to pursue, with debates about which options are optimal. Whichever form it takes, whether through open deliberative process or through emotional appeal or incentives, leaders actively engage other members within a collective to support specific actions. This is what occurred with the HJC when they made the decision to act publicly on the housing needs assessment issue discussed in the previous chapter.

Jano, as the lead coordinator of the early (pre) HJC meetings, began to sense the possibility to do more than just convene to share the problems that attendees were experiencing in their work. He began to introduce to the regular monthly meetings conversations about systemic causes for some of the issues participating organizations were experiencing, in this way opening the possibility for strategic action field recommendations later. According to Jano, he and a couple of other HJC leading voices with whom he had a relationship began to sense early on that these convenings would indeed turn into a relevant collective of organizations who cared about affordable housing, as was quoted in the previous chapter.

Relying on his deep knowledge about the New Orleans and Louisiana housing fields, particularly regarding the actors involved in affordable housing development and policy setting, Jano saw opportunities to challenge the field through the gathered actors working as a collective. He set about prepping participants for this potential, broaching the idea of forming a coalition and pushing for change over a series of meetings until he gained support from a handful of the monthly participants to create a policy subcommittee.

While Jano was forming the policy committee, the housing needs assessment discussed in the previous chapter came to their attention. Jano presented the flaws within the copy of the Louisiana Housing Finance Agency's (LHFA) drafted needs assessment they had received and connected the potential impact of the document to affordable housing development work that the majority of monthly participants cared about. The new policy committee tackled researching and providing written revisions and commentary that the group would send to the LHFA as a unified voice, in public, for the first time, as a collective.

Jano identified this issue as the first action by the HJC as a collective, which he discussed over the span of the first two interviews. Previous to this moment, the actors who participated in monthly meetings were no more than that, a loose combination of housing actors who came together monthly. Collective will activation in this instance took two forms: first as an agreement to publicly announce the creation of the collective and each organization's participation within it and second as a specific strategic action field aimed at achieving changes to an official document that once published in final form would have an impact on housing affordability work in the New Orleans housing field.

Without Jano's insistence that the gathered actors form a collective that worked on the very issues they were experiencing, and without his decision to establish a policy committee, Jano would have found it a much more difficult road to getting folks to do more than just show up to a meeting to complain. Indeed, this is the conundrum of many a would-be contentious collective leader, how to activate a disgruntled group into a functioning collective that engaged in strategic action.

Again, just because everyone at the table is equally upset about the same things does not mean that this will translate into the creation of a collective-informed strategic action field. Jano correctly identified an attainable action that many who had come to the monthly meetings saw as beneficial to their work; thus, he used an incentive-oriented ask that garnered support. In addition to this, Jano also provided a route (the policy committee) by which most participants could engage without having to dedicate too many resources, which was critical to many of the actors who already worked well beyond their budgeted means.[7]

In providing a policy committee that focused on conducting the necessary work, Jano deployed operational *know-how* (discussed in more detail below) that enabled him to provide the additional incentive of added value. By putting together a small team who could analyze, research, and provide corrections to the housing needs assessment and then presenting this as a collective response, participating members who did not do the policy work could benefit as having been involved in the development of a meaningful response in housing simply by being members. Finally, Jano's proposal to do the work through the policy committee also enabled him to invite actors to act with minimal effort and time commitment, an added incentive that made the switch to activation less painful.

Unfortunately, this successful first-ever strategic action field by the HJC, which achieved its desired result of making necessary changes to the housing needs assessment, would not be easily replicable. While the initial foray into public contention as a collective on the housing needs assessment helped Jano both activate the group as a collective and activate the collective to act on the specific strategic action field aimed at the report, the work to maintain sustained activation of members in different strategic action fields would prove far more challenging.

Around the same time that the newly formed HJC was developing its response to the housing needs assessment, a New Orleans quasi-government agency called the Finance Authority of New Orleans (or FANO at the time – it has since changed its name to Finance New Orleans) invited housing actors to participate in discussions aimed at creating a new housing assistance program. Originally created to issue bonds that helped reduce mortgage rates in the late 1970s and early 1980s, FANO had morphed into a commercial development bond financing arm for the city prior to Katrina. In 2009, it was exploring how to turn housing funding it had received from the state into a meaningful program for homebuyers. While the agency did not have recent experience with homebuyer assistance, it did offer a down payment and closing costs assistance program in the 1990s. Around this same time, FANO became a key partner of the first-time homebuyer training effort, connecting the banks it worked with to the trainings provided by area housing educators.

This pre-Katrina history and deep relationship between FANO and the homebuyer educators would prove to be too entrenched for HJC, affecting Jano's ability to fully galvanize the collective into shared a strategic action field directed at FANO's new soft second program.[8] We had been meeting for 2 months now, and each time we sat down together, Jano fully relived the moments he recounted as if it had taken place the day before. In our fifth interview, still inside his office, with the door closed to the large open room where the cubicles and the conference table is situated, Jano asserted that the ideas being floated by the then-FANO director were not going to work for the target population who would apply for the soft second:

> *Jano:* Okay. So yeah, all this happened around the same time because this is what we did. I will tell you what happened with [LJ] .... So [LJ] gets the 27 million dollars. [Mayor] Nagin matches it, I am going to match your 27 million dollars with my 27 million dollars. So, we got a 56, 54 million dollar fund, right? Then Nagin starts going, "Well, we were going to do different things with the money. Is that all going to be soft second? We were going to do all this owner occupied stuff, blah blah blah." So instead of doubling [LJ]'s investment, he is now putting on LJ all the programs that he is going to have to run, right? So, we were all watching this as the train wreck that it is because Ray [Nagin] is insane by this point, right? Nagin is just out to lunch and these idiots he had over there, they did not know what the hell did they were. I mean, this part largely, this is [Ed] Blakeley too because Nagin made the initial commitment, the very rash commitment and I think Blakeley and them were like, "Well, no, let us see figure out what we can do." So, in the meantime, in between time, [LJ] who is beloved by mostly people who do not know me from Eve, is starting to explain how his program is going to work. So, he is in these meetings and he is explaining them and I am going, that was not a soft second. That was a hard second. What he wanted to do was take the money allocated and have it be repayable in full when the first mortgage was paid. So in 30 years if you got $30,000 second mortgage, when your first mortgage

was due, you would owe the Finance Authority $30,000 in 30 years. Right, but it is not a soft second.

Jano and other members of HJC proposed a different set of solutions that would ultimately be dismissed by the FANO director. In this same interview, when I asked what went wrong in this endeavor that yielded such a different outcome than the housing needs assessment action, Jano summed it up this way:

Lucas: Do you remember what you wanted to accomplish when you brought him to your meeting?

Jano: We wanted him to change these stupid rules.

Lucas: You agreed on that?

Jano: Yes.

Lucas: You were like, "This is what we want this guy to do."

Jano: Yes, that was right. We wanted to be a soft second. We wanted Section 8 people to be able to participate and there was something else that he did that we were like, "Fuck, what is wrong with him?"

Lucas: So, you wanted to change his mind.

Jano: About his program.

Lucas: That day you did not succeed.

Jano: No, he was still we could tell like I think he was a little overwhelmed to see so many people ....

The "so many people" Jano is referring to here is the collective members, whom he had informed about the shortcomings of the soft second program design. While LT's (the FANO director) arrival to the HJC meeting indicates the collective's ability in 2009 to get a local government actor to attend their meeting, the plan did not go as desired. Part of the reason this tactic failed is because having the full collective membership present seems to have created a problem for the targeted actor. At the same time, as Jano further explains, one key member, who had a long-standing relationship with LT, disagreed with Jano's assessment. It is possible that these two factors contributed to this strategic action field not achieving success. Compare this assessment with how Jano assessed what enabled him to have success with the housing needs assessment:

Jano: Part of the reason so many of the members responded [s]o positively to this is because the threat of that document made it difficult for them to get an allocation of tax credits and resources and things like that in New Orleans, which is where most of them were trying to work. They had deals they were trying to put together, and this document was going to make it hard.

Lucas: It directly was going to affect them.

Jano: That's right.

In Jano's view, the field-wide threat posed by a housing needs assessment that found no affordability issues in New Orleans post-Katrina boosted Jano's collective will activation efforts, making it easier for him to sell his strategic action field tactics to everyone. Whereas in the FANO situation, only a small subgroup of housing actors cared deeply enough about FANO's program design to weigh in, and these were of three camps, newcomers to the New Orleans housing field who had more abstract social justice interests in good housing programming, developers who wanted more development funding assistance, and pre-Katrina housing educators who had a vested interest in keeping the doors open.

The broad interests of a broad-based collective, at least in this instance, proved too great to overcome. Jano could not get the collective to agree on the shared strategic action field he proposed. Instead, key members of the collective who had their own relationships with FANO engaged directly with the quasi-government agency while Jano was trying to present a unified HJC response, effectively undermining any hope for the HJC to achieve its desired outcome of challenging FANO to revise its soft second program.

Here it is important to point out that despite the fractured interests relative to the FANO housing assistance program, Jano did represent a large portion of the collective's interests, not just his own ideas about what should be done. Having undergone a process of debate and deliberation about the impacts of various solutions, Jano was charged with promoting to FANO the solution that the HJC felt would have the greatest immediate impact on access to affordable housing. Indeed, he was able to effectively activate a significant portion of the collective in support of a specific strategic action field, but he could not galvanize the entire membership. Collective will activation *know-how*, in this instance, helped him get a large component of the HJC on the same page, but not enough, leaving those who did not see their interests met in the HJC solution to seek their own solutions, particularly if they had relationships that could assist them in this, which turned out to be the case.

Jano's assessment offers an interesting insight into the potential limitations of collective will activation *know-how*. No amount of high-level *know-how* is a guarantee of success. An actor can do everything right to build relationships, frame issues with allies and collective members, work deliberatively to arrive at consensus, and so on in preparation for strategic action field activation on a shared agenda and not achieve the desired outcomes, even when other structural and cultural factors are aligned favorably in a field, such as a conducive social environment to a given issue and its accompanying solution. The human contingency component always leaves open the possibility that a public leader, or a group of leaders, will derail a collective's efforts in favor of more immediate, singular interests, even when these leaders are members of the same collective.

Of course, it should be noted here, as analysis throughout this and the other chapters reveals, that *know-how* is no panacea. When it comes to human involvement in interpretation, decision-making, interaction, and implementation, the more *know-how* that actors bring to the effort, the better for them, as this increases their opportunities for success. But this is all it can ever be, an increased prospect of winning, but never a guarantee. There are no guaranteed wins in political contention of any type, as even the most seemingly simple fields with wide open opportunities at local levels are fraught with complexities of actors, processes, histories, meanings, structures, and power relationships.

On how the uneven distribution of social know-how interacts with successful outcomes attainment. Compared to the HJC, the NNG represents a significantly different type of collective. Unlike the HJC's professional collective of organizations who all work in housing, the NNG is a neighborhood group whose members are residents from the neighborhood and who represent a wide range of individual (and not organizational) interests, abilities, and socioeconomic status. Operating in a mixed neighborhood that includes African American, white, and Latino working-, middle-, and upper-class families, the NNG presents a different set of challenges to broad base organizing. While geographically concentrated, the base is more diffuse and diverse relative to interests, abilities, and knowledge.

From building the collective to activating it, bringing together organizations is a far less complicated endeavor when compared to the work of bringing together individuals who are not affiliated with an organization, even if these individuals live within two square miles of each other. Where organizations have stated goals and public mission statements that they use to guide their work, individuals without this level of organizational logic operate from a much broader and more fluid approach to public contention, making it much more challenging to build collective shared interest.

As a city bureaucrat who was responsible for working with neighborhoods, I witnessed no shortage of neighborhood group infighting in my nearly 3 years of service. Intra-neighborhood squabbles often paralyzed any attempt to implement collective action. Despite these common issues, the NNG was one of the most successful neighborhood groups in the city in the immediate years after the storm, achieving many of the desired outcomes they pursued much quicker than similar neighborhoods who faced the same threats in New Orleans.

Similar to a number of neighborhoods in the city, the NNG galvanized as a collective upon learning of the city's plans to convert their area into a water retention green space.[9] The threat of being erased as a community under the Nagin administration served as a significant influencing factor that helped residents of the Nearby Neighborhood to put aside any differences that would typically get in the way, as they endeavored to focus on the singular task of fighting city hall's plans.

In such a situation, it would seem that broad base development *know-how* would be irrelevant, given that the external threat from city hall was significant enough to potentially give rise to spontaneous collective formation, but this would be an imprecise observation. One simply has to compare the NNG's early success to that of similar neighborhoods under the same threat at that time in the city to see that the NNG was an anomaly and not the norm. That is, given the immediate potential threat of erasure for select neighborhoods throughout the city, one would expect to see similar collective formation and activation resulting in similar success to that displayed by the NNG, but this didn't occur in mixed income neighborhoods similar to the Nearby Neighborhood.

Instead, it is more likely that some level of broad base development and collective will *know-how* played a role in NNG's successful strategic actions. Interviews with two resident leaders, a neighborhood ally, and the director of the group in 2016 certainly points in this direction as each consistently references and gives credit to two neighborhood leaders, named Nona and Jonas, who initiated regular meetings, organized task forces, communicated externally on behalf of the group, secured resources, provided strategic direction, and more.[10]

Sammie, whose home sat on the higher income side of the neighborhood, fully supported the direction and endeavors of the NNG, which according to him provided the needed structural supports to just do his job, which he punctuated during our April 2017 interview in his home:

Lucas: [The NNG] was just volunteer run?

Sammie: It was volunteer run.

Lucas: And, who led these meetings?

Sammie: Nona

Lucas: She led them?

Sammie: She led them and Jonas led the meetings.

Lucas: So, she and Jonas led the meetings?

Sammie: Yeah.

Lucas: So, basically they organized the activities, they gave you responsibilities-

Sammie: Yeah. Yeah.

Lucas: They had the meetings, they held them?

Sammie: Right.

Lucas: They created the agenda.

Sammie: Yeah. Yeah.

Lucas: They did all of that?

Sammie: They did all that.

Lucas: Okay.

One of the allies of the NNG is a well-established church that was highly active in the Nearby Neighborhood, becoming a volunteer center for out-of-town volunteers. Its priest, a local product named Kurt, met with me for his singular interview on a warm spring day in 2017. He had a two-story center in a converted home with tight spaces filled with materials used for nonchurch-related activities, which were still active at the time of the interview, such as continuing to house out-of-town volunteers, developing buildings, building urban gardens, and conducting other neighborhood beautification projects. When I stepped into the building, there were crammed spaces filled with young people hard at work on some project or other. It almost felt as if the bustle of the immediate post-Katrina years were still alive and palpable in this space. Despite Kurt seeming quite capable as a leader of volunteers, he agreed with Sammie's view about the two leaders who directed the NNG.

> *Kurt:* We always joked that when Jonas came over, it was cause he was trying to take something we owned. It's kind of true, but it's also what makes Nona and Jonas really great at it, because they were shameless. Like, "You should give us two million dollars." And then at the end, you want to give them more than two million dollars.

In all instances in which the NNG developed and implemented strategic action fields that was designed to move forward a desired political outcome for the neighborhood, Nona and Jonas are referenced as being responsible for bringing folks together and positioning individuals to act. In other words, both Nona and Jonas were able to bring the disparate voices of a mixed neighborhood together, get them to see themselves as a cohesive collective, and activate them into a unified body capable of initiating a host of strategic action fields. But before the NNG took on any of the specific activities that pitted them contentiously against local government, the group required that someone, or some group of people, took the anger and fear and turned it into an organized group.

Again, the threat and fear of erasure could not by itself, as a motivating factor, give rise to a successful organized neighborhood collective. While the field created the opportunity for many people to experience the same frustration, the same pain, and the same fear, it did not create a unified collective. Someone with broad base development *know-how* had to step in, take advantage of the opportunity created by the field, and fashion a true organized base of people, which is what Nona and Jonas did when they organized the neighborhood, created working committees, galvanized outside allies and resources, and provided direction.

While charisma or personability certainly can aid a public leader's efforts to bring people together and get them to work on a shared agenda, these traits cannot, on their own, fully account for Nona and Jonas' success in building a broad neighborhood base that successfully engaged in contentious collective activities. In the case of the Nearby Neighborhood, the opportunity created by the field has to be properly understood as a significant factor that potentially boosted Nona and Jona's efforts to unify an already largely angry neighborhood.

That is, it is possible that had the city's threat of erasure not included the Nearby Neighborhood, which was severely devastated by the flood waters after the storm, this neighborhood may not have experienced the success it did. Without this immediate threat, people wouldn't have had a unifying sense of urgency, and without this, it is possible that Nona and Jonas would have been less successful in convincing people that their involvement was needed. Effectually, the threat of erasure served to provide a strong incentive for involvement, which the leaders of NNG used to its full advantage.

Once the threat of erasure was successfully challenged and the neighborhood began to re-establish a sense of normalcy in the years further removed from the storm, keeping people involved in the NNG became a great deal more challenging. According to the group's director at the times of the interviews, this was one of his main struggles between 2016 and 2017. He shared the following during our first interview in September 2016:

> *Lucas:* So there's some kind of message you're trying to connect people to, that I think you alluded to earlier, may have been lost along the way, or maybe it's not as urgent as used to be…could you talk about that…
>
> *Linas:* Yeah, both of those things. I think one major piece of it is the urgency. We knew that [we] were fighting, that was going to be an uphill battle because we're not face with the same realities…
>
> *Lucas:* Back then the green dot…we need to say we exist, F-U the green dot
>
> *Linas:* Well, I mean this was in 2010, so this was 4–5 years after the neighborhood had been doing the work. But, people were seeing progress in very tangible ways. There was major trust in the leadership…
>
> *Lucas:* But still connected to that threat, right?
>
> *Linas:* Yeah, still connected to that threat. Still galvanized, and involved, and proud of the progress that the neighborhood had made in the face of that threat. So, so I think, what was it? I think it was 67, 68 approved the referendum in 2010. Um, and then I would say in the 5 years after that, 2010–2015, is when we had these suborganizations operating separately, and there was a lot of leadership change…. Um, the board of commissioners, like the neighborhood association's board had people in leadership positions who…were just not, up really for the task of leading, and didn't know how to really bring people together and isolated people.

All of the individuals interviewed from the NNG were convinced by either Nona or Jonas to put in the time and energy to help the organization achieve its desired outcomes. Each of them attributed to both Nona and Jonas a special ability to communicate and convince people to come together and work toward a shared vision of the future for the neighborhood. The exogenous threat of erasure from city hall certainly aided these two individuals' efforts, but it required some level of broad base development and collective will activation *know-how* to take advantage of this threat in a way that no other neighborhood in New Orleans was able to realize, nor any subsequent leadership at the NNG (as the quote above suggests) after that.

At NBHI, neighborhood-oriented collective-building work looked different. For this organization, which worked in another part of New Orleans, the work of bringing affordable homes to the neighborhood also meant going in and building relationships with residents. They hired a professional community organizer, named Phin, whose job was to create organized neighborhood groups that could advocate for their needs on their own and challenge city hall on blight and other housing-related matters, as well as support NBHI's affordable housing goals. While NBHI is not a collective that offers direct comparison to the HJC and the NNG, it is an actor that conducts its work within the housing field, is a member of the HJC, and has been a challenger in the New Orleans housing field on its own (outside of HJC membership). One of the more interesting aspects of their work as a new housing developer was their intentional investment in organizing communities (which is not a typical strategy for nonprofit community development organizations).

Phin, as a professional community organizer, was steeped in the knowledge of community organizing tactics and strategies. When we sat down for our single interview, he was particularly despondent about how the work was becoming more difficult the further away life moved from Katrina. We met in the NBHI offices, which at the time were located in one of the rooms that used to serve as a school for the church that founded NBHI. In our interview, he reflected at length on the type of training he had received and how he used this training to help stand up three distinct neighborhood associations in the geographic area where NBHI operated. He explained his work this way in our singular interview in March 2016:

> *Phin:* I like to say is that organizers have an attitude, or swagger. I will say this, engagement, I define as, you have an agenda, and you're getting the community to buy into your agenda. Organizing is, you take people, and you take their agenda, and you figure out how to connect the dots for their agenda. You know, I do a little bit of here, a little bit of there, but our community building, so you know, it's organizing with a bit more attitude.

As a professionally trained public leader employed by a housing organizational actor, Phin possessed a great deal of knowledge about building a base of people into a collective and organizing them for action. In building three distinct neighborhood groups that represented small, disconnected geographic boundaries within a larger neighborhood area, Phin understood his work as being focused on the micro level of base building. Phin was able to not only build three distinct bases in three distinct areas, but he was also able to help these new groups successfully challenge city hall on a number of quality-of-life issues that required sustained strategic action fields just to get the city to step in and provide a needed but long-neglected service. His work, while successful in standing up three distinct groups, points to one of the challenges that *know-how* can present if it is not widely distributed among members of a collective.

At the time of the interview, Phin was already in the process of removing himself from an active role with the three neighborhood associations he had helped create. This removal meant that his role as coordinator, trainer, and all-around guide, in other words, as the person with extensive knowledge and *know-how* about collective contention, would no longer be as readily available to the three groups he helped stand up.

Without Phin's *know-how* about bringing people together and activating them in a manner that sets them up for potential success, the associations declined in both resident participation and ability to act, something Phin lamented often before, during, and after the interview (as well as in other conversations he and I have had between 2015 and 2018). Despite Phin's efforts to "train up" resident leaders so that they could act as challengers in strategic action fields that they design and implement for themselves, it would appear from his own assessment that the trainings weren't sufficient to position these three new groups as effective challengers (at least in his estimation during this interview).

Unlike the NNG, which relied on resident leadership with social *know-how* who lived in the Nearby Neighborhood, Phin was a community outsider to the three areas he organized. He was not a neighbor but a professional from an organizational neighbor that brought outside knowledge and *know-how* for a specific amount of time. When he stepped back, Phin also removed access to his abilities for all three of the groups he helped create. This decision was largely made for him, as NBHI could no longer afford to keep Phin as a full-time employee. As such, the paid-for knowledge and social *know-how* that helped create three new neighborhood associations also resulted in these organizations taking a step back.

The case of NBHI's paid expertise being used to build a collective base is one that reflects a standard practice in social justice fields across the United States. Issued-based nonprofit organizations secure funds for professional organizing, deploy these individuals in an organization's target community, only to have any attained success jeopardized when funding runs out. This issue of funding sustainability for professional support is one of the key reasons that "micro" (to borrow Phin's terminology) organizing at the super local level often fails to build a sustained collective base that is able to engage in sustained strategic action fields capable of achieving desired outcomes in local governance. While the groups that Phin helped create continue to exist, their success as challengers in the New Orleans neighborhood field has not risen to the levels they were able to achieve when Phin was actively involved.

Similar to the NNG, the neighborhood groups that Phin helped create experienced a small return to normalcy as the years post-Katrina added up and fields in New Orleans stabilized. More stable fields translate to less opportunities for successful challenges, as stability also implies entrenched incumbents who become harder to challenge. Both the NNG and the neighborhood groups created by NBHI show that as fields stabilized and threats minimized throughout the city, keeping neighborhood collectives active with participating members and getting these members to continue to engage in contentious collective politics became increasingly more difficult to accomplish. Combine stabilizing fields in New Orleans with the loss of leadership who have high-level collective contention knowledge and *know-how* (not just of the social dimension), and the resulting potential exists for groups to become less effective challengers (at best) or fully demobilized challengers (at worst).

On the limits of broad base development and collective will activation know-how in collectives. One of the last collectives, the Citizen Rights Collective (CRT), I participated in during the time I served as director of a nonprofit in the New Orleans area failed to accomplish any of its desired outcomes despite having professionally trained members with broad base development and collective will activation *know-how*. The CRT sought to affect key government practices at the local and state levels, but it failed to accomplish any of its desired outcomes, which were directed at government accountability and transparency processes. This analysis perceives two factors that contributed to this group's lack of success that is worth discussing here: the creation of a collective artificially brought together by national funding and the racialized and gendered hierarchies that permeated group dynamics.[11]

In 2009, I was invited to a handful of meetings organized by a local consultant who was working with a national foundation (which will remain unnamed for the purposes of protecting individuals involved in this effort) about people-centered government accountability and transparency. This consultant was not a community organizing expert, but rather a professional connector who raised money for local groups. I learned from these meetings that the consultant represented a significant national foundation that was interested in investing in a people-centered coalition that could keep local and state government accountable. The coalition would bring together "expert" organizations and engage the general public in its work. The organization I directed was invited as a "community" partner, that is, as a group that worked directly with community. This very beginning framework for how the coalition was to be organized created the seeds for its own ineffectiveness.

The group that was brought together to form the CRT never transitioned out of the initial impetus that brought them together, which was the promise of funding. There was a shared body of work, certainly, that was promoted and offered as an area of focus by the funder, in which the members of CRT all engaged and agreed to tackle, but this wasn't driven by the type of unifying exogenous threat experienced by the NNG or by the shared experiences of powerless challengers that saw value in forming a collective. There were discussions, of course, of advancing within this "collective-from-above" a more community-oriented, bottom-up, relationship-building working model, but this was repeatedly rejected by the more "professionally" oriented organizations in the group, which included research, legal, and journalism-based organizations.[12] After 3 years of funding, the group never built the type of people-oriented collective it desired, nor did it affect a single government policy that it could count as a success.

Within 5 years, the group ceased to exist as a collective, maintaining the work and the name but representing only the singular interests of two organizations. Not only did the initial framework that brought the organizations together fail to serve as sufficient "glue" for maintaining the group, it also served to eventually undo the very type of collective it hoped to create, primarily because the professionally based organizations prioritized the funding stream from the national foundation rather than the collective they agreed to help create. When the community-based organizations proposed immediate expansion and other strategies that would help build a true people-oriented and people-informed coalition, the professional-based organizations balked at these ideas, citing concerns about funding limitations.

As the professional-based organizations expressed, the pie was only so big. The problem with their assessment was that they believed it would be sufficient for the collective to remain small (there were less than 10 founding organizations) while the funding was available. Effectively, the collective remained small, which in turn hindered its ability to grow any power as a challenger. The CRT largely disbanded after the national funder pulled out. The community-based organizations, recognizing this potential problem early on, offered solutions based on their broad-based development and collective will activation *know-how*. Unfortunately, the CRT professional-based members refused to accept the expertise offered by the members that possessed the requisite *know-how*.

When collectives are artificially created via outside funding in the same manner as the CRT, the likelihood for success is diminished when there is no allowance for broad-based development and collective will activation *know-how* within the group to direct strategic action. Relative to the CRT, the national funder, unaware of the on-the-ground dynamics it had created by working through a consultant who was ill-equipped to deliver what was promised, failed to support the growth of the very coalition it hoped to create by simply playing its role as a national funder – offering funds with certain strings that only served to constrain the work.

Secondly, the demarcation of professional-based vs community-based also tracked racial lines, with white men running the professional-based organizations and people of color and women primarily running the community-based organizations. This racialized difference influenced how knowledge and *know-how* was received and valued within the collective, with the knowledge and expertise of the professional-based leaders having far more value than the knowledge and expertise of the community-based leaders.[13] The community-based leaders were fully aware of this dynamic and once attempted to present this issue in a meeting with the funder. The meeting didn't go as planned, as any mention of racial dynamics in this work befuddled the national funder's professional staff, creating further de-valuing of the very community-based groups that the national funder espoused to want to include in the work it was funding. This de-valuing of the community-based organizations translated to a devaluing of the social *know-how* that these organizations brought to the collective, resulting in a top-down collective that remained disconnected from the average New Orleans resident.

Is it possible that the community-based organizations could have put their broad-based development and collective will activation *know-how* to bear on the CRT in such a way that it may have helped it achieve some of its desired goals? Perhaps, but regardless, what is observable from this example is that there can be a certain level of *know-how* within a collective that is never allowed to contribute because of the internal dynamics and structural frameworks of that collective. In the end, collectives that engage as challengers in contentious politics that close their proverbial eyes and ears to any amount of social *know-how* within their midst run the risk of failing to advance their desired outcomes because they failed to tap into valuable expertise from within.

Notes

1. These public meetings, created by Mayor Ray Nagin and supported by the New Orleans City Council, began less than 2 months after the storm and were designed to create a comprehensive rebuilding plan. See "Bring Back N.O. Commission takes lead role" by Deon Robert in the *New Orleans CityBusiness* on Feb. 8, 2006.
2. The collective of housing educators prior to the storm can be considered a field governance unit that was in place pre-Katrina for the purposes of certifying first time homebuyer training in the New Orleans area. This collective's highly limited focus contributed to this group's inability to form a broader collective of housing actors.
3. See the Data Center's Katrina-related research for local data on Katrina's impact here: https://www.datacenterresearch.org/data-resources/katrina/facts-for-impact/
4. Then Lt. Governor Landrieu would later become Mayor Landrieu in 2010.
5. As mentioned in the previous chapter, the BYHH organization was formed by the largest faith-based charitable organization in New Orleans, which remains un-named in this study for the purposes of protection.
6. These tenets are foundational elements to the IAF's community organizing training. For more information on the IAF training tradition, see Alinsky and Chambers.
7. In any given nonprofit field at the local level, the majority of nonprofits will typically be small, with budgets less than $250K annually, with underpaid and overworked staff who pull double and triple duty. This was certainly the case with housing leaders who were busy trying to develop homes or get people back into homes.
8. As mentioned above, a soft second is a forgivable second mortgage offered as gap financing to qualifying first-time homebuyers. Often, soft second programs target working-class families who earn enough to afford a qualifying mortgage that is based on an area median income but don't have the deposit and closing funds to secure these loans. Nonprofits and local government agencies secure funds to offer prospective working-class homebuyers a forgivable loan that helps them meet these cash gaps.

9. See endnote 2 in Chapter 3.
10. I was not able to interview either of the two individuals who led the NNG during the interview time period, as both individuals proved to be difficult to track down. However, during my time as a nonprofit director and a city hall bureaucrat in New Orleans, I interacted with both on many occasions. Ultimately, I made the design decision to use the data provided by those from NNG whom I did interview and use that to deduce what *know-how* these two leaders deployed in specific strategic actions.
11. For an excellent discussion on both the racialized and gendered dynamics of collective building, see *Garza, Alicia. 2020. The Purpose of Power: How We Come Together When We Fall Apart. Random House Publishing Group.*
12. The terminology "from above" refers to top-down arrangements rather than bottom-up arrangements in which national or powerful actors direct the flow of money and strategic action priorities rather than those on the ground who do the work or who experience the issues being addressed, who are referred to as those "from below," or at the bottom.
13. This is an additional research and theory development opportunity within any focus on *know-how* that I believe merits further consideration.

Chapter 5

No Directions Given

Without real-world narratives from actors directly involved in contentious collective politics, one would be mistakenly led to believe that most collective contention efforts have clear road maps. The type of driving directions that drivers use in mapping software, which plots a course with way signs on a digital screen, just doesn't exist for challengers within a field whose aim it is to undo, upend, or create a new a field. The spaces in which collective contention takes place is public space, a highly contingent social space that offers little in the way of guidance and direction for challengers (though incumbents do know the circumscribed contours of field structures and processes that enable them to occupy the role of incumbents within their field).[1] There is no tourist map that helps a collective actor navigate the various traps and dead ends that inevitably arise unannounced when strategic action fields are implemented. Everything from jealousy and fear to feeling direct existential threats, and more, can overcome individual actors, be they challengers, incumbents, or governance units in a field.[2]

The matter of where to direct action is made evident at the individual resident level. Consider New Orleans, a small city that has a population slightly under 400K. A resident experiencing crime, blight, poor performing schools, flooding, low wages, and housing insecurity who decides to become active politically and challenge for better quality-of-life outcomes will find herself overwhelmed by the complexity of systems and structures in place at the local level. Where does she begin? With the legislators in city council? The chief executive office, which is the mayor? How about the school board or the sewerage and water board? Which departments report directly to the mayor, maybe that's the place to start? Each of these options represents different subfields with their own complexities of individuals, structures, histories, etc. Such complexities in processes and structures within fields at the local level can certainly seem daunting, particularly if actors enter contention without sufficient information and skills to engage the different organizational actors in each field.

Modern governance and modern urban centers have become such complex webs of fields and networks, even in small cities such as New Orleans, that deciphering which one is the correct network and, or field toward which one can direct energy is just the beginning of an ever-changing and partially completed road map that would-be challengers self-build as they progress in their work.[3] When actors self-build without prior experience of the road, the road map can be filled with errors, wrong turns, and wasted trips that sap the life-energy right out of any contentious collective effort. However, even actors with high levels of *know-how* find that putting together a road map that will lead to success comes with many unknowns.

Let's assume that a challenger possesses high-level field knowledge. As such, the challenger knows the types of authority incumbents have, the power levers that may exist within and outside of a target field, the influence of adjacent fields, and all the bureaucratic complexity within a target field. This challenger will be in a strong position to map out a potential set of steps for strategic action. But even with a great deal of knowledge, there remains contingent unknowns, such as hidden power figures who inform the known actors, or the flow of influencing money from powerful interests outside the field, to a name a couple, which are much more difficult to tease out by the average collection of people grouped together as challengers to local fields. Therefore, it would be naïve to expect a clear linear path from start to finish in any political endeavor.

Political contention rarely moves in a simple linear fashion from a call-to-action to achievement of a desired outcome. Every step of the way, actors are actively making strategic choices, using whatever information and abilities they possess to achieve the change they seek. Having knowledge of the field and its issues as well as knowing how to bring people together are invaluable abilities that enable human beings to enter existing fields as collective challengers or fashion new fields out of the rubble from vanquished fields. However, having the ability to convert field knowledge and social skills into *know-how* does not guarantee a collective's ability to move toward its desired outcome, much less accomplish it.

Collective actors require an ability to analyze the field they are challenging, then use this analysis to devise a set of steps that the collective will take toward achieving their desired outcome. The ability to do this and keep a collective on track toward its intended target demonstrates strategic *know-how*. For the purposes of this study, the analysis operationalizes two types of strategic *know-how* that are vital in contentious collective politics: consequence *know-how* and action-to-goal congruence *know-how*. In demonstrating consequence *know-how*, collectives make strategic action plans and decisions knowing exactly what they want to achieve, as well as what potentially undesired outcomes may arise. When deploying high-level consequence *know-how* in both design and implementation of strategic action fields, actions are selected because of their anticipated value in advancing a collective's work toward attaining its desired outcomes within a specific field.

As collectives implement their strategic activities, however, changing realities within the field (or within the collectives themselves) often forces a change in the direction and scope of previously planned strategic action fields. Collectives that possess action-to-goal congruence *know-how* demonstrate a distinct ability to keep a collective on track, which becomes critical for groups that encompass diverse interests attempting to work on a shared agenda. Congruence *know-how* is critical because groups engaged in contentious politics are certain to experience turbulence along the way, as any number of curveballs and unexpected land mines arise, posing the threat of derailing planned efforts. Encountering these types of issues requires that collectives possess the ability to recognize when they are meandering off course and conduct course corrections. Without the ability to recognize when implemented activities no longer contribute to advancing a group's originally desired outcome(s), collectives sputter in circles, never achieving the changes they seek within their target fields and never growing the power they need to influence field incumbents.

In this chapter, I examine situations in which the Housing Justice Collective's (HJC's) deployment of strategic *know-how* interacted in different ways with the collective's ability to achieve desired outcomes. This chapter also compares the HJC's deployment of strategic *know-how* with that of the Nearby Neighborhood Group (NNG) and note any differences or similarities. Finally, this chapter explores an episode from my work as a former nonprofit director in the New Orleans Latinx social justice field during which I chaired an action committee for the (pseudonymously named) Alliance for Language Access for All People (ALAAP).

On the interaction of strategic know-how *in HJC's efforts to advance changes within the affordable housing field in New Orleans.* Before the HJC came into existence, a disparate group of housing actors in the post-Katrina New Orleans housing field were beginning to dialogue with each other, primarily to share difficulties and explore ways they could advance their work of bringing residents back, getting homes rebuilt, and creating new, affordable units. This is the environment into which Jano, the leader of the HJC during the 2016 and 2017 interviews, entered.

As was mentioned in the previous chapter, the HJC was not originally created for the purposes of engaging in contentious collective politics, but rather for the purposes of bringing housing actors together to network and share resources, with the hope of alleviating rebuilding issues. Sinu's decision to form the group and take ownership of forming the group demonstrates consequence *know-how* that warrant discussion here (despite this specific application of *know-how* not necessarily being used for political contention) because it was the first critical step that gave birth to a subsequently politically oriented collective and because it shows by way of example how consequence *know-how* can lead to both intended and unintended consequences.

According to Sinu, when he decided to invite other housing actors to a first-ever convening to discuss ways they can help each other, he was simply doing it because it made sense. However, as a participant actor in the years post-Katrina who worked alongside Sinu, I perceived a degree of subterfuge in his response that is informed by his own perspectives on such an action and those offered by Jano. As Jano informed me on several occasions, he learned from Sinu in their one-on-one conversations as subordinate and supervisor that their organization, the Bring You Home Housing (BYHH), needed to get scattered site development moving if they were to ever succeed in securing funding for the public housing campus because the two were part of a single package being sold to funders.[4] In other words, to achieve their desired ends of redeveloping the public housing complex in their purview, the BYHH also needed to demonstrate progress on the scattered sites surrounding the campus.

Sinu saw an advantage to convening the disparate housing developers throughout the city, which he perceived would provide a strategic benefit to their own work. By convening other housing developers and engendering cooperation and dialogue, he hoped to enhance BYHH's processes and find ways to speed up the bottlenecks BYHH was also experiencing, and in doing so directly benefit BYHH. His desired outcome, a direct benefit to BYHH's own work, would indeed be realized by the creation of this monthly convening of housing actors, as the work they pursued as challengers did benefit BYHH, as well as other housing actors. At the same time, Sinu did not anticipate the shift that the monthly convenings would take, as actors began to speak more about systemic issues within the broader housing field and less about the direct work of developing homes near the BYHH's areas of interest. Once this began to happen, Jano points out, Sinu relegated the coordination and facilitation of the monthly convenings to Jano:

> *Jano:* Yeah, within a year the two of them ... It was really funny. I think with [Sinu] it was, not intentional. I think he was bored with it, frankly.... I think what happened was is that he didn't see ... it's not that he got bored with it. I don't think he could get out of it what he wanted to get out of it. Then that's why he shifted focus....

Again, though Sinu's strategic decision-making in this scenario is not used in service of a strategic action field that advances contentious collective politics, it does demonstrate how consequence *know-how* can interact with desired outcomes. In this situation, the creation of the monthly convenings with other housing actors resulted in both wanted and unwanted outcomes, which enables analysis to connect deployment of consequence *know-how* in playing a contributing role in the future development of scattered site housing (which BYHH desired) and a contributing role in the creation of the HJC (which BYHH did not necessarily desire), which would go on to become a significant housing challenger in the New Orleans housing field in its own right. The benefit realized by the BYHH did not come from better coordinated housing development in the geographic areas that interested BYHH, but rather from the political strategic actions the HJC implemented.

Can it be said that there was deployment of consequence *know-how* when the creation of the HJC and its political activities were not a desired intent? The answer is affirmative because deployment of consequence *know-how* doesn't only exist when an actor confidently anticipates what will occur in the future, but rather it is demonstrated when an actor makes a strategic decision that is specifically designed to achieve an intended result out of perceived real-world possibilities in a field. Strategic decisions are little more than highly educated guesses about possible futures. These educated guesses attempt to weigh the potential responses by other actors in a given field. Public leaders then uses these calculations to inform decisions on different tactics and activities they will implement in a given strategic action field.[5]

No matter how much information an actor may acquire, however, strategic decision-making about which steps to take in a strategic action field will always be accompanied by contingent elements. This contingency, which is ever-present in human social interactions of any type, doesn't negate strategic thinking, as it is through application of consequence *know-how* that actors attempt to minimize the effects of the unknown elements in the field that will have an impact on their actions.

When the HJC made the calculated decision to publicly tackle the housing needs assessment report as a collective, it did so because it perceived this specific strategic action field as an instrumental step in presenting the group as a challenger within the Louisiana and New Orleans housing fields while also disrupting these fields in a way that would benefit the HJC members. The HJC was little more than a collection of housing actors who convened together, shared information, and assisted each other with program delivery issues at that time. But as was pointed out in the informational *know-how* chapter, a small group of leaders within the HJC viewed the growing conversations about systemic issues as an indication that the group had the potential to become more than just a monthly gathering of housing actors, something he elaborated on in the first interview, which took place in December 2016.

Lucas: Who started to think about being strategic, you did?

Jano: Me. And [Sis].

Lucas: But at the same time you're saying, thoughts are coming out and conversations are happening about, "We need to be strategic?"

Jano: Right.

Lucas: About what?

Jano: Road Home.

Lucas: Okay. So Road Home was a big deal.

Jano: Mm-hmm (affirmative).

Lucas: And what were the issues with Road Home? That you're like, "Okay we need..."

Jano: The program wasn't moving. We had a number of the members who were working to help people rebuild.

Lucas: So let me ask, so Road Home started to force you to start thinking as a group?

Jano: Mm-hmm (affirmative).

Lucas: To start thinking about what can we due to affect this program to work better?

Jano: Yeah.

Lucas: So you started thinking that?

Jano: Yes, exactly.

Lucas: So you're learning things now and you're thinking ... and since you're running these meetings you're thinking "Okay, there's something here we could do."

Jano: Mm-hmm (affirmative). Oh, we need to be doing this. The stuff with [the statewide group] ... it's like, well they're occupying the space, that's fine. But what can [HJC] do ... not necessarily to aid, but what issues should we be looking at? So it did prompt some thoughts like that, because I'm not such a compartmentalized soul that it goes, "Oh, I'm doing this and this has nothing to do with all of that."

Lucas: Right.

Jano: But you're sitting with people every month who have real, identifiable needs who want help with addressing it. It's not systemic yet, I'm not processing it to systemic, because you know that's how I think. They can't do the systemic stuff yet.

Lucas: You mean your [HJC members]?

Jano: Yes! Yeah, they weren't ready for it.

Neither Jano nor any of the other leaders who at that time encouraged him to convert the monthly meetings into an organized collective knew with certainty that they wouldn't lose a substantial number of the participating actors with a push to become an organized group. What they did know was that there was an opportunity in the field to offer a new voice, that the public leaders attending regular convenings had the potential to become that voice as a unified collective that could enter the housing field as a challenger, and that conversations about systemic housing issues in the months before taking their first action on the 2009 housing needs assessment hinted at the possibility that actors would support and remain with the new collective.

Recognition of different interests at play in a newly formed collective also requires that actors have the ability to apply consequence *know-how* to the working relationships with other members, particularly for a newly formed group. Before any strategic action can be implemented that targets incumbents in a field, the collective itself can be the target of the first order of strategic action field activities. In other words, there is some level of strategic *know-how* that is applied in enabling the creation, maintenance, and growth of a collective. Consequence *know-how* in this sense is directed at the desired outcome of establishing a strong unified voice within the newly formed collective that will be able to engage publicly as a challenger.

Gamu, an HJC member who worked for another housing actor during the activities he highlights in our interview, and who worked directly with Jano on various strategic action fields, was working at a new organization at the time I interviewed him. His role within this new organization was oriented toward housing, but the organization he worked for during the time of the interview in April 2017 was not a housing organization but a service organization that focused on a specific population who had housing concerns. We met in his office, situated on the upper floors of a multi-organizational 10-story office building. Our conversation was less fluid than those I had with Jano, as Gamu repeatedly stated that he had not thought about specific events in some time. Still, he offered some insight into how he and Jano approached strategic action fields directed at the collective itself:

> *Lucas:* How did that go, and who took the lead for that, and how did the alliance organize that? It was just somebody would say something from time to time, was it [Jano] only, was it ... How would that happen?
>
> *Gamu:* I think we were ... We brought it up. There was definitely, at different points trying to be strategic about who brought what up.
>
> *Lucas:* Oh, you were?
>
> *Gamu:* Yeah. I don't remember if it was about that particular issue, but [Jano] and I would conspire, as we still do on the HANO board, you know?
>
> *Lucas:* So that means you ... So you would sit down ... Not sit down, but you may have a phone call. But you would plan beforehand about language and about what to say, and who would say it?
>
> *Gamu:* And I can't ... I honestly can't remember if we did that with the consolidated plan, but we've definitely done that with the QAP meetings..., and various things, and trying to be thoughtful about who says what and all that kind of stuff. There's some strategy that happens.

Such an admission may sound like manipulation to the untrained observer but is in fact normative strategic choices actors in leadership positions make regularly as they look for ways to ensure a group moves toward its intended goals. Both consequence and action-to-goal congruence *know-how* are applied by actors as they devise and implement strategic moves that are designed to strengthen the collective as an organized unit. While it is not impossible for a collective to organically self-organize in such a way as to be leaderless, the normative path toward collective cohesion and effectiveness relies on the leadership of an individual or a small few who apply what they know to building an organized group. Even if an external threat, as was the case with Katrina and the failed levees, serves to bring people together, there remains a need to organize people in such a way that they become a truly unified collective with a shared agenda.

As a collective, the HJC was not unique in its need to continually engage in strategic action fields aimed at its own members. In my own participatory work with the HJC that began in earnest as a participant observer in 2015, Jano called upon my knowledge about nonprofit lobbying and asked me to create and deliver an educational presentation on the matter in 2017.

The overt intent was to provide factual information from the Internal Revenue Service about the do's and don'ts of nonprofit lobbying and advocacy in an effort to demystify any concerns HJC actors had about engaging in direct lobbying and other advocacy activities. Behind the overt intent, however, Jano had more covert reasons for doing this.

First, the collective in 2015 was transforming. Many of the initial nonprofit housing developers had closed their doors and those left were winding down to the point that they, too, would soon be on their way to closing their doors. At the same time, new housing groups not involved in the business of developing housing were propping up, and the collaborative of housing educators that existed pre-Katrina was in the process of folding into the HJC. Additionally, Jano had expanded participation (though not voting membership) to organizations who had interests in housing issues, which included organizations working on homelessness, criminal justice, and environmental justice, to name a few, but who did not directly work on housing policy. With this new mix of actors joining the HJC, Jano found himself needing to "reorient" the collective's new members in how participation in the HJC could be maximized from an advocacy/political challenger perspective, which made some of the new members uncomfortable.

Not only did the HJC advance political challenges within the housing field on behalf of its members, it also needed individual organizations to pursue, when and where possible, actionable tactics when called upon to do so. Gamu provides an example of how this worked:

Gamu: And so, you need the people who actually engage in the services, and then you partner with them, and you help them and you educate them enough, and you make the technocrat policy speak make sense to them, so that they can then speak and then they can take their personal experience. And they bring the personal experience that I don't have. And it's very powerful.

Lucas: So, you mean the full spectrum, meaning everything from folks who know nothing about the technical stuff, but they're experiencing it, and then all the technical folks and everything in between.

Gamu: Mm-hmm (affirmative).

Lucas: So full spectrum being anyone who can help in this arena, who is involved in one way or another, would be great if we're all together working on this.

Gamu: Yes.

Lucas: Is that what you're saying?

Gamu: Yes.

When the HJC took up an issue, such as the Qualified Allocation Plan (QAP) in 2012 in which the HJC wanted to get certain stipulations added to the final document that was critical to how tax credits were doled out, it deployed a multiple-actor strategy.[6] This multiple-actor strategy stipulated that not only would the leadership of the HJC do its part to advance the interests of the collective (through a variety of tactics, such as meeting with incumbents, publishing editorials, and pushing their agenda at public meetings, to name a few), but it also meant that organizational members would complement the HJC's strategic action tactics with their own set of activities as separate organizational actors, wherever this was appropriate and helpful.

For example, if a member had a strong relationship with a target incumbent, this member would be relied upon to both advance the HJC's agenda directly in its own one-on-one meetings with the incumbent, as well as connect the HJC publicly by confirming participation within the collective and helping the HJC establish a relationship with the target incumbent. Under this strategy, a field incumbent who is challenged by the HJC also hears from relationships it has with single organizational actors, making it more apparent that there is a united front of actors who are challenging on the same thing. This was a common strategy used by the HJC in other strategic action fields the HJC initiated between 2009 and 2015, but as the HJC membership transformed and the housing field stabilized, Jano increasingly engaged in strategic action fields without the benefit of a multiple-actor strategy simply because new members were more hesitant to engage in activities that might affect their 501c3 status.[7]

By planning for the educational workshop, Jano sought to eliminate any direct engagement with a member about federal regulations. His hope was that the presentation would enable him later to make an action-oriented ask. In other words, he could spend less energy convincing a member that the law allowed certain political activities and more time on the specific task he wanted a member to undertake. Using a PowerPoint presentation, I presented the information in March 2017, at one of HJC's regularly scheduled meetings to a room of about 30 individuals from various organizations, who were all seated in a semicircle around me on folding chairs. As is typical with HJC meetings, this particular meeting was held in a member's space (meetings initially were held at BYHH, but after separating from BYHH, meetings roved around the city, taking place in members' spaces) that was slightly too small for the number of people attending. Aside from a few clarifying questions from attendees, the presentation did not appear to generate any strong reaction, positive or negative, but Jano affirmed afterward that it accomplished what he wanted.

By having an outside consultant (that was my role, though as a volunteer) present the information, it provided Jano and other HJC leadership members a position of authority on matters of 501 c3 lobbying regulations, which they could then turn into a sort of capital that enabled them to engage their members more easily on strategic action fields that required public political tactics. As such, Jano could ask a member to follow up with a political actor on a specific issue without having to enter into a difficult dialogue about whether or not the HJC was asking the member organization to occupy a precarious political space.

Regardless if the HJC ever asked any of its members to engage in direct advocacy or lobbying, as regulated by the Internal Revenue Service's (IRS') 501 c3 code, the educational seminar contributed to the HJC's ability to continue on its political challenger trajectory uninterrupted. This was a key concern because new members can sometimes result in collectives moving in new directions that are less politically contentious in practice, particularly if there isn't a shared heightened sense of threat. Jano indicated as such in conversations we had throughout the data gathering period that were not recorded in interview fashion. By simply offering the educational presentation, Jano felt the green light to push on members to take on politically oriented strategic actions.

As New Orleans moved further and further away from the devastation of Katrina's levee floods, the urgency for housing, particularly for affordable housing for working-class and low-income families, diminished (though not the real, on-the-ground need). This loss of threat urgency occurred in most, if not all, New Orleans social justice fields and translated to a decrease in participation for many organizations that engaged in contentious collective politics, as well as a devaluation of any power that challengers had when the Louisiana and New Orleans housing fields were still somewhat unstable.[8] Such changes were not lost on Jano, who was constantly looking for ways to maintain and increase HJC's power within the Louisiana and New Orleans housing fields.

While more immediate and organizationally oriented in nature, applying strategic skills, abilities, and/or tactics toward one's own collective members, particularly when the members are by-and-large organizational, may not appear, on first assessment, to qualify as a strategic action field because it doesn't seem directly associated with field outcomes. However, as the examples above reflect, collective strategic action fields require multiple actors within a collective to engage directly in designed activities. While there may be instances in which actors within a collective readily and easily comply with requests for their time and energy on specifically planned activities, more often than not leaders within a collective have to convince other actors to lend time, energy, resources, power, and reputation.

The simplest method for achieving the desired participation on any strategic action field is to simply ask outright for volunteers to take on specific tasks, but this method fails to maximize the strategic potential that a collective is supposed to offer. Collective leaders who deploy strategic *know-how* will direct usage of this *know-how* toward their own collective, as needed, when activities don't move forward as expected. But even when leadership does all that it can strategically to both engage its own members in collective activities and engage the target incumbent on a specific strategic action field, it can result in failure.

By 2012, the HJC was on its way to incorporating as a 501 c4 organization, finalizing a formal and legal structure that could enable the HJC to establish itself as an independent collective.[9,10] At the same that it was doing this, the HJC was involved in various strategic actions, some aimed at the New Orleans housing field and some aimed at the Louisiana housing field. One that stands out as an example of a failed outcome despite a high-level of strategic *know-how* is the attempt to include language in the state's Qualified Allocation Plan (QAP) that would benefit nonprofit developers.

The QAP is a tool designed by states as part of their requirement for offering tax credits to developers.[11] Essentially, the QAP is designed to set the parameters under which tax credits are allocated. Housing justice advocates use QAP's to include affordability criteria for developers looking to tap into the tax credits in their market-rate developments. Out of discussions among the HJC members between 2009 and 2010, the collective agreed to pursue challenging the QAP, with the intent of including as much language as would be allowed that resulted in affordability allocation stipulations for future developments that would pursue the use of tax credits.

As Gamu recalled during our interview, the issue was that in the years immediately after the storm, tax credits had sufficient stipulations that appeased affordable housing advocates and developers, but at some point, when the Louisiana Housing Corporation (LHC) issued a new round of tax credits, the previous stipulations had disappeared:[12]

Gamu: And after Katrina, the gulf coast got flooded, which is how all the buildings got bumped up. So, any ... Pretty much any housing that happened had tax credits associated with it. And what they did was built it into qualified allocation plan that if you're gonna ... If you get tax credits, a certain percentage of the units have to go to these permits in support of housing units. Meaning that 200 permits had permanent support of housing, deeply affordable units for that population. So, it's across disabilities, low income, all of that.

Lucas: Mm-hmm (affirmative).

Gamu: And that was in it for a couple years, because of the work of advocates. And then it conveniently dropped out.

Lucas: When you say it was in it for a couple of years, immediately after the storm and then dropped out around –

Gamu: I don't know if it was immediately.

Lucas: But at some point during recovery?

Gamu: During recovery, yeah.

Lucas: It dropped out, do you remember when? And this was a state policy that changed?

Gamu: Yeah. I mean it's ... Right. The staff of the LHC get to determine it. And then it's approved by their board.

Lucas: So, you noticed that there was a change.

Gamu: Mm-hmm (affirmative).

The HJC became quickly aware of these changes, which they anticipated to some degree, stemming from a general anticipation of major policy changes throughout all Louisiana fields upon the re-election of the state's governor, Bobby Jindal, in 2011.[13] Indeed, this election would create new challenges for the HJC that it did not face during Jindal's first term, primarily because Jindal's first administrative term operated largely under the same instability affecting the majority of the state after two major hurricanes in 2005 (Katrina and Rita) and a third major hurricane in 2009 (Gustav).

During Jindal's first term, between 2008 and 2012, the LHC (called the LHFA before 2012) operated with relative autonomy from the governor, guided in large part by a professional director who had arrived post-Katrina from D.C., where more progressive housing development ideas existed when compared to Louisiana at that time. It is under this director that the tax credit stipulations referenced by Gamu above were instituted, and it is under this director that the HJC was able to succeed in challenging for the changes they wanted to the housing needs assessment.

However, as Jindal's first administration ended, it gravitated toward more extreme conservative fiscal policies that affected the states' ability to raise the needed revenue for its annual budget.[14] The Jindal administration advanced fiscally conservative policies immediately upon winning re-election in 2012 and instituted an effort to garner greater control over its agencies, resulting in significant changes at the LHC beyond just its name change.

> *Jano:* Yes. So, the state, Bobby Jindal, had decided in a purely political move to reorganize into the Louisiana Housing Corporation. It was the Louisiana Housing Finance Agency, an independent quasi-governmental arm. And he changed it to the Louisiana Housing Corporation, which was an arm of the state. This was done purely so that Bobby Jindal could access their significant reserves and he ended up raiding them for about $63,000,000.

It is unclear from my interviews with the HJC leaders and members, or from my participation with them between 2008 and 2018, or during the interview period, if they actively calculated how the Jindal administration's changes would affect their work. What is clear is that they recognized that changes were happening and mobilized to address these, deploying all the strategic *know-how* at their disposal:

> *Lucas:* ... so what happened then? So, you got involved in the policy committee to deal with this change.
>
> *Gamu:* Mm-hmm (affirmative).
>
> *Lucas:* And what was the goal?
>
> *Gamu:* The goal ... So, the goal was to get the coalition to agree on the things that we wanted on it. And initially that was kind of a laundry list, and it was everything from smart growth, green energy.... What we

wanted was ... What the qualified allocation plan is, is actually like saying [to] developers, that you want these tax credits. These are the requirements and the criteria that you need to abide by. And you get a certain number of points in your application for tax credits if you say you're gonna do renewable energy or be a green building. You get a certain number if you say you're gonna have a certain number of slots for people with certain incomes, or certain demographics....

Lucas: Mm-hmm (affirmative).

Gamu: But that wasn't based on data on [our] end. And part of the challenge is, there's always a tension between New Orleans getting the resources versus other parts of the state, so they decided that in their infinite wisdom, the best way to allocate all of this was based on a congressional ... Areas. So, each one would get a certain number. It was the dumbest thing.

Lucas: So that was the decision they made, and you saw that, and [were] like oh, no?

Gamu: Right. Well, it was just ... My guess is some developer lobbyists from other parts of the state had gotten in there and run amok with what they wanted. And so ... So initially, it was the laundry list of what all the members wanted, including the things that I cared about, but also some of the things that other members cared about. Which are fine.

Lucas: Some [HJC] members, yeah?

Gamu: Mm-hmm (affirmative).

Lucas: So, you had to do that work first, to get them all on-[board]

Gamu: Yeah. And [Jano], [he] definitely ... And there were other people. I was just a part of it. So, the work was to get all of us on the same page, and get your piece in here.

Lucas: And then what, take this to the state?

Gamu: Right. So, we submitted written comments, because they would come out ... Like a lot of things, they would come out with a draft and people can comment on it. And then we also separately I think submitted some other stuff. So there was stuff that we did as [HJC], and then there was other stuff that [Jano] and I, and these lawyers committee folks, were also pushing. That not ... That we couldn't necessarily get everybody from [HJC] on board with. And we ended up meeting ... I feel like at least once, maybe more than once, with [LHC] staff. So some of the other parts of the work were relationship building.

As this passage highlights, the HJC deployed a mixture of tactics as part of their strategic action to ensure that the latest round of state tax credits included stipulations that benefitted low-income housing needs. From dividing the work among allies to engaging in a set of activities that were not agreed upon by the collective, Gamu points to the work that he, Jano, and other leadership members engaged in to achieve their desired outcome. Unfortunately, this work, which spanned over 2 years of effort, yielded little return:

Gamu: And didn't help then that the guy was removed, [Bam Smith]? He had worked for HUD and come on, and then there was some sexual scandal and he got ... Yeah. He's a good guy, and it seemed to be headed in the right direction. So a lot of staff turnover and disfunction.

Lucas: And so, you intentionally needed to go work with the staff, because the other ones drafted stuff together. And you had a strategy to organize your own members, get their report together in here. But then also separate strategy to go out and work with the actual staff of LHC to try to get to some understanding, try to get to ... What was that about? Just trying to get to know each other?

Gamu: I mean, it was ... Yes, there was relationship building. But it was for them to actually include our comments, and actually change the way the QAP was allocating points.

Lucas: Yeah. And how long did this last? Like doing this kind of work, do you remember?

Gamu: Probably a good 2 years.

Lucas: Wow, that long?

Gamu: Yeah.

Lucas: On what, building relationships and talking to them?

Gamu: Yeah. Because then they ... They delayed putting out the QAP. Yeah, it was a while that we were working on that.

Lucas: And what happened ultimately?

Gamu: Not much.

Here, Gamu reveals that despite all their work, they were unable to move the needle in this specific strategic action field, which resulted in failure to secure the HJC's desired outcome. Both consequence and action-to-goal congruence *know-how* were deployed in this endeavor at a relatively high-level. This means that the actors knew what they were doing, understood what they needed to do and how to do it, and implemented a set of tactics to achieve their desired outcomes on a specific action strategy. In this planning, these actors envisioned a specific result within the Louisiana and New Orleans housing fields that ultimately failed to occur.

Despite having the ability to plan and implement accordingly, the HJC was unable to obtain its desired outcomes on the low-income tax credit stipulations. Does this instance indicate the ineffectiveness of strategic *know-how*? It does not, but it does point to its limitations. As was discussed previously, no amount of *know-how* will enable challengers in a field to succeed if the opportunities are closed or closing. As regards the LHC, Jindal was already in the process of stripping the organization of its autonomous power while also plundering its coffers for the purposes of balancing budget shortfalls elsewhere, which combined to make the LHC, as an organization, less willing to make changes requested by nongovernment challengers.

Additionally, in this telling of the work to push for desired language in the QAP, it is possible that Jano and Gamu exhausted all avenues available to them to get their language included, but it is also possible that they focused too much energy on too short a list of actors affiliated with the LHC in their relationship-building work. Knowing how to balance which actors within an incumbent organization and how many to challenge and/or build relationships with is highly subjective, as challengers have to weigh oversaturating their requests with different incumbents across various government agencies, which can create more problems than solutions.

While not successful with the QAP, the HJC leadership on this strategic action demonstrated consequence *know-how* and action-to-goal congruence *know-how* that enabled it to stay on track over the course of 2 years. As circumstances change over time and new difficulties arise, staying on track with one's desired goals can become more challenging as the months turn into years. For the HJC, having consistent leadership for a prolonged time (from 2008 until the time of this study's data gathering period) certainly can aid a collective's ability to maintain its broader strategic direction over the span of years (at the same time, such longevity can also serve to stunt growth – depending on the leadership and organizational culture).

As the initial coordinator, turned-chairperson, turned-executive director, of the HJC, Jano ensured that the collective's initial goals of tackling inequitable housing, particularly as that relates to housing affordability, have remained the focus of all strategic actions. One of the most successful examples of his ability to deploy both consequence *know-how* and action-to-goal congruence *know-how* toward advancing the HJC's desired outcomes can be observed in the soft second opportunity that eventually found its way into the hands of first-time homeowners.

As was explained previously, a soft second is a forgivable second mortgage offered as gap financing to qualifying first-time homebuyers. Often, soft second programs target working-class families who earn enough to pay a mortgage but don't have the deposit and closing funds to secure these loans. A faith-based group in New Orleans who had successfully challenged the Road Home program in 2008 to set aside $52M for renter assistance soon after found that it needed to redirect these newly allocated funds toward other housing initiatives. In four of the 11 interviews conducted at his office between 2016 and 2017, Jano discussed the strategic action work that HJC put in to get the soft second released in the manner that HJC thought would work best for New Orleans.

> *Jano:* Actually, we started with [The Faith Leaders] group to get the money allocated in the first place.
>
> *Lucas:* You were working with the organizing group on the rental thing?
>
> *Jano:* Yeah. Actually, I am the one who, when they came up with the idea to take some of the rental money to help first-time homeowners and ... and they were, what should we do with this money? And I said, we should do soft second.

Urged by the HJC's recommendation, this organization worked with the state of Louisiana and the City of New Orleans to redirect funds toward homeownership, resulting in the creation of a $52M pool of cash for homeownership assistance. The New Orleans agency set to receive these funds was the Finance Authority of New Orleans (FANO). As was discussed previously, the HJC had little success in challenging this agency on its design of the soft second program under its initial iteration at FANO.

Taken as a singular episode, as was the case in analysis previously, the HJC indeed failed to achieve their desired outcome of a true soft second program. However, the soft second program did not fare well under FANO, and in 2010, when Mayor Mitchell Landrieu took office, the program was moved to a new housing bureaucrat who worked with the HJC to relaunch it, largely with the elements that the HJC asked to be included originally. By expanding analytically to include the multiyear trajectory of the soft second program, one can see how years later, the HJC did achieve its desired outcome of getting a program that maximized buyer opportunities, as per the HJC's view.

Previously, the analytical focus on the HJC's actions and activities with FANO limited conversation to that singular episode of events. However, while the HJC experienced setbacks in its FANO-aimed efforts, it did not walk away from continued engagement on the future design and implementation opportunities on this matter. While FANO did finalize design of its version of the soft second program and implemented it, making it available for broad public use, the program proved to be too cumbersome and onerous for first-time homebuyers to benefit from it, resulting in a stalled program that the incoming Landrieu administration wanted to fix and push forward. During this period of stalled implementation, the HJC continued to push FANO to reconsider changes to the program that the HJC felt would better benefit prospective homeowners, but it wasn't until actors in leadership positions changed at city hall that the HJC was able to experience some success.

By the time newly elected Mayor Landrieu took office in 2010, the program had become a negative PR headache for the city due to FANO's inability to move the funds into prospective homebuyer's hands. Pantu, a newly installed city hall bureaucrat who had the responsibility of fixing the program, is an individual I worked with during my tenure in Landrieu's administration. When I interviewed Pantu in May 2017, he was still in the same office location he occupied when I last worked with him as a colleague in 2013. Pantu's entire department was situated in a commercial building across the street from city hall. The city rented this space for various agencies due to a shortage of city-owned office spaces. In his office were stacks of reports and memos related to housing that Pantu was constantly working with, as it was his responsibility to direct local government housing policies and programs. Pantu recalled the issue with the soft second this way:

Pantu: So when I came, I found out the big program that they recruited me to administer was the soft second. So had a [50] million-dollar program that they had been trying for, back in the Nagin days, to get off the ground and never could.

Pantu had come to New Orleans from New York. He was a government veteran, having worked both for New York City and New York State. He entered New Orleans post-Katrina as a housing government actor and brought a more open sensibility to his government work than his predecessors in New Orleans. Again:

Pantu: And when I started…, my first thing is well, we gotta get all the stakeholders around the table to find out what was wrong with the first attempts and figure out what we can accomplish and talk them through.

This strategy expressed by Pantu requires further discussion. The idea that a new government bureaucrat will seek stakeholders to engage in the work under his charge is nothing new. However, what was new in the New Orleans field, at least as regards the office that Pantu led, was that the "stakeholders" he sought would not be the traditional clientelist stakeholders that typically benefitted from close relationships with city hall in New Orleans politics. For Pantu, the work of identifying stakeholders relied on identifying representative voices belonging to housing actors who had a real stake in the New Orleans housing field and who seemed to be capable of occupying a professional relationship role. The HJC, in Pantu's opinion, fit that bill:

Pantu: My success in New York was really the result of working with stakeholders…. Because I knew that this city really needed to … my strategic plan as to how to get things done was you can't really do creative things unless you have a firm foundation. Like you have to have partners and they all have to be strong enough to hold onto whatever you want to build on top, whether it's a house, a program, a neighborhood, a block.... So to [the HJC], what I had learned in New York was you cannot talk to each individual organization that is out there, whether they are private developers, lenders, whatever. You need a organization that speaks for them and communicates for you.... And [the HJC] was an organization that City Hall had dealt with occasionally but not ... I don't think they really gave them a true seat at the table. And [Jano] was the head of it there, and [he] had experience in government and kind of went all in. And [the HJC] and [Jano] were one of the ones that were the first ones that were receptive and said okay, let's see if we can build a relationship cause we want this program to work.

An interesting note about Pantu's observation here is his recognition of the HJC's strategic move in recognizing his role within city hall and the New Orleans housing field. In Pantu's estimation, the HJC presented the type of partner that could be deeply involved in the future direction of city hall's role in housing affordability. Over the course of 2 years, Pantu built a relationship with Jano, allowing the HJC, when invited, to partner on housing programming ideas. One of these housing programming ideas was the soft second, but even here, with Pantu's opening and invitation, tensions arose.

Jano recognized that under Pantu's charge, the soft second would be shut down and redesigned. He saw this as an opportunity to inform the decision-making agency now in charge of the program (the program was taken out of the hands of FANO by Mayor Landrieu) of HJC's design ideas and how these would maximize the benefit to prospective first-time homebuyers. From 2010 to 2012, through ongoing negotiations, group meetings, and many tense and difficult discussions, Jano remained committed to helping the city move the funds into the general public's hands. There were instances of confrontation over different ideas during the ongoing development of the new design, but contention was minimized because Jano perceived in Pantu's work a true interest in delivering a program that would benefit New Orleanians, unlike the previous iteration, which sought to have the money returned.

Many other challenges occurred, of course, such as disagreements with the first-time homebuyer educators and with members of the HJC, particularly those who did not like having city hall bureaucrats participate in HJC meetings (after they established a working relationship, Jano invited Pantu and his staff to join in regular meetings).

Despite all this, Jano remained focused on the ultimate desired goal, a program that focused on helping families in New Orleans tap into financial assistance so that more working families could purchase homes. Eventually, Jano's perseverance in keeping this goal in sight paid off, as the soft second program successfully launched, which the HJC openly championed and promoted (despite Jano disliking some elements of the program).

This ability to remain focused, playing a long game, if you will, that spanned 4 years (from 2008 to 2012), was possible because Jano and other leadership members of the HJC deployed both consequence and action-to-goal congruence *know-how* in their strategic action fields, which targeted affordable housing opportunities for working-class families in New Orleans. This singular focus, established in 2008 when conversations for the potential soft second began, guided the HJC's decision-making and participation, as they remained clear in their desire to see the allocated funds make it into the hands of the general public in the way that it was intended. Along the way, there were numerous pitfalls that could have easily derailed the HJC's ability to participate in this work and play a key role in its development. However, a recognition by actors such as Jano, who took on leadership roles within the collective, about the need for the program, its impact on the growing housing affordability crisis, and the need to be the voice that remained committed to a final program design that worked for families, combined to enable the HJC to remain engaged on this action despite setbacks and pitfalls.

Across all its endeavors from its founding in 2008 to its incorporation in 2012, and its growth after that, the HJC has demonstrated a strong ability to remain on task. To this day, at the time of writing, the HJC continues to focus on building power within the Louisiana and New Orleans housing fields, with a steady aim toward affecting the state of Louisiana's housing affordability issues, which it currently frames as a crisis. This long-term consistency in its pursuits has aided the HJC's development as a recognizable actor capable of challenging the Louisiana and New Orleans housing fields on issues affecting housing affordability. Demonstrated in the housing needs assessment, the soft second effort and QAP efforts, and other initiatives, the HJC's deployment of action-to-goal congruence *know-how* has been one of the key abilities that has enabled the organization to grow in budget, reach, and abilities. This ability to stay on track is highly underestimated and under-assessed by outside observers, as there tends to be an assumption that there is an automatic-like linear flow to contention.

The ability to recognize when an idea is not worth the trouble because it has the potential to derail the trajectory of work already in play is not something that comes easily to many public leaders. As a nonprofit advocate, I experienced this firsthand as soon as I had the budget to bring new individuals on board. Fresh ideas from new faces were the order of the day whenever I hired new individuals to work at the organization. Sometimes, an idea made sense because it would support and/or enhance our ability to reach our stated organizational goals. For me, this was the criteria for new pursuits: did they add or detract from our stated work goals? If they detracted, and they often did, I shot the idea down. Unfortunately, these exchanges with staff, and sometimes with board members, were not always pleasant, which is another important component to discuss here.

As leaders of a group effort, or of an organization, individuals don't get to make decisions in a vacuum. Others in the group have ideas about the direction of strategic action, and as one can imagine, if the leadership isn't capable of maintaining a clear direction or isn't positioned strongly enough within a group or an organization, to hold off internal challengers, then one can visualize how easy it becomes for new directions to formulate. If, however, leaders of a collective or of an organization have the ability to navigate internal challenges as they arise without letting these moments undermine group cohesion, then ongoing internal agitation for new pursuits that detract from stated goals become easier to manage.

Even so, the act of listening to someone who wants something that won't be allowed creates significant tensions. Assuming an individual's best intentions, a push for a new direction that has the potential to derail strategic action (regardless if the individual advocating for the idea doesn't realize this potential) requires that group or organizational leadership have the ability to listen in such a way that doesn't create additional tensions and issues for the group while simultaneously deterring continued challenges. While this study does not focus on the value of emotional maturity and/or intelligence in collective formation and maintenance, it is a critical factor that can also contribute to the success or failure of a collective achieving its desired outcomes (Goodwin & Jasper, 2004), as it is a contributing component to action-to-goal congruence *know-how*.

On how strategic know-how *interacts in other groups' abilities to secure desired outcomes.* Similar to the HJC, the NNG experienced its share of successes and failures in achieving its desired outcomes. As a challenger, the NNG successfully fought city hall on many fronts. The NNG defied any plans for converting the Nearby Neighborhood into greenspace by; occupying the neighborhood school and rebuilding it, securing funding for a shuttered library and bringing it back with more resources than it had before the storm, and articulating a vision for neighborhood resilience and engagement that would become a model for other neighborhoods to copy.

But channeling the energies of a diverse membership of residents who represented significant class and ethnic differences into targeted strategic actions didn't happen simply because everyone shared the same external threat from city hall. The NNG's ability to secure extensive buy-in from its residents on a set of singular activities is indicative of a leadership team capable of understanding what strategies aligned with which consequence and what strategies would keep them on track to achieve their goals. In other words, consequence *know-how* and action-to-goal congruence *know-how* were key abilities used by the two leaders who helped the NNG achieve its desired outcomes.

This is an ability that Kurt, the priest in charge of the church that was an ally to NNG, noticed and admired, summed up in the following statement:

> *Kurt:* New Orleanians are great at community. They're great at listening to their neighbors, I think, but they also can become paralyzed, because they want to satisfy everybody. And that's where [Nona's] great, "cause she goes, 'Well, I can't make everybody happy.'"

Such an observation underpins how general members appreciated these abilities because without this type of leadership maintaining a strategic direction on course, it is possible that the Nearby Neighborhood may not have experienced similar success. Indeed, in my experiences as either a complete member, active participant, a government facilitator, or a research observer of a variety of collectives and community meetings within New Orleans between 2007 and 2018, I observed countless scenarios in which the direction of a collective was continuously a matter of debate. That is to say, keeping the ship on track is not a given. Simply because people come together out of shared frustrations does not mean that adequate direction for action will automatically follow. A single public leader, or a group of leaders, has to provide the ability to navigate and steer.

Within a collective, not everyone wants to lead and provide the group's broad strategic directions. When folks come together, as they did in the Nearby Neighborhood, someone (or a small group of people) must be able to organize them into a cohesive unit that is working toward a shared goal, and then must be able to implement strategies and tactics that have a demonstrable ability to bring the work closer to fruition.

Similar to the HJC, the NNG enjoyed consistent leadership for a prolonged period of time, with both Nona and Jonas serving as cochairs from 2005 until 2013. This consistency in leadership, which could deploy strategic *know-how*, while not a sole contributing factor, contributed to NNG's ability to achieve some of the critical goals it had targeted as important to getting the neighborhood back on track.

In my own participation with various coalitions and alliances, I witnessed firsthand all too often how easily strategic efforts were derailed by public leaders who felt the group's energies should be directed in different directions. In one particular alliance, called the ALAAP, that came together in 2007 to address language access for non-English speaking people, I spent a full year (from 2008 to 2009) attending meetings in which alliance members argued about the direction for action. Nothing happened during this period, and as I quickly learned from actors who would become my colleagues in the field, the alliance had been meeting for 2 years prior without articulating a clear direction for action before I joined in 2008.

What I observed during those early meetings was the group's inability to articulate a clear strategic action that aligned with a clear desired outcome, led by a leadership group that wasn't quite ready to orient the many voices that had agreed to come together into some form of unified direction. The initial ALAAP members were like-minded individuals, most of them mid-level managers of color (mostly Latinx and Vietnamese individuals) who worked in New Orleans area nonprofit organizations across various fields, such as education, health, immigration, criminal justice, youth services, and housing. Many of these members didn't have decision-making authority within their respective organizations, making it more difficult for ALAAP to secure organizational commitments. As a result, a great deal of opinions were offered in these meetings about what needed to be done with little to no actionable decisions being made and no subsequent actions being taken.

By the time I had begun attending the ALAAP meetings in 2008, the group had yet to formalize any sort of leaderships structure. It relied on the two founding members who continued to initiate monthly gatherings, but who through their lack of action on issues also contributed to the creation of a growing leadership void in the face of increased interest to do something about the lack of language access for non-to-limited-English speakers.

Similar to the HJC, the ALAAP came together to learn about language issues from each other and collaborate on potential solutions. By mid-2008, it had become clear to many of the actors involved that the New Orleans area needed an organized voice on this issue, particularly since the storm had served as a catalyst for a new wave of limited English proficient speaking immigrants arriving to the area. It was during this time that conversations began about having a clear set of desired outcomes that the alliance could focus on. After several deliberation meetings, the group agreed to focus on three areas, education, criminal justice, and health language access, and created a simple structure of committees and committee chairs. I chaired the criminal justice committee. Each committee was tasked with creating the trajectory for its work.

The committee I led included a number of attorneys and criminal justice advocates who knew the New Orleans criminal justice field. They also had extensive knowledge of the language access issues and opportunities within the field. We evaluated different strategic directions for action, weighing the potential for each and arrived at a strategic action we believed had the best chance of having system-wide impact within the New Orleans criminal justice field. The strategic action field we created focused on convincing the Louisiana Supreme Court to adopt a standard for interpreter services in Louisiana courts.[15]

This committee stumbled a bit in the early meetings because I made a strategic decision to allow the individuals who knew the most about the field to lead with their ideas about what should be the plan of action. The majority of meetings took place in the offices belonging to the nonprofit organization that I led, with typically 7–10 lawyers from different organizations participating. Often, those who couldn't attend in person participated via conference calls that we put on speakers. In the initial months, we met every other week, but as directions became clear and tasks were assigned, our meetings shifted to once every 3–4 weeks. Initial discussions centered around the value of one goal over another. Throughout this process, my only input was to remind those with extensive knowledge about the language access issues in criminal justice to consider each idea in terms of its ability to be attained in a timely manner and its ability to serve as potential foundation for further systems-wide change down the road.

As the chair of the committee, my concern was getting to a plan that could be implemented and that aligned with the desired goals of bringing about equitable access to limited-to-non-English speakers in New Orleans courts. I listened to the lawyers as they debated the merits of different goals and strategies, asked probing questions, and regularly reminding everyone of the criteria of a winnable goal. In the span of 6 months, the group chose a direction.

In this scenario, I played the role of group convenor, facilitator, and in some ways, strategic coach. As strategic coach, I helped keep ideas for strategic action aligned with the overall collective's desired goals, oftentimes by simply reminding everyone to consider certain criteria. While the lawyers and criminal justice advocates were significantly more knowledgeable about the field than me, they tended to either focus on hyper-specific issues they were accustomed to working with or on overly ambitious programmatic ideas that required certain structures and practices to be in place that didn't exist within the criminal justice field. We were able to pool our combined field and strategic planning knowledge in deploying both consequence *know-how* and action-to-goal congruence *know-how* that played a key role in aiding our success.

Knowing what we wanted as a desired outcome – a truly equitable language access process and structure in Louisiana courts that ensured due process for limited-to-non-English speaking defendants – enabled the committee to focus on the initial element needed to move the field in that direction. With clarity about what to change in the field and clarity about what existed (and didn't exist) in the field, the committee was able to design a strategic action field that focused on the chief authority in the state, the Louisiana Supreme Court, which could install changes without legislation. With this in view, the committee designed a set of steps, which included researching the first steps that other states took, reaching out to prospective allies, and exploring options for a meeting with the Louisiana Supreme Court. Achieving these steps kept the work on track, which the committee conducted over the course of a year until it achieved the adoption of interpreter standards at the Louisiana Supreme Court in 2011.

This achieved outcome was in part aided by three factors arising from strategic decisions made by the committee, which were: (1) to conduct the research and draft the complete document that we wanted the Louisiana Supreme Court to ultimately approve, (2) to secure inclusion in the Louisiana Bar Association's upcoming legislative agenda, and (3) to identify and meet with an individual within the Louisiana Supreme Court who could aid the process. Success in these three strategic actions enabled this small committee of less than 15 people to achieve a significant change in how the State of Louisiana considered language access in its courts.[16] The strategic *know-how* the committee deployed enabled the committee to move from discussion to achievable actions, which then set the wheels in motion toward successfully attaining the originally established desired outcome.

Notes

1. See Alinsky (1946, 1972) and Chambers (2003) for the IAF's view of power in the public realm.
2. As Fligstein and McAdam point out in *Theory of Fields* (2012), existential threat is a significant aspect of any form of political contention, and I would add here that the degree to which an incumbent or a governing unit feels that a challenger's interests will result in either substantial changes to the status quo or loss of power is directly proportional to that actor's response to a challenger. The more existentially threatened an incumbent or governance unit feels, the more potential exists that a strong reaction to protect the status quo will take place.
3. Networks can occur within and across fields. Where a field is a social circumscribed area, as Fligstein and McAdam describe in which a variety of actors play roles that maintain a field or reorders it, networks are social or institutional relationships irrespective of a field (see Fligstein & McAdam, 2012). A field may contain hundreds of networks, and a network may span across several fields. For example, as a member organization of a national Latino advocacy group, the

150   The Know-How of Public Leaders in Collective Politics

organization I led benefitted from membership that provided access to a vast network of other Latino organizations throughout the United States, but this did not translate to any strategic action within a field in which other member organizations engaged in contentious politics.

4. The BYHH was not only awarded the major contract for redevelopment of a large public housing campus but also awarded over 100 individual lots (some with properties on them and some without) owned by HANO for redevelopment, which folks at the BYHH referred to as their "scattered sites," which surrounded the main public housing site.
5. Here, it is important to reiterate that these calculations cannot be fully understood via the rational actor model, as such a model is too limiting in scope in terms of explaining the different reasons human beings take action on any matter, be it personal and individual or collective and public. Additionally, the rational actor model fails to account for the role contingency plays in actors' decisions.
6. The QAP is a tool that states use to determine how they will share their allocated low-income housing tax credits. Whenever such tax credits are provided to a state by the federal government, states must prepare QAPs, which advocates typically challenge during the drafting period.
7. The United States' IRS code that creates the 501 c3 establishes that these organizations can only allocate a small percentage (typically less than 10%) of their total budget to lobbying, but it does not prohibit lobbying outright. Despite this, many organizations believe the code prohibits lobbying (see https://www.irs.gov/charities-and-nonprofits for a complete description of allowable activities by nonprofit activities within the Internal Revenue Service Tax Code).
8. Whatever power challengers were able to garner during the more uncertain times in the years immediately after Katrina, this diminished gradually as fields restabilized, and incumbents resettled into positions of power. With stable fields, incumbents could assess more clearly the likely threat offered by a challenger, something which would have been murkier during the unstable years closer to the aftermath of Katrina.
9. While classified by the Internal Revenue Services as a social welfare organization, the name is misleading as this classification allows for the expenditure of funds on lobbying and advocacy activities without the restrictions placed on 501 c3 organizations. Many groups throughout the United States use this IRS nonprofit designation as a funding mechanism for the lobbying needs of 501 c3 organizations.
10. Until this incorporation, the HJC remained a loosely organized group without legal standing. Complicating matters for the HJC as it grew in reputation and power was the fact that Jano continued to coordinate it while still an employee of the BYHH. He remained an employee of the BYHH until resigning in 2015 to serve as the full-time leader of the HJC.
11. The National Low Income Housing Coalition (https://www.nlihc.org/) provides a useful reference tool on QAP's, located here: https://nlihc.org/sites/default/files/2014AG-259.pdf
12. The LHC is the new name of the LHFA, which was introduced in the informational *know-how* chapter. The name change occurred in 2012 under then-Governor Bobby Jindal at the onset of his second term.
13. See https://www.reuters.com/article/idUSTRE79M07V/ for a report on Governor Jindal's 2011 election victory.

14. See this Times Picayune article for a summary of Governor Jindal's fiscal policies: https://www.nola.com/opinions/article_39311716-bbf6-5bb9-a0b3-be098fce9d83.html
15. At the time of this action, Louisiana was one of 13 states without an official statewide standard for court interpreters. Without this standard in place, it would be impossible to get any true traction going in any court in the state.
16. At the time of its creation, this was a significant foundational step, designed to allow future advocacy efforts to build upon in the work to bring actual implementation changes within the local courts in New Orleans.

Chapter 6

Without Clear Roles and Processes, They Suffer

Participation in group activities, regardless of the type of activity, has added value to human life since the dawn of man. Group life has enabled civilization to advance technologically and culturally, enriching our existence on earth. What we know now from over a century of social, biological, and psychological science research and theory development is that human beings flourish precisely because group life provides meaning via a combination of rituals, symbols, and formal and informal social structures. Through informal social structures, such as those that inform normative understandings about how a society functions (what is often termed "common sense"), we make our world understandable within our families and in the general societies where we live. Through formal structures, we learn our roles and that of others at work, in sports activities, and in politics, to name a few spaces. At the same time, social structures (particularly informal) are not always evident. In newly formed groups, such as in those that endeavor to engage in contentious collective politics, social structures do not self-realize, as if ready-made. Instead, social structures require some intentional work if a group is to find its footing and progress in its work to become challengers to existing fields.

In the Industrial Areas Foundation (IAF) tradition, community organizers are trained to "organize" their target communities. The central idea of "organizing" within this tradition refers to the establishment of a people's organization that provides the structure and processes resident leaders can then use to effectively participate and build power (Alinsky, 1972; Chambers, 2003). Building and/or maintaining successful collectives that can engage in strategic action that pursues a unified agenda requires an ability to install and maintain operational structures and processes that give people clarity about their roles and how to go about acting out these roles.

In this chapter, I explore how actors' operational *know-how* interacts with a collective's ability to pursue its desired outcomes. As discussed in the analytical framework chapter, operational *know-how* refers to actors' abilities to build and maintain structural and procedural paths for participation within collectives. When people come together in a group, if they have any intention of engaging in some form of action, they will require some form of social structure. A public leader, or a group of leaders, in a leadership position with knowledge about structures and processes will typically organize a chain of command and internal rules for engagement, at the very least, to enable more effective group functionality. Actors' abilities in setting up these structures have typically been the domain of institutional and organizational theories and not so much collective contention theorists (Fligstein, 1997; Fligstein & McAdam, 2012).

This chapter explores two types of operational *know-how*: structure and process creation *know-how* and structure and process maintenance *know-how*. The two types of *know-how* work hand-in-hand but aren't always needed together, depending on the situation. For example, a public leader (or group) observed in a collective may simply inherit a structure already in place. Therefore, this public leader would need to know how to maintain structures and processes that work. On the other hand, a public leader (or group) may create a new collective, and in doing so will need to install new structures and processes that others can follow.

At the same time, actors who can create structures and processes that enable the operation of a collective may not necessarily know how to maintain them. For example, a public leader (or group) may know that certain structures and processes are known to work, based on her (or their) experiences in other groups, but may not have any experience with how such processes and structures are maintained. Without this know-how she runs the risk of being unable to sustain these structures and processes after installing them. Combined, a collective's ability to create and install, as well as maintain, operational structures and processes enhances a collective's potential to enjoy a long-term existence in which others are able to enter and participate. While not the sole reason for a collective's success, having structures that define roles and processes that clarify how action is undertaken within and outside of the collective enhances a group's ability to create a long-term unified voice, one that is able to continue beyond the initial energy that created it.

On how the HJC's operational know-how played a role in the collective's pursuit of its desired outcomes. It didn't take long for Jano to realize that the organic structure offered by the loose monthly convenings would be insufficient for the future potential of affecting change in the New Orleans and Louisiana housing justice fields. In the second interview in December 2016, meeting in his office, he offered the following observation:

> *Jano:* Yeah, so we're sitting at the table, and again, these tables are still … We're sitting at a table like that out there. You remember with [HJC] meetings, now it's 40 people in the room set up classroom style. But then we were sitting very much around a table and talking to folks about how we assemble this and how we organize this. That was in my mind through a corporation, which in '08, we're still moving it. We're starting to talk about how do we respond to policy, how we have the policy question. We formed a policy committee.

Between 2007 and 2008, the Housing Justice Coalition (HJC) was not yet the HJC. In this first year of existence, the HJC was little more than a monthly gathering of housing actors who were interested in getting houses back online in post-Katrina, New Orleans. Between 2008 and 2009, when Sinu relegated convening and facilitation duties to Jano, this coincided with a shift in conversations that was also taking place within the collective. Conversations were evolving from discussions about who had access to the cheapest wood to discussions about systemic bottlenecks that made building affordable homes in the new post-Katrina environment challenging.

While still not exactly an organized collective, there was already an understanding by these individuals and Jano that a specialized structure focused on policy opportunities would be required. It was clear to the initial participants in the collective that not everyone who participated in the regular monthly meetings was interested in policy research and action strategizing. It was also clear to Jano that occupying the monthly meetings with policy conversations would detract from the possibility of building a collective.

A policy committee, therefore, was created to provide a separate space that would be understood as part of the monthly meetings but that would conduct its own work outside of these regular gatherings and report any opportunities worth exploring at the monthly meetings. As such, the HJC deployed structure and process creation *know-how*, which manifested in their assessment of the need for, and subsequent implementation of, a separate committee. But to Jano, this was just the beginning of what would be needed, as he indicated in our second interview in 2016:

> *Jano:* In 2008, we started doing the committee thing, right? And started looking at how do we start reviewing things to prepare a response. Still no formal structure. Even in 2012, when we finally incorporated, it was 2010 when we made the decision to incorporate, it took us about 18 months working with the lawyer's committee for civil rights under law to write the by-laws and everything like that. It says explicitly in the by-laws to be a voting member of [the HJC], you have to be a developer. You have to be someone who is attempting to create housing.

As the selection above highlights, the HJC incorporated as a formal independent organization in 2012, electing to do so as a 501 c4 rather than a 501 c3 for the express purpose of pursuing community improvement outcomes via political activities.[1] Between 2008 and 2012, the HJC created additional committees and established a chairmanship, which Jano occupied from its inception until an executive staff structure was created for incorporation in 2012, at which time a board was established, with the chairmanship role moving to the new organization's board structure. More importantly, as Jano shares above, the HJC instituted a voting structure for strategic direction and action that restricted the collective's voting power to organizations that were involved in building homes, which by 2012 included both nonprofit and for-profit developers.

While establishing this voting restriction limited the HJC's ability to grow as a collective somewhat, the structure and procedural processes they implemented enabled the group to solidify its New Orleans base of invested actors who represented a part of the solution to housing affordability in the field. Instead of relying on groups or individuals who cared about housing but had little stake in the field, such as individual activist actors, the HJC looked to strengthen the ability of those groups who were focused on providing affordable housing.

This restriction stems from the HJC's original founding, which ties back to the nonprofit developer that created it, the Bring You Home Housing organization (BYHH) as well as to a leadership group whose primary experiences in the housing field had been informed by housing development. Given this, it makes normative sense, if not exactly strategic sense, that the HJC would initially restrict strategic action voting to a specific type of housing actor. Additionally, this decision benefitted the type of leaders that ran the HJC precisely because the majority of individuals involved belonged to housing development organizations, which as a group engaged in highly technical housing policy–related communications and actions that tended to have strong opinions about what approaches were best for addressing housing affordability.

However, this voting restriction did not limit participation by other housing actors, particularly in the monthly convenings that have become a standard in the New Orleans field since they began in 2007, or in the ongoing working committees. Indeed, anyone interested in housing has always been (and remains) welcomed to attend the HJC's monthly meetings, which continue as of the time I write this in 2022. But as one can imagine, not too many public leaders want to give time and energy to ideas that they don't get to vote on, so inevitably, the HJC opened its voting membership to include housing educators in 2014, community development financial institutions in 2016, and building contractors in 2018.[2]

By creating a clear leadership structure and process for voting, the HJC facilitated the collective's ability to pursue its ongoing desired goals of bringing housing affordability to the New Orleans and Louisiana housing fields in a manner that suited the HJC's leadership and minimized newcomer agitators.[3] These initial voting restrictions were indicative of a need for the group to first focus on a solid, long-term trajectory that could be safeguarded (in as much as voting restrictions to housing developer organizations could offer such a safeguard) in such a way as to enable the growth of a cohesive base of housing actors that could build a shared agenda.

While this strategy worked for a time, as was indicated above, the collective did have to eventually accept other housing players into its voting structure. The primary reason for expansion stemmed from ongoing participating housing actors' desires to have input in the overall direction of the HJC's political work, but an important external factor also played a key role in this expansion: the shuttering of nonprofit housing developers. As the years stretched further away from the devastation caused by the failed levees after Katrina, New Orleans area, nonprofit housing developers began to close their doors due to dwindling funds. As the influx of cash from outside sources slowed down, many post-Katrina organizations were forced to close or consolidate, which resulted in a gradual attrition of voting members for the HJC.

The piecemeal approach to expanding access to voting, however, worked to the HJC's benefit, as it served to strengthen and maintain the value of the voting structure, ensuring its ongoing maintenance by future voting members. By the time the HJC was ready to expand voting beyond housing developers, the structures and processes for strategic action were solidly in place, making it more challenging for any new member to push for significant changes in this regard. In this manner, operational *know-how* played a key role in not only helping the HJC to implement it desired strategic directions but eventually succeed in achieving some of its desired strategic outcomes.

By establishing structural processes of research and evaluation that begin in committees, which then provide recommendations to the full voting membership, the HJC was able to implement strategies that were supported by housing actors who had the most stake in any given strategic action field. From a structural perspective, the HJC created the needed structures and processes that enabled the multiple-actor strategy mentioned above to take place. The important role of such operational structures and processes cannot be undervalued, as they too often are when discussing group behavior in contentious collective politics.

Without these structures and processes, the act of prioritizing step *A* over step *B* can easily devolve into a battle of wills, as it cannot be assumed that in the absence of clear internal structures and processes, groups will self-organize according to some mythical natural order, as was once assumed by 19th and early 20th century natural and social scientists (Banton, 1998). This may sound tongue-in-cheek, but it is far from it, as 19th and early 20th century thinking about natural order continues to inform under-analyzed normative dynamics in group settings, particularly in newly formed political collectives, where often internal structures and processes don't exist until actors in leadership roles create them.

Operationally, a collective with well-defined structures and processes has one less item to tackle on its change-making agenda, that of deciding how to decide. This may seem trivial, and as such is a highly underappreciated element in building and sustaining collectives. In my time as a social justice actor and a city bureaucrat, I experienced firsthand moments and situations in which individuals have single-handedly destroyed a group's momentum simply because the structures and processes were either inadequate or nonexistent. When there is no clear path for decision-making, participants in a collective run the risk of engaging in highly charged arguments about items and topics that sap the energy out of the group, which can in turn leave those who witness such situations frustrated or "turned off."[4]

As the HJC embarked in the various strategic directions discussed in the previous chapters, it relied on structures and processes that enabled it to focus its energies on researching and voting on opportunities and designing and implementing strategic action fields in a manner that became (over time) systematic and (eventually) institutional. The ability to institutionalize structures and processes provided clear paths for participation for collective members, with those interested in pushing a particular agenda urged to do so via committee work. In this way, whenever newcomers would show up and demand an action of some sort (which is an ongoing phenomenon) during the monthly meetings, their concerns could be channeled into the collective structure and explored on its viability relative to the collective's established agenda. For any collective, the ability to stay on course over the long haul, particularly when incumbents in a target field continue to stay in power and yield only small concessions along the way, is a critical factor in being able to achieve desired outcomes, when doing so may take years of consistent challenge.

Despite the HJC's successful creation of, and subsequent revisions to, a clear set of processes and structures through which members could advance ideas for strategic action fields on housing affordability, the collective did not offer a space for the average resident to be involved. When the collective embarked upon the creation of a citywide housing strategy, it recognized this shortcoming and endeavored to begin exploring how to incorporate everyday residents.

Between 2013 and 2015, the HJC held numerous community meetings throughout the city, inviting resident leaders to convenings about housing. These meetings proved to be beneficial to the HJC, as they provided the collective with a good deal of information that they were able to incorporate in the final housing strategy published in 2015.[5] Out of this experience, they recognized a need to build a resident involvement structure, which they included as part of a new organization, a 501 c3, which they created to provide an institution for professional staff that could focus on housing research, education, and resident involvement. During the study's data gathering period between 2015 and 2018, Jano led both the HJC and the newly formed organization, Homes for Us New Orleans (HUNO).

Through HUNO, Jano created resident-led advisory committees that served to inform the programming and direction of the new organization, eliminating any concerns about politically oriented strategic action decisions at the HJC proper. Through this two-organization structure, Jano was able to expand the work conducted, as well as create a new actor in the New Orleans housing field in which residents could get involved. Part of my participatory work with the HJC has included participating in the resident involvement work at HUNO since 2015. While there has been real struggle to expand everyday resident involvement, Jano has been able to successfully create the spaces in which nonhousing professionals can and do engage (though not yet in large numbers as of 2022).

Additionally, establishing HUNO has expanded the pool of resources that Jano can pursue, which has enabled him to develop a full-time operational staff from 2016 onward. This added benefit is worth discussing further. When researchers examine a collective's ability to mobilize resources, specifically cash resources, there are many factors at play. Structurally, however, one factor specifically stands out. In the United States, cash donations require a legally registered nonprofit organization to which funds can be delivered and through which they can be administered.

Without such a structure, a collective will be hard pressed to raise the needed cash to engage in desired strategic activities. While there are successful instances in which specific actions can occur without any of these structures (consider reactionary, local public demonstrations, for example), most of the strategic action fields conducted by collective challengers within a field are supported by structures and processes that both provide clear paths for participation to members and help secure the needed resources to support the work.

The HJC's ability to engage in a nearly 2-year long process of developing a citywide housing strategy, which included numerous community meetings, extensive research, and marketing dollars, was aided in large part by the structures and processes they built over time. General participation, voting, and leadership structures and processes, in particular, enabled the HJC to continue to provide clear paths for member participation while establishing the long-term viability of an institutional actor that has the potential to exist long after the founding individuals move on.

Finally, the creation of a citywide housing strategy, which HJC intended for local government to adopt, was a significant undertaking that required the mobilization of a considerable number of resources that would have been more challenging to secure without the support of established structures and processes in place. As a challenger in the New Orleans housing field that had engaged in various strategic actions form 2008, the HJC had developed deep knowledge and expertise on housing affordability strategies, policies, and solutions. The years of participation and experience in the New Orleans housing field led it to ascertain a need for a citywide housing strategy that was assumed would never be developed by government agencies.

HJC's ability to deploy high-level operational *know-how* served as a contributing factor to not only the organization's ability to continue to exist as a collective from 2008 until the present (as of 2022) but also to its ability to initiate various strategic action fields that challenged incumbents in the New Orleans and Louisiana housing fields. While the collective's deployment of operational *know-how* did not interact directly with a specific strategic action field in such a way as to be understood as having some direct impact on success or failure, it can be said that the collective's general ability to engage in contentious politics continuously and consistently over its 13-year span is due, in part, to its creation and maintenance of structures and processes that fostered and aided ongoing membership participation.

On how other collectives and organizations' operational know-how *interacted with their desired outcomes.* Similar to the HJC, the Nearby Neighborhood Group (NNG) shows how the ability to create and maintain structures and processes interacted in a positive way with this collective's ability to secure its desired outcomes. For the NNG, which was an already legally established neighborhood association before Katrina, the matter was not about needing to create a legal structure but about creating working structures that would allow resident volunteers to lead the work in their charge. This approach worked well with the school agenda, enabling resident leaders who led this strategic action field to fully pursue the work. However, the NNG committee process differed from the HJC in one key fashion.

While both collectives' committees consisted of volunteer work (nonpaid work) conducted by their members, the NNG more heavily relied on the direct leadership and direction of the two resident leaders who led the association from 2005 until 2013, while the HJC relied on a mixed leadership structure that included: the director (called the chairperson before incorporation) and the board (after incorporation) informed by committee work and membership votes. In the HJC, committees were led by experts in their field who volunteered their time to advance work that could become potential strategic action. Whereas in the NNG, committees were led by resident leaders who were not professional experts in the work they conducted as volunteers.

At the NNG, the direction of strategic action fields was largely led by one of the two resident leaders, Nona and Jonas. This more top-down approach in terms of the direction of strategic action fields didn't hinder the NNG in its efforts to challenge city agencies. Instead, it provided the guidance and support that resident volunteers needed to feel confident about the work they conducted. Linas recalled how these worked in our first interview in 2016:

> *Linas:* ...then there were some people who weren't as much like the face of the movement, but who played an extremely active role...and so, but you know, and then there were all these committees. There was a library committee, and an education committee, and a community development committee, and a crime committee, and all these different, you know, that were born in this process....
>
> *Lucas:* As a support role, did you get to see how any of those decided things and what did they do and what did you observe?
>
> *Linas:* Yeah, so when I would come down, um, I would attend some of the community meetings, and the committee meetings, um...and sometimes we would do, like, small projects, for a subcommittee, like I remember, um, well, with the surveying, that was the repopulation committee. That was a support role for the repopulation committee... then we did, we do, like data input sometimes, you know, it's different, it's hands-on roles...that could help support the role of the committee.... [the NNG] was really good about, with all of the partners that it brought it, um, contextualizing the work.

The simplicity of the structure benefitted resident leaders, such as Sammie, who were less interested in debating the merits of one strategic action over another and more interested in doing the work they volunteered to do, particularly because of his limited time in the city (when he lived between Texas and Louisiana, as many poststorm residents did during the rebuild process).

> *Lucas:* Then the committee, your role as a committee member in that topic. Do you remember, is it just be available or-
>
> *Sammie:* Be available, discuss the pros and cons. What we had discussed at the meetings. You know, I'd bring my perspective.
>
> *Lucas:* Yeah.
>
> *Sammie:* I guess most of the committee members, when we would have those monthly meetings, we would give some background to the rest of the community. So they'd know. In the capsulated form instead of us going through the whole-

Lucas: Right.

Sammie: Months and months of debate.

Lucas: Right, right.

In the school-related strategic action fields, the NNG relied on assignments and direction given to volunteers by the two resident leaders. Strategic action succeeded in challenging the relevant local government agency and enabling the school's reopening. Another major effort, NNG's work to address housing affordability in the Nearby Neighborhood, ultimately failed, however. While the work to purchase, rehab, and provide housing differed greatly from the more direct work of bringing back online a neighborhood government service, the NNG's approach to the structures and processes needed for this work, which relied less on the resident volunteer energy that worked for the school and the library and more on housing expertise, may have contributed to this work not advancing as desired.

Lucas: So, you were on the development. So what did you have to do there? What did you do there?

Sammie: Well, yeah, it was kind of a, it was a difficult committee in a way. Not really difficult, but we were trying to acquire property.

Lucas: Mm-hmm (affirmative).

Sammie: And then renovate that property. Again, there was some conflict about, well, and this is the part where it's kind of like, not controversial, but like okay. [James], great guy, amazing man, said, "Listen, I don't know if I want to be in this committee because I'm not really in the market to redevelop houses," because he didn't know how successful it would be.

Lucas: Yeah.

Sammie: We weren't as successful as we had thought we would be. Because redeveloping property to that extent really required much more funding than we had.

Beyond gutting and cleanup work, the NNG offered little participation mechanisms for neighborhood leaders to engage in the affordable housing work, opting instead to create new legal structures, such as a community development nonprofit, that would ultimately fold into the neighborhood association structure after it became unable to conduct its work. While the difference in scope and scale of the work matters significantly here, contributing to the NNG's inability to advance its desired outcomes in this endeavor, it raises the question about both the potential and limitations of resident involvement in certain strategic action fields.

Could the NNG have been more proactive in its participation structures and processes relative to its affordable housing strategies? Or is it simply that the housing focus may have been far less galvanizing than the unifying cause of reopening the local school, which was a strategic action field designed, in part, to challenge city hall's plans to convert the area to green space? Perhaps no type of structure and process would have been sufficient to overcome the challenge of unifying a mixed working- and upper-class neighborhood on work that dealt with housing affordability, particularly as this term in the years immediately after Katrina still elicited visions of slumlord housing in New Orleans middle class minds.

In my work heading a language access criminal justice committee for ALAAP, the ability to deploy operational *know-how* can be observed as serving a critical role in this committee's ability to achieve a desired outcome. As previously discussed, Alliance for Language Access for All People (ALAAP) had been meeting for 2 years without much progress on any form of strategic agenda. It wasn't until we established clear committee leadership roles based on advocacy areas that strategic action fields began to take shape and traction. I credit this to ALAAP's deployment of structure and process creation *know-how*, evidenced in the decision to install three 2-year termed committee chairs roles that had the responsibility of pursuing a strategic agenda in its issue area.

Establishing these committees enabled ALAAP to spend less time on broad arguments and opinion-making across fields at monthly meetings. Anyone who wanted to opine, complain, or advance their recommendation for strategic direction could do so at one of the three issue-based committees. If the language access area of concern did not fit within one of the three issue areas, then it would be tabled for future consideration, enabling ALAAP to remain focused on the three issue areas it had agreed to pursue.

Committee chairs had the responsibilities of coordinating meetings with those interested in the issue area and make decisions about strategic action fields. As a committee chair, I also had full discretion as to how I should facilitate committee meetings and manage decision-making. My approach was simple: let the experts in the field, the folks with knowledge about the systems, explore a viable opportunity and help guide their efforts toward that opportunity. This approach, combined with the flexible committee structure, enabled the criminal justice committee I led to design a strategic action field that ultimately succeeded in getting the Louisiana Supreme Court to accept and adopt a set of standards for court interpretation services (a much-need first step in Louisiana at the time).

The Citizen Rights Collective (CRT) in which I participated, failed to provide clear structure and voting processes, resulting in ongoing confusion and (rather consistent) tensions among collective members about who decided the direction of work. Initially invited by a third-party consultant who ultimately became the collective's coordinator, the CRT never moved from this initial loose structure. Throughout my time with this collective (from 2009 to 2011), monthly meetings would yield little in the way of unified strategic direction, stymying strategic action decision-making and implementation.

Without Clear Roles and Processes, They Suffer   163

While it cannot be established that this lack of clear structure and processes is the cause of the CRT's inability to achieve its stated desired outcomes in local governance practices, it can be established that failure to deploy operational *know-how* in this instance contributed to the group's ultimate demise. As a participant in this effort, I found that our monthly meetings often reiterated unresolved issues within the collective itself, never quite fully gaining the needed traction to simply direct our efforts collectively on a single action item. Of course, there were other dynamics at play, such as what I discussed previously about racial and gender power issues, but it is possible to establish here that some clarity and acceptance in a structure and process that the collective members could have agreed upon would have benefitted the group by simply enabling it to create shared strategic action fields. When the collectives' energy is consumed with unanswered questions about **who gets to decide what** for the collective, it leaves little room (and little confidence) for strategic action field decision-making.

Notes

1. See endnotes 7 and 9 in Chapter 5 for explanation of 501 c3 IRS code information. The 501 c4 code provides greater flexibility in terms of lobbying activities, but it does not provide the charitable deduction that philanthropists and general public donors use for tax write-off purposes.
2. Building contractors should not be confused with developers, who often are not contractors. For example, the majority of nonprofit developers relied on for-profit contractors to build homes for the developers. Developers typically focus on the deal and the structural designs, then hire contractors to build the structures. Sometimes a developer has an in-house contractor, but not typically.
3. The description "newcomer agitator" refers to new individuals to the collective who push for strategic action that the collective is either incapable of or unwilling to pursue in the manner desired by these individuals. Unfortunately, collectives do find themselves excluding actors who champion their individual or organization's goals over those of the collective in a manner that detracts from the collective being able to advance its work.
4. In my experiences as an advocate across various fields in the New Orleans area, I observed numerous instances in which individuals simply discontinued participation because they did not enjoy being a part of confrontational arguments that led nowhere. Oftentimes, such moments of disagreement would turn hostile and unprofessional, which inevitably left an impression of disorganization on those not directly involved in the fray.
5. For the purposes of protecting the study case, this report is not made available here but can be furnished upon request.

Chapter 7

Know-How Conclusions

Research Recap

This study gathered qualitative data from third-party reports and articles, interviews, research participant-observer experiences, and practice in the field (as a complete member) to explore how actors in the New Orleans area post-Katrina pursued social justice change from 2007 to 2018, with a focus on organizations operating in the New Orleans area. Applying Fligstein and McAdam's Strategic Action Field (SAF) theory (2012), this study was able to place observed, documented, and shared events into the context of the relevant fields in which actors engaged in political action.

While SAF theory articulates how these fields provide actors the circumscribed social spaces in which they engage in contentious collective political activities (Fligstein & McAdam, 2012), the theory does not limit an actor's ability to effect change as being nontransferrable from one field to another. In other words, while some abilities may be field specific, such as knowledge about a field's contours, issues, and actors, other abilities will be readily transferrable across fields, such as the ability to influence people to participate and become active members of a collective.

These abilities, whether field specific (certain information specific to a field) or general (certain abilities that can be applied across various fields), are used by public leaders who engage in contentious collective politics to affect some sort of change in the fields in which they operate. As such, this study explores the interactions between what public leaders know how to do (their *know-how*) to achieve the outcomes they desire in their social justice agendas and their success or failure to do so. Sociologically, this study asks: *can the know-how public leaders deploy in contentious collective politics play a role in achieving outcome success or failure? And if so, what are the ways that such know-how can interact in success or failure?* Put another way, I explore how *public leaders' know-how can play a vital role in either enhancing or limiting the potential for outcome success in local contentious collective politics.*

To explore this, I operationalized nine types of *know-how* that correspond to four broad *know-how* dimensions: informational, social, strategic, and operational.

Analysis was divided among the four dimensions, with a chapter dedicated to each of the four dimensions.

Findings

As a qualitative design I am not "testing" causal relationships, which is something sociologists and political scientists love to do. Instead, I provide thick descriptions of the data, which I then interpret via the SAF theory frame and my application of *know-how*, showing how *know-how* interacted in such ways as to either enhance or limit a group's ability to achieve its desired outcomes. This is not to say that *know-how*, regardless of dimension, could be singled out in any situation as the factor that contributed to outcomes' success or failure. The study does show, however, that public leaders' *know-how* across all four dimensions does play a role in a group's (be it a collective or a nonprofit organization) ability to achieve its desired outcomes in contentious politics.

Across the four *know-how* dimensions, there are varying levels of abilities, as *know-how* is not evenly distributed, which this study understands to represent a snapshot of society in which the same will be the case. There is no even distribution of *know-how* when it comes to public leaders' abilities to successfully lead contentious collective politics in the same way that individual talents and abilities are not evenly distributed in any general population. Some have more and some have less *know-how* in specific issues and fields. Those public leaders who have been trained to develop specific *know-how* either through formal training or on the job opportunities tend to deploy higher level *know-how* in their contentious collective politics planning and implementation decision-making.

On how actors' informational know-how *either enhanced or limited the prospect for outcome success in local contentious collective actions.* What contentious collective challengers know about a field, its contours, its actors and their power, its historical trajectories, and debated issues matters significantly in contentious collective politics. Without this type of knowledge, public leaders who challenge existing incumbents within fields run the risk of misdirecting their contention toward futile ends.

Public leaders who possess a substantial amount of knowledge about the field in which they are actively engaged in contentious collective politics increase their opportunities to achieve their desired outcomes. They do this by using their knowledge in deploying informational *know-how* that informs their decision-making about which tactics to pursue and when to pursue them. Knowing who or what to target, as well, requires that public leaders deploy informational *know-how*, which relies on public leaders being able to bring to their decisions all the information they can muster about the field in which their contentious activities are directed.

At the same time, sometimes they fail. A group's *know-how* may play a key role in helping the group develop into a collective, plan decisive and meaningful strategic action fields and relevant tactics, and still fail to achieve success. This is because while high levels of *know-how* can interact in such a way as to enhance a group's ability to achieve its desired outcomes, this is not a straightforward causal relationship.

For example, I explored a situation in which high levels of *know-how* still weren't sufficient to enable the Housing Justice Coalition (HJC) to achieve its desired outcomes in the short term on the soft second mortgage program. Sometimes, the opportunities within the fields are such that no matter the amount and level of *know-how* applied, contentious collective actors just won't win. Of course, the opposite was also found to be true. Sometimes, the field is so unstable and so favorable or the opportunities are such that even low-level *know-how* will be sufficient to enable a group's attainment of its desired outcomes.

Public leaders involved in ongoing efforts to challenge the fields in which they operate require informational *know-how* before, during, and after the creation of strategic action fields. Without knowledge about the field, its actors, the issues and debates, and so on, the effort to create a collective that will be capable of challenging a given field will yield very little in the way of progress. Public leaders need to know something about the fields in which they intend to challenge, even if at the very least to point toward their general targets. Public leaders who lack informational *know-how* run the risk of wasting a great deal of energy pursuing dead ends and achieving little to nothing.

Finally, informational *know-how* can be of little use if collectives don't have the ability to deploy the other dimensions of *know-how*. Knowing a great deal about a field isn't sufficient for public leaders engaged in contentious collective politics. They must know how to "make use" of the information, deploying this as *know-how* when creating strategic action fields that must account for a wide range of factors before a group can engage in political contention. In other words, informational *know-how* is intricately interwoven into public leaders' deployment of other dimensions of *know-how*, as it informs what actions to take and who to target when pushing for change.

Additionally, in a contentious collective politics situation between an incumbent and a new collective challenger, the incumbent in a field is much more likely to know most, if not all, of what he needs to know to remain an incumbent within his given field when compared to a new collective challenger. Typically (of course, not necessarily always), new challengers will possess less informational *know-how* relative to a given field than incumbents within that field. While it is not out of the realm of possibility that the opposite can be true, this assertion highlights how informational *know-how* across field actors cannot be assumed to be of equal degree.

It would then seem that an important element to consider when determining what contributes to successful outcomes in contentious collective politics is having some understanding of the knowledge and *know-how* challengers possess. Along the informational dimension of *know-how*, this means that challengers must know something about a field's purpose, its related content, both internal and external, that corresponds to the field, the political debates within the field and about the field, the historical development of the field, the positions of power within the field and who holds these, the positions of maintenance and who does this, and more.

On how actors' social know-how *either enhanced or limited the prospect for outcome success in local contentious collective actions.* This book does not assume that collectives form out of thin air, as if by some magical unknown force people simply coalesce, unify, and act with a shared vision. As discussed above, I assume that it takes the work of specific individuals, or a group of individuals, with the requisite social *know-how*, to bring people together, encourage them to unify under a shared vision, and convince them to act on this vision via a series of political activities. In other words, it takes *knowing how* to engage, organize, and activate people if a collective is to form and participate in contentious political activities.

The cases analyzed in this study demonstrate that social *know-how* can indeed interact in such a way to either enhance or limit a group's ability to succeed, as it can serve as a contributing factor to a group's ability to act as an organized collective. Even when an exogenous shock significant enough to galvanize people in shared anger occurs, deployment of social *know-how* is required if this anger is to be converted into an organized collective that works in a unified manner toward a shared political goal. The cases explored in this study show that the majority of individuals interviewed and observed were called to political action as a direct result of the levee failures after Katrina. However, it took more than just feelings of anger and frustration to convert these new political actors into effective participants and members of organized collectives. Some public leader with the social *know-how* either invited interviewees to participate in organized activities or the interviewees themselves acted as public leaders and invited others to join organized groups.

At the same time, the exogenous shock of Katrina's aftermath does reveal that in times of great crisis, when large numbers of people are experiencing shared frustrations, anger, and fear, an opportunity is created for public leaders with social *know-how* to bring people together in an organized fashion. As the Nearby Neighborhood Group (NNG) case showed, when threat urgency diminishes, even public leaders with high-level social *know-how* struggle to engage and activate individuals.

The HJC case offers a similar interpretation. Actors involved in forming and joining the HJC were all "activated" by Katrina's aftermath, with new groups forming in the housing field at a time when the field was highly unstable between 2005 and 2008. Yet, it took the efforts of the BYHH leader to bring these actors together and then subsequently the efforts of the HJC leadership to continuously engage and organize this newly formed collective. In the final analysis, exogenous shocks may galvanize generally shared anger and fear, but they don't create collectives – public leaders with social *know-how* form collectives, sometimes made easier by exogenous shocks.

Yet, as with all types of *know-how*, the wisdom that public leaders have about bringing people together and how to put this into practice cannot be considered a panacea for understanding why some collectives achieve their outcomes and some don't. Instead, what this study does show is that any strategic action field that a collective embarks upon will require some level of social *know-how* if this collective is to achieve some level of success in attaining their desired outcomes as a group. The reason for this is shown in analysis as being related to power and the ability to influence incumbent actors in a field. Collectives have far more power when compared to individuals, generally speaking (that is, when one omits wealthy elites and other similar individual power brokers from this consideration). As such, the social *know-how* that public leaders use to build an organized collective, capable of acting on a shared politically contentious agenda, has the ability to enhance (not guarantee) a collective's chances to succeed in achieving their desired outcomes.

Indeed, the majority of wins considered in this study occurred because an organized collective, with a shared, unified agenda was able to work cohesively toward its desired outcomes. In the cases discussed in this study, it took the involved work of a variety of participants within a collective to achieve the wins they enjoyed. Without this level of organization and collective will activation, it would have been much more challenging for these groups to succeed, as the work conducted by many would not have been possible if it was not organized in such a way as to feed into a collective's agenda.

However, the cases analyzed also showed that social *know-how* doesn't end with simply bringing people together and motivating them to engage in a unified direction. There is ongoing maintenance of a group, and as time passes, actors change, with new ones entering and old ones leaving, creating an ever-changing dynamic that warrants attention. For public leaders without sufficient social *know-how*, such fluidity can overwhelm, and if left unattended can result in splinter groups forming out of collectives or even internal coups, in which groups of actors redirect a collective if the opportunity arises. As a specific strategic action field conducted by the HJC revealed, a small group within the collective that did not agree with the direction of this strategic action field ultimately undermined this effort because it benefitted the small group. Thus, organizing collectives can be a double-edged sword, with the successful deployment of social *know-how* creating an opportunity for new actors to gain advantage in a way not originally intended by the initial creators of a group.

Similarly, public leaders may possess and deploy high levels of social *know-how* and still find themselves unable to detect (sufficiently in time to combat this) when an internal member is acting in a way that is counterproductive to the collective's stated goals. Hidden agendas, emotional instabilities, and generally irrational behaviors are all elements that human beings have the potential to bring to a collective, and even the highest skilled public leader may find it difficult identifying and dealing with such elements.

Or, as the case of the Citizen Rights Collective (CRT) showed, even when there is sufficient social *know-how* within a collective to expand and bring others onboard to grow the power and reach of a group, this will not result in any successful attainment of desired outcomes if this *know-how* remains sidelined by leadership. In other words, groups may form without much deployment of social *know-how*, as in the case of the CRT, which was formed out of a funding priority by a national funder. But once formed, if they have a desire to build a true collective, as the CRT did, then social *know-how* will be needed to engage other actors and include them as new members. Such *know-how* was present in the CRT but was actively devalued and dismissed, resulting in the original size of the coalition to remain in place for a few years until it eventually disbanded once funding ended.

Similar to the exogenous shock of Katrina and its levee failures, external funding in this case was insufficient to form a significant collective. The external funding was enough to bring a small group together that were funded out of the same pool of money, but the allotted money would not be enough to pay others to join and as such created a limitation to who could join. Without usage of the social *know-how* already in place, this group was unable to grow, build power, and engage successfully in strategic action fields, resulting in little to no desired outcomes achieved.

Finally, the study showed that there are instances in which the social *know-how* needed to form a collective may sometimes be external to the group being formed, such as was the case for the Neighborhood-Based Housing Initiative (NBHI) which hired a professional organizer who organized three neighborhood associations. With the help of external social *know-how*, residents were brought together into a collective through the creation of new neighborhood associations. However, despite the professional organizer providing some training to individuals in these new collectives, these groups' social *know-how* diminished considerably once the professional organizer was no longer actively involved with them. As such, a group's inability to maintain the needed level of social *know-how* runs the risk of failing to engage actors sufficiently to keep them involved in ongoing collective contention, which in turn has an impact on a group's ability to achieve desired outcomes.

Ultimately, leaders with social *know-how* matter a great deal when getting people to join and act as a group. Without social *know-how*, groups may find themselves challenged to secure the adequate resources that may be needed for strategic action fields, be that in the form of cash, time on specific tasks, or expertise. When collectives come together to form a group for the purposes of participating in contentious politics, it is likely that such collective building is taking place because people share a sense of powerlessness about the way things are and perceive the potential value of increased power in working collectively. When this is the case, social *know-how* plays a significant role in a contentious collective's ability to build a sufficiently viable collective capable of planning and implementing successful strategic action fields that yield that group's desired outcomes.

On how actors' strategic know-how *either enhanced or limited the prospect for outcome success in local contentious collective actions.* When public leaders in collectives engaged in contentious politics know the ins and outs of the fields in which they are challenging and know how to bring people together to form a unified group with a shared agenda and goals, the work of deciding upon effective strategic action fields requires that someone, or a group of people, can evaluate one strategic direction over others. Such an ability is typically described normatively as strategic thinking. In this study, strategic thinking is part of a skill that is used when strategic *know-how* is deployed in collective contention, which the analyzed cases show is a critical component of any successful attainment of desired outcomes.

Similar to other forms of *know-how* discussed so far, analysis does not find a direct causal relationship between strategic *know-how* and achieved desired outcomes, but it does find that this type of *know-how* is a necessary element in strategic action fields implemented by public leaders engaged in contentious collective political activities. As such, strategic *know-how* cannot eliminate the contingent unknowns waiting behind each politically oriented action, but its deployment can help public leaders mitigate this contingency, helping to direct activities in such a way that attempts to maximize effectiveness and maintain focus. Hence, even with high-level strategic *know-how*, nothing may go right.

In order for strategic *know-how* to have a high chance of contributing to success, however, a great deal of many other factors must be in place, as well, such as a collective having requisite informational and social *know-how*. Strategic *know-how* uses both social and informational *know-how* to arrive at decisions about actionable steps. Public leaders who do not know much about the field they want to challenge and who do not know how to bring people together but may have a keen eye for strategic decisions will be hard pressed to deploy strategic *know-how* in strategic action fields (lacking both awareness of where to point an action and lacking the group of people needed to execute desired tactics).

The cases in this study also show that strategic *know-how* is critical to internal group dynamics, as sometimes it takes ongoing strategizing directed at one's own members to be able to continue to pursue the development and implementation of strategic action fields that aim to challenge incumbents. Such *know-how* becomes even more critical when external threats are less urgent, which fosters a greater potential for internal disagreements on strategic direction. As the HJC showed, collectives with high-level strategic *know-how* can withstand the vicissitudes of changing fields, changing society, and changing actors (within and outside a collective), as it is through this dimension of *know-how*, most of all, that collectives stay on track over long periods of time. As such, the ability to deploy strategic *know-how*, in service of remaining consistently oriented toward a group's stated desired outcomes over prolonged periods of times (sometimes decades), contributes to a collective's abilities to achieve its desired outcomes, particularly if such outcomes take years to accomplish.

At the same time, even with great strategies, collectives can fail to achieve desired outcomes, often because other exogenous forces come into play, such as changing fields and societal norms. The HJC presented an episode in which its 2-year work on a specific strategic action field failed to yield the desired outcome because of external changing landscapes in the Louisiana governance field when Governor Jindal's second administration pursued more centralized oversight of the agencies under its purview. There are times that, despite a collective's high-level deployment of strategic *know-how*, the field simply changes so drastically or quickly that it results in months and even years of work achieving little to nothing of its desired outcomes.

The ability to deploy strategic *know-how* can indirectly benefit a collective's ability to achieve desired outcomes on any given strategic action field it implements when such *know-how* signals to other actors that a collective is highly capable and well-organized. In other words, belief in a collective's ability to be a sound strategic partner, as demonstrated by a collective's actions can lead to increased recognition of value by incumbents, making the work to challenge existing systems and policies less confrontational (though not less contentious). In such a scenario, it is possible that a collective challenger increases the likelihood of being received by incumbents in a manner that may facilitate the collective's ability to achieve its desired outcome, as occurred with the HJC's second attempt at a soft second strategic action field targeted at new local government leadership.

Finally, strategic *know-how*, when deployed in a way that it enables a collective to achieve desired outcomes in a local field, contributes directly to the accumulation of social capital within that field. That is to say, the more successful a politically contentious group is in achieving its desired outcomes, the better able it will be to engage incumbents in future strategic action fields because such a group would have built value in recognition and reputation, which then translates to perceived power by incumbents. This perceived power becomes a contributing element to a collective's future potential to achieve its desired outcome, acting in a manner similar to compound interest (though not always, of course). Such accumulation of social capital can also have a negative effect on a collective by moving them closer to incumbents and risking the threat of being co-opted under the guise of being recognized. As such, groups that deploy strategic *know-how* successfully try to avoid such pitfalls by continuing to apply strategic *know-how* to their ongoing efforts to affect change in the fields in which they operate, particularly after having achieved some level of success.

On how actors' operational know-how *either enhanced or limited the prospect for outcome success in local contentious collective actions.* To say that operational structures and processes are critical to any group endeavor is akin to saying that structural frames are critical for buildings. It goes without saying, one might imagine. However, analysis of collective contention has tended to inadequately explore this critical component of any collective endeavor. For critical analysis of group structures and processes, one must typically look to organizational and/or institutional researchers. While this study does not conduct an in-depth analysis of the different types of structures and processes used by actors in collective contention, it does show that public leaders who have the ability to deploy operational *know-how* overwhelmingly succeed in creating a unified group capable of acting on a shared agenda, which in turn helps increase a group's potential to achieve its desired outcomes in social change efforts. The cases analyzed in this study help show how collectives involved in contentious politics increase their likelihood of achieving their desired outcomes if they have installed adequate structures and processes in place that help direct how actors engage in and how the collective decides on strategic action fields.

Creating such structures and processes requires someone, or a group of people, to deploy operational *know-how* of the sort needed to establish and maintain a collective. Within any group, duties have to be assigned, a decision-making structure and process has to be established, and responsible parties have to be set up. Without these basic structures and processes in place, a group will simply exhaust itself battling over miniscule items that fail to accomplish any field changes. While the establishment of operational structures and processes does not guarantee the achievement of desired outcomes, failure to deploy this type of *know-how* can have a crippling effect on a collective's abilities to act.

This study shows that among all of the cases analyzed, the case with the least ability to deploy operational *know-how* was unable to achieve any of its desired outcomes. Similar to the other *know-how* discussed above, this is not to say that there is a direct causal relationship between having and not having operational *know-how* and a collective achieving its desired outcomes, but it does establish that without adequate *know-how* in this dimension, the road forward for a collective will be much more difficult than it already is, given a group's position as a challenger to a field.

Needless energy will be spent, as discussed in analysis, arguing about how to decide and who gets to decide, when structures and processes aren't clear for actors involved in a collective. For collectives involved in political contention, the less energy they can spend fighting on internal processes and instead spend it on designing and implementing strategic action fields, the better positioned they will be to potentially achieve their desired outcome.

Again, having and deploying operational *know-how* does not guarantee success for any politically contentious collective, but such *know-how* does enhance a group's ability to plan and act. As such, when all else is equal (including just and equitable inclusion of voices), the group unable to deploy operational *know-how* increases the potential for failure to achieve desired outcomes. At the same time, operational *know-how* can also over-paralyze actors when processes are too complex or actively dissuade actors when processes and structures are too opaque. In both cases, collectives may have the ability to deploy operational *know-how*, installing structures and processes, but these may either be limited in scope (in terms of who gets to decide) or too vague to be of any use, thereby contributing to a group's inability to pursue strategic action fields at all.

Conclusions and Discussion

This research has sought to bring attention to a missing factor in the contentious collective politics literature by exploring the *know-how* that public leaders bring to their efforts to create social justice change in the New Orleans area. The ability to deploy *know-how* does not come from everyone within a collective, but rather from the select few who either step up to take a leadership role or are elected by the group into leadership roles. Analysis shows how public leaders with informational, social, strategic, and operational *know-how* have a far better chance of experiencing some level of success in their collective contention efforts. Such success is multidimensional, as it can occur internally to the collective itself along different aspects of group-building and maintenance as well as externally in the form of expanded alliances and/or attained outcomes. As such, it is possible to assert that public leadership matters in collective contention. Whether one or many public leaders in a group, what these leaders know how to do to affect change matters more than has been previously recognized.

At the same time, this study does not establish any causal linkages between a specific deployment of *know-how* and desired outcomes attainment, but it does show that *know-how* requires more attention when making observations about a collective's ability to achieve its desired outcomes. The entire research project and analysis assumes democratic opportunity structures are in place, enabling people to envision a different social order. Through this open structure that enables this type of visioning, actors embark upon creating strategic action fields that are aimed at creating a group's desired change.

Using Fligstein and McAdam's SAF theory (2012), one can perceive all efforts, no matter how uncontentious these may look in real-world observation, aimed at changing status quo social orders as contentious when incumbents do not want the existing order from which they benefit to change. Such an analytical positioning and understanding then enables this book, for example, to see contention at play even when actors sit amicably down with field incumbents to dialogue about policy changes. It may not be loud and full of masses on the street, but it is no less contentious in that a push is being made that is aimed at changing the status quo.

Sometimes, shifting status quo may happen in the very meanings we share collectively in a given geography. For example, the HJC in this study was able to shift the commonly understood, normative meaning of the term *affordable housing* within both the New Orleans and Louisiana housing fields from that of the typically pejorative slumlord housing that was prevalent in 2008 to that of safe, clean, and sound housing one can afford in 2022. While this study cannot assert with concrete causal relationships that such a shift in meaning can be attributed solely to the HJC's work, what can be established is that the HJC did its part to contribute to this shift (which, in fact, was an intentional strategic action field on their part that was not discussed in the analysis chapters).

Such a shift signals how contentious collective political efforts attempt to affect normative meanings that are part of a field's overall culture. Indeed, the work by collective challengers to change social orders is also cultural in nature. That is to say, the contours of a social order, how policies are defined, how laws are written, how governance occurs, and so forth create a cultural arena in which societies function within geopolitical borders. Fields exist within these geopolitical borders and typically express the cultural milieu represented within such borders. This study hints at the possibility that earlier views on social movement frames can be connected to broader inquiries about cultural shifts within circumscribed arenas, much in the manner that the HJC was able to contribute to the shifting meaning of affordable housing in the New Orleans field.

An element of inquiry requiring further study and theorizing is the connection between opportunities and acquisition of skills and abilities and traditionally disadvantaged communities. While this book does not focus on a particular demographic, there is a running undercurrent about racialized and gendered social orders that position people of color and women at the bottom of social hierarchies in the United States. As such, I do want to raise the question about how such disparities may affect certain groups' access to the needed *know-how* that can help a group more effectively create change in a field. We need more research on how socioeconomic disparities along racialized and gendered lines contribute to *know-how* disparities in political contention.

As I discussed in this book, SAF theory (Fligstein & McAdam, 2012) has enabled analysis to place public leaders' *know-how* within circumscribed social arenas called fields. Through this theoretical application, this study has been able to show how fields matter in the development of better-informed knowledge about public leaders' potential impacts on their own success. I show this by presenting and analyzing how public leaders' *know-how* interacts within a target field, paying attention to public leaders' articulation of specific desired outcomes that belong within the fields in which they engage. While most *know-how* deployed can be generally transferrable, such as the ability to activate others into collective action, the application of *know-how* will reflect contextual differences that are structurally circumscribed by the fields in which these occur. In the same way that averages differ in sports precisely because it is the rules of the game in a sport that dictates the value of a 0.333 batting average or a 47% three-point shot, so do fields. The circumscribed spaces of fields provide the "rules of the game" in which public leaders engage to pursue their desired outcomes.

Finally, I also aim to inform how academia can better engage and encompass knowledge from the field, and how practitioners in the field can better engage and encompass knowledge generated in academia. Bringing these two into better conversation with each other has the potential to more effectively assist future collectives interested in challenging outdated, inequitable, and unjust governance structures and processes not just in the United States but anywhere in the world where the structural opportunities allow.

Parting Thoughts

I would like to close with some thoughts on what both practitioners and scholars may be able to do with this book. First, to the practitioners, I would like to say that I do hope the analysis chapters, in particular, provided some insight worth reflecting upon as you move forward in helping people form well-organized collectives that seek to make the world a better place. I don't touch on all the complex skills and scenarios that you may encounter, but my hope is that by bringing *know-how* to your attention, you begin to consider how this gets developed, who gets to develop it in your collective, group, or organization, and when obtained, do you allow it to guide decision-making? Too often, people in leadership position shoot down ideas that may come from people with deep *know-how* about what they are saying, and it will take public leaders with active listening skills and inclusive practices to allow these voices to offer solutions. Indeed, I hope that public leaders everywhere who get a chance to read this book walk away with a greater understanding of the diverse capacities needed within their group/organization and how it will be impossible to imagine or expect that one individual can possess all the needed abilities. The potential for effectiveness in a group will be deeply connected to that group's ability to foster diverse development of *know-how* among its members and in this way prepare future leaders to move the baton further.

In the same vein, I would like to offer to scholars, particularly the qualitative researchers out there who engage with community directly, that they consider the arguments I made about *know-how* not fitting into the mainstream rational models of human behavior. Not just as social scientists but as human beings, I'm certain you have come to realize that life is messy, so why would political contention conducted by collectives be any different? A more meaningful approach to analysis and interpretation exists within the pragmatist tradition that I touch on and I encourage better theorists and thinkers than me to continue this exploration and build upon the idea that indeed it is the knowledge that we create that we put into action (informed as it may be by existing cultural norms and values). In this way, we begin to more openly accept that when we observe our research subjects, we are not actually perceiving something so foreign as to require some reality-detached model of human action. What we are observing, analyzing, and struggling to interpret is nothing more than a reflection of ourselves, of the human endeavor to make life meaningful, even if the process is full of contention. In this regard, I hope scholars across the social sciences consider how *know-how* can help enrich analysis and interpretation of human social interaction in our public lives.

References

Agre, P. E. (2004). The practical republic: Social skills and the progress of citizenship. In *Community in the digital age* (pp. 201–223). Rowman and Littlefield.

Alinsky, S. D. (1946). *Reveille for radicals*. University of Chicago Press.

Alinsky, S. D. (1972). *Rules for radicals: A practical primer for realistic radicals*. Vintage Books.

Amenta, E., Caren, N., Chiarello, E., & Su, Y. (2010). The political consequences of social movements. *Annual Review of Sociology, 36*(1), 287–307.

Anderson, B. R. O'G. (2006a). *Imagined communities: Reflections on the origin and spread of nationalism* (Rev. ed.). Verso. (originally published 1983).

Anderson, L. (2006b). Analytic autoethnography. *Journal of Contemporary Ethnography, 35*(4), 373–395.

Anderson, C., & Brown, C. E. (2010). The functions and dysfunctions of hierarchy. *Research in Organizational Behavior, 30*, 55–89.

Andrews, K. T., & Edwards, B. (2004). Advocacy organizations in the U.S. political process. *Annual Review of Sociology, 30*(1), 479–506.

Andrews, K. T., Ganz, M., Baggetta, M., Han, H., & Lim, C. (2010). Leadership, membership, and voice: Civic associations that work. *American Journal of Sociology, 115*(4), 1191–1242.

Arce, M., Rice, R., & Silva, G. E. (2019). Rethinking protest impacts. In *Protest and democracy* (pp. 195–213). University of Calgary Press.

Battilana, J., Leca, B., & Boxenbaum, E. (2009). How actors change institutions: Towards a theory of institutional entrepreneurship. *The Academy of Management Annals, 3*(1), 65–107.

Banton, M. (1998). *Racial theories* (2nd ed.). Cambridge University Press.

Baranowski, M. (2019). Sociology of knowledge in times determined by knowledge. *Society Register, 3*(1), 7–22.

Beckwith, D., & Lopez, C. (2013). *Community organizing: People power from the grassroots*. Center for Community Change.

Benford, R. D., & Snow, D. A. (2000). Framing processes and social movements: An overview and assessment. *Annual Review of Sociology, 26*(1), 611–639.

Berger, P., & Luckman, T. (1966). The reality of everyday life. In *The social construction of reality* (pp. 19–28). Doubleday.

Bingham, L. B., Nabatchi, T., & O'Leary, R. (2005). The new governance: Practices and processes for stakeholder and citizen participation in the work of government. *Public Administration Review, 65*(5), 547–558.

Bosi, L., Giugni, M., & Uba, K. (Eds.). (2016). The consequences of social movements: Taking stock and looking forward. In *The consequences of social movements* (pp. 3–37). Cambridge University Press.

Bosi, L., & Uba, K. (2009). Introduction: The outcomes of social movements. *Mobilization, 14*(4), 409–415.

Bottery, M. (2003). The end of citizenship? The nation state, threats to its legitimacy, and citizenship education in the twenty-first century. *Cambridge Journal of Education*, *33*(1), 101–122.
Bourdieu, P. (1977). *Outline of a theory of practice*. Cambridge University Press.
Bourdieu, P. (1992). *Language and symbolic power*. Polity Press.
Boyte, H. C. (2000). Civic education as a craft, not a program. In *Education for civic engagement in democracy: Service learning and other promising practices*. ERIC Clearinghouse for Social Studies/Social Science Education.
Boyte, H. C. (2004). *Everyday politics: Reconnecting citizens and public life*. University of Pennsylvania Press.
Boyte, H. C. (2005). Reframing democracy: Governance, civic agency, and politics. *Public Administration Review*, *65*(5), 536–546.
Boyte, H. C. (2013). *Reinventing citizenship as public work: Citizen-centered democracy and the empowerment gap*. Kettering Foundation Press.
Brady, H. E., Verba, S., & Schlozman, K. L. (1995). Beyond SES: A resource model of political participation. *American Political Science Review*, *89*(2), 271–294.
Brookes, S. (2014). Is selfless leadership an impossible ideal for public leaders? *The International Journal of Public Leadership*, *10*(4), 200–216.
Brubaker, R. (2009). Ethnicity, race, and nationalism. *Annual Review of Sociology*, *35*, 21.
Brungardt, C. (2011). The intersection between soft skill development and leadership education. *Journal of Leadership Education*, *10*(1), 1–22.
Burns, P. F., & Thomas, M. O. (2011). *Uneven recovery: An examination of public safety, education, housing, and economic development in post-Katrina New Orleans*. APSA 2011 Annual Meeting Paper. https://ssrn.com/abstract=1901270
Burns, P. F., & Thomas, M. O. (2016). *Reforming New Orleans*. Cornell University Press.
Carpini, M. X. D., Cook, F. L., & Jacobs, L. R. (2004). Public deliberation, discursive participation, and citizen engagement: A review of the empirical literature. *Annual Review of Political Science*, *7*(1), 315–344.
Chambers, E. T. (2003). *Roots for radicals: Organizing for power, action, and justice*. Continuum.
Chambers, S., & Kymlicka, W. (2002). *Alternative conceptions of civil society*. Princeton University Press.
Chrislip, D. D., MacPhee, D., & Schmitt, P. (2022). Developing a civic capacity index: Measuring community capacity to respond to civic challenges. *International Journal of Public Leadership*, *19*(1), 14–30.
Cohen, J. L., & Arato, A. (1992). *Civil society and political theory*. MIT Press.
Cohen, J., Pickeral, T., & Levine, P. (2010). The foundation for democracy: Promoting social, emotional, ethical, cognitive skills and dispositions in K-12 schools. *Inter-American Journal of Education for Democracy*, *3*(1), 74–94.
Colapietro, V. (2009). A revised portrait of human agency. *European Journal of Pragmatism and American Philosophy*, *I*(1/2).
Cowan, M. A. (2017). Inclusiveness, foresight, and decisiveness: The practical wisdom of barrier-crossing leaders. *New England Journal of Public Policy*, *29*(1), 1–10.
Curtis, J. E., & Petras, J. W. (1970). Community power, power studies and the sociology of knowledge. *Human Organization*, *29*(3), 204–218.

Cuthill, M., & Fien, J. (2005). Capacity building: Facilitating citizen participation in local governance. *Australian Journal of Public Administration, 64*(4), 63–80.

Daas, R., ten Dam, G., & Dijkstra, A. B. (2016). Contemplating modes of assessing citizenship competences. *Studies in Educational Evaluation, 51*, 88–95.

Dahlgren, P. (2006). Doing citizenship: The cultural origins of civic agency in the public sphere. *European Journal of Cultural Studies, 9*(3), 267–286.

de Freitas, R. S. (2020). The sociology of knowledge and its movements. *Sociologia & Antropologia, 10*, 267–287.

de Souza Briggs, X. (2008). *Democracy as problem solving: Civic capacity in communities across the globe*. The MIT Press.

Dewey, J. (2016). *The public and its problems: An essay in political inquiry*. Ohio University Press. (Originally published 1927).

Dewey, J. (2017). *The essential John Dewey: 20+ books in one edition*. Musaicum Books.

DiMaggio, P. (1988). Interest and agency in institutional theory. In L. Zucker (Ed.), *Institutional patterns and organizations: Culture and environment* (pp. 3–21). Ballinger Publishing.

DiMaggio, P., & Powell, W. (1983). The iron cage revisited: Institutional isomorphism and collective rationality in organizational fields. *American Sociological Review, 48*(2), 147–160.

DiMaggio, P., & Powell, W. (1991). Constructing an organizational field as a professional project: US art museums, 1920–1940. In *The new institutionalism in organizational analysis* (pp. 267–292). University of Chicago Press.

Douglas, N., & Wykowski, T. (2011). What does it mean to know? In *From belief to knowledge: Achieving and sustaining an adaptive culture in organizations* (pp. 23–44). CRC Press.

Edwards, M. (2014). *Civil society* (3rd ed.). Polity Press.

Emirbayer, M., & Maynard, D. W. (2011). Pragmatism and ethnomethodology – ProQuest. *Qualitative Sociology, 34*(1), 221–261.

Fields, B. (2009). From green dots to greenways: Planning in the age of climate change in post-Katrina New Orleans. *Journal of Urban Design, 14*(3), 325–344.

Fligstein, N. (1997). Social skill and institutional theory. *American Behavioral Scientist, 40*(4), 397–405.

Fligstein, N. (2001). Social skill and the theory of fields. *Sociological Theory, 19*(2), 105–125.

Fligstein, N., & McAdam, D. (2012). *A theory of fields*. Oxford University Press.

Forestal, J. (2016). *"Midwife to democracy:" Civic learning in higher education*. Stockton University William J. Hughes Center for Public Policy.

Fourcade, M. (2010). The problem of embodiment in the sociology of knowledge: Afterword to the special issue on knowledge in practice. *Qualitative Sociology, 33*(4), 569–574.

Freire, P. (2005). *Pedagogy of the oppressed* (30th Anniversary Edition). Continuum.

Fung, A. (2004). *Empowered participation: Reinventing urban democracy*. Princeton University Press.

Fussell, E., & Diaz, L. (2015). *Latinos in Metro New Orleans: Progress, problems, and potential*. The Data Center.

Gamson, W. A. (1990). *The strategy of social protest* (2nd ed.). Wadsworth. (1st edition published 1975).

Gamson, W. A. (1992). *Talking politics*. Cambridge University Press.
Ganz, M. (2009). *Why David sometimes wins: Leadership, organization, and strategy in the California farm worker movement*. Oxford University Press.
Garza, A. (2020). *The purpose of power: How we come together when we fall apart*. Random House Publishing Group.
Gecan, M. (2002). *Going public*. Beacon Press.
Gist, M. E., Locke, E. A., & Susan Taylor, M. (1987). Organizational behavior: Group structure, process, and effectiveness. *Journal of Management, 13*(2), 237.
Giugni, M. G. (1998). Was it worth the effort? The outcomes and consequences of social movements. *Annual Review of Sociology, 24*, 371.
Goodwin, J., & Jasper, J. M. (1999). Caught in a winding, snarling vine: The structural bias of political process theory. *Sociological Forum, 14*(1), 27–55.
Goodwin, J., & Jasper, J. M. (Eds.). (2004). *Rethinking social movements: Structure, meaning, and emotion*. Rowman & Littlefield Publishers.
Gross, N. (2009). A pragmatist theory of social mechanisms. *American Sociological Review, 74*(3), 358–379.
Gross, N. (2010). Charles Tilly and American pragmatism. *The American Sociologist, 41*(4), 337–357.
Gurr, T. R. (2016). *Why men rebel*. Routledge.
Habermas, J. (1998). *Between facts and norms: Contributions to a discourse theory of law and democracy*. MIT Press.
Hartley, J. (2018). Ten propositions about public leadership. *International Journal of Public Leadership, 14*(4), 202–217.
Hurrell, S. A., Scholarios, D., & Thompson, P. (2013). More than a 'humpty dumpty' term: Strengthening the conceptualization of soft skills. *Economic and Industrial Democracy, 34*(1), 161–182.
Jain, S., & Anjuman, A. S. S. (2013). Facilitating the acquisition of soft skills through training. *IUP Journal of Soft Skills, 7*(2), 32–39.
Jasper, J. M. (2005). Culture, knowledge, politics. In *The handbook of political sociology: States, civil societies, and globalization*. Cambridge University Press.
Jasper, J. M. (2006). *Getting your way: Strategic dilemmas in the real world*. University of Chicago Press.
Jasper, J. M. (2011). Emotions and social movements: Twenty years of theory and research. *Annual Review of Sociology, 37*(1), 285–303.
Jasper, J. M. (2015). Playing the game. In *Players and arenas: The interactive dynamics of protest, protest and social movements* (pp. 9–32). Amsterdam University Press.
Jasper, J. M., & Goodwin, J. (1999). Trouble in paradigms. *Sociological Forum, 14*(1), 107–125.
Joas, H. (1996). *The creativity of action*. University of Chicago Press.
Johnston, H., & Klandermans, B. (1995). The cultural analysis of social movements. In *Social movements and culture. Social movements, protest, and contention* (Vol. 4, pp. 3–24). University of Minnesota Press.
Kamel, N. (2012). Social marginalization, federal assistance and repopulation patterns in the New Orleans metropolitan area following Hurricane Katrina. *Urban Studies, 49*(14), 3211–3231.
Kilpinen, E. (2009). The habitual conception of action and social theory. *Semiotica, 2009*(173), 99–128.

Kirlin, M. (2003). *The role of civic skills in fostering civic engagement*. CIRCLE Working Paper 06. Center for Information and Research on Civic Learning and Engagement (CIRCLE).

Kirlin, M. (2005). Understanding the relationship between civic skills and civic participation: Educating future public managers. *Journal of Public Affairs Education, 11*(4), 305–314.

Kuklick, H. (1983). The sociology of knowledge: Retrospect and prospect. *Annual Review of Sociology, 9*, 287–310.

Lafont, C. (2015). Deliberation, participation, and democratic legitimacy: Should deliberative mini-publics shape public policy? *The Journal of Political Philosophy, 23*(1), 40–63.

le Bon, G. (1931). *Psychology of crowds*. The Viking Press.

Levine, P. (2007). Collective action, civic engagement, and the knowledge commons. In *Understanding knowledge as a commons: From theory to practice* (pp. 247–276). The MIT Press.

Lichterman, P., & Eliasoph, N. (2014). Civic action. *American Journal of Sociology, 120*(3), 798–863.

Lichterman, P. (2020). *How civic action works: Fighting for housing in Los Angeles*. Princeton University Press.

Lukes, S. (2005). *Power: A radical view* (2nd ed.). Palgrave MacMillan. (Originally published 1974).

Marcy, R. T. (2023). Reflections on gaps in public sector leadership development theory. *International Journal of Public Leadership, 19*(4), 261–275.

McAdam, D. (1982). *Political process and the development of black insurgency, 1930–1970*. University of Chicago Press.

McAdam, D., Tarrow, S., & Tilly, C. (2001). *Dynamics of contention*. Cambridge University Press.

McCarthy, E. D. (2000). The sociology of knowledge. *Encyclopedia of Sociology, 2*, 2953–2960.

Meyer, J. W., & Rowan, B. (1977). Institutionalized organizations: Formal structure as myth and ceremony. *American Journal of Sociology, 83*(2), 340–363.

Mouffe, C. (1991). Democratic citizenship and the political community. In *Community at loose ends* (pp. 70–82). University of Minnesota Press.

Omi, M., & Winant, H. (1994). *Racial formation in the United States: From the 1960s to the 1990s* (2nd ed.). Routledge.

Opp, K.-D. (2009). *Theories of political protest and social movements: A multidisciplinary introduction, critique, and synthesis*. Routledge.

Paschel, T. S., & Sawyer, M. Q. (2008). Contesting politics as usual: Black social movements, globalization, and race policy in Latin America. *Souls, 10*(3), 197–214.

Pedwell, C. (2017). Habit and the politics of social change: A comparison of nudge theory and pragmatist philosophy. *Body & Society, 23*(4), 59–94.

Pensoneau-Conway, S. L., & Toyosaki, S. (2011). Automethodology: Tracing a home for praxis-oriented ethnography. *International Journal of Qualitative Methods, 10*(4), 378–399.

Power, E. M. (1999). An introduction to Pierre Bourdieu's key theoretical concepts. *Journal for the Study of Food and Society, 3*(1), 48–52.

References

Robert, D. (2006, February 8). Bring Back N.O. Commission takes lead role. *New Orleans CityBusiness*. https://neworleanscitybusiness.com/blog/2006/02/08/bring-back-no-commission-takes-lead-role/

Rogers, M. L. (2016). Introduction: Revisiting *The public and its problem*. In *The public and its problems: An essay in political inquiry* (pp. 1–43). Ohio University Press.

Romania, V. (2013). Pragmatist epistemology and the post-structural turn of the social sciences: A new kind of non-Aristotelean logic? *Philosophy Today*, *57*(2), 150–158.

Ron, A. (2008). Power: A pragmatist, deliberative (and radical) view. *The Journal of Political Philosophy*, *16*(3), 272–292.

Ross, L., & Nisbett, R. E. (2011). *The person and the situation: Perspectives of social psychology*. Pinter & Martin Publishers.

Ryfe, D. M. (2002). The practice of deliberative democracy: A study of 16 deliberative organizations. *Political Communication*, *19*(3), 359–377.

Sennett, R. (1977). *The fall of public man* (1st ed.). Knopf.

Shmueli, D., Warfield, W., & Kaufman, S. (2009). Enhancing community leadership negotiation skills to build civic capacity. *Negotiation Journal*, *25*(2), 249–266.

Silva, E. (2015). Social movements, protest, and policy. *European Review of Latin American & Caribbean Studies*, *100*, 27–39.

Smelser, N. J. (2011). *Theory of collective behavior* (Kindle Edition). Quid Pro Books. (Original publication occurred in 1963).

Smilde, D. (2004, mayo–agosto). Los evangélicos y la polarización: la moralización de la política y la politización de la religión. *Revista Venezolana de Economía y Ciencias Sociales*, *10*(núm. 2), 163–179. Universidad Central de Venezuela Caracas, Venezuela.

Smilde, D. (2007). *Reason to believe: Cultural agency in Latin American evangelicalism*. University of California Press.

Smilde, D. (2013). Beyond the strong program in the sociology of religion. In *Religion on the edge: De-centering and re-centering the sociology of religion* (pp. 43–66). Oxford University Press.

Snow, D., Rochford, E., Worden, S., & Benford, R. (1986). Frame alignment processes, micromobilization, and movement participation. *American Sociological Review*, *51*(4), 464.

Stahler-Sholk, R. (2010). The Zapatista social movement: Innovation and sustainability. *Alternatives: Global, Local, Political*, *35*(3), 269–290.

Stanley, J. (2011a). *Know how*. Oxford University Press.

Stanley, J. (2011b). Knowing (how). *Noûs*, *45*(2), 207–238.

Tarrow, S. G. (2011). *Power in movement: Social movements and contentious politics* (Rev. & updated 3rd ed.). Cambridge University Press. (originally published in 1998).

Tilly, C. (1978). *From mobilization to revolution*. Addison-Wesley Pub.

Tilly, C. (1986). *The contentious French*. Belknap Press.

Toyosaki, S. (2011). Critical complete-member ethnography: Theorizing dialectics of consensus and conflict in intracultural communication. *Journal of International & Intercultural Communication*, *4*(1), 62–80.

Turner, R. H., & Killian, L. M. (1972). *Collective behavior*. Prentice-Hall.

Van Dyke, N., & Dixon, M. (2013). Activist human capital: Skills acquisition and the development of commitment to social movement activism. *Mobilization: An International Journal, 18*(2), 197–212.

Verba, S., Schlozman, K. L., & Brady, H. E. (1995). *Voice and equality: Civic voluntarism in American politics.* Harvard University Press.

Warren, M. R. (2001). *Dry bones rattling: Community building to revitalize American democracy.* Princeton University Press.

Weber, M. (1946). Politics as a vocation. In H. H. Gerth & C. W. Mills (Eds.), *From Max Weber: Essays in sociology* (pp. 77–128). Oxford University Press.

Weil, F. D. (2011). Rise of community organizations, citizen engagement, and new institutions. In A. Liu, R. V. Anglin, R. Mizelle, & P. Allison (Eds.), *Resilience and opportunity: Lessons from the U.S. Gulf Coast after Katrina and Rita* (pp. 201–219). Brookings Institution Press.

Westheimer, J., & Kahne, J. (2004). What kind of citizen? The politics of educating for democracy. *American Educational Research Journal, 41*(2), 237–269.

Whitman, G. (2018). *Stand up! How to get involved, speak out, and win in a world on fire.* Berrett-Koehler Publishers, Inc.

Yang, K., & Pandey, S. K. (2011). Further dissecting the black box of citizen participation: When does citizen involvement lead to good outcomes? *Public Administration Review, 71*(6), 880–892.

Printed and bound by CPI Group (UK) Ltd, Croydon, CR0 4YY
19/11/2024

14595509-0001